Rivers of Darkness, Visions of Light

From Extortion to Salvation

Larry A. Whited

WestBow
Press
A Division of Thomas Nelson

WestBow Press books may be ordered through booksellers or by contacting:

WestBow Press
A Division of Thomas Nelson
1663 Liberty Drive
Bloomington, IN 47403
www.westbowpress.com
1-(866) 928-1240

ISBN: 978-1-4497-0742-2 (sc)
ISBN: 978-1-4497-0743-9 (dj)
ISBN: 978-1-4497-0610-4 (e)

Library of Congress Control Number: 2010939287

Printed in the United States of America

WestBow Press rev. date: 11/23/2010

Dedicated to...

My sister, Kathy, who has had to share a difficult journey;

Jennie and Harold, who made the journey bearable;

But mostly, simply to my Lord. This is His story more than mine.

Contents

Preface

When writing the story of a life, one must have a reason. When the person is famous, the reason is obvious. But when the person is otherwise obscure, we wonder about the merit of the story and if it warrants our time. This is absolutely a fair thing to consider.

Had certain happenings in the story that follows made the news when the events took place, there would be a natural curiosity about the more sensational aspects—the extortion of a public utility company and FBI involvement in the investigation are not small matters. Furthermore, a nighttime five-mile swim down the Mississippi River with its deceptively powerful current to evade capture is hardly a typical escape plan. This story has quietly lain dormant for over thirty years, but it refuses to go away.

Yet crime alone is an unworthy story if achieving sensationalism is the only intended goal. By necessity, this writing develops the crime along every step of the way, laying bare the motivations, planning, and execution. This is a documented story told as openly and honestly as possible. It is not a story of excuses or justifications; it is instead a story of truth. This truth encompasses far more than a criminal act, for it is an exploration of darkness and light in a sometimes painful revelation of the soul and spirit.

There is a greater story here than that of the extortion. In a very real sense, the story is timeless. This is a journey through parallel spiritual waters where the dangers were every bit as real as those encountered during the commission of the crime. Eternity hung in the balance, and time was suspended for me as I lived out a forbidden adventure. I walked the rim of hell and stepped back as a strong hand rested on my shoulder and kept me from falling. It is a frightening and humbling realization.

I have written boldly of thoughts and happenings where the lasting impressions are unquestionable and remain with me today as clearly as they did years ago as a child and later as a young man. Where there was no recollection, there was no license taken. Also, I was fortunate to have saved my records from my years as a deep sea diver in the Gulf of Mexico, thus allowing me to accurately capture certain time windows. For the criminal events that occurred in 1973, I had solid references: FBI reports released to me under the Freedom of Information – Privacy Act. Those FBI reports jogged my memory where needed, and the resulting story follows truth with an accuracy that I could not have otherwise achieved.

For legal reasons and in some cases to protect the privacy of others, certain names have been withheld or changed. To the best of my knowledge, this is the only compromise that I have made in telling this story. There has been no professional editing as per my choice and not the publishers. Where there are shortcomings with writing substance or style, they are mine. I wanted the writing to be real, to be authentic, to be as from a friend still subject to failings. I am grateful for the liberty given me by the publisher.

I ask you to join me in what is more of a letter to you than it is a book. This is personal, and I have told you all that seems fitting and appropriate. It is my greatest hope that you, the reader, will find yourself touched and blessed by the true story that follows.

Chapter One

Unholy Foundations

Strange, this compartmentalizing of the mind and heart, soul and spirit, that we can know even in childhood. There are no clear boundaries, but there are clear differences. Good angels and bad angels perched on opposite shoulders competing for the soul afford an imperfect understanding of the divisions and resulting struggles, although there might well be some truth to this notion.

In the 1950's and 1960's the Beartooth Bar was located mid-block on Broadway, known to us simply as Main Street. This was the street with the businesses that sliced through the center of town in Red Lodge, Montana. The town of some 2,000 people was a shadow of what it once had been when the area's coal mines were active before the Smith Mine disaster decimated Bearcreek, a rugged western mining community six miles east of Red Lodge. Seventy-four lives were lost on February 27, 1943, when an explosion ripped through the Smith Mine, eventually closing it forever. The disaster left fifty-eight widows and one hundred twenty-five children without fathers. Bearcreek faded into an undeserved obscurity, although tenacity still keeps it alive. Red Lodge, one of the gateways to Yellowstone National Park, fared better.

At least ten bars that I can recall still populated Main Street in the 1950's—relics of a time when hard-working miners and ranchers had shared beers, brawls, and a tough but good life. Red Lodge was a town comprised mostly of European immigrants drawn by the work in the mines. They were hard workers. Nearly everyone in those days seemed to be a hard worker.

Our second-story home over the bar had an inside stairway descending to Main Street. The door opened onto the city sidewalk, and it was only a matter of a few steps to then enter the bar through its front door. This was the way to work for my parents, and sometimes for play for me and my sister, Kathy, who was four years older—although all I can honestly remember about any play in the bar with my sister involved our few spooky trips together into the dimly lit basement. Usually I was there alone, but at times there were shared dares with friends to walk to the back of the long, narrow basement with lights on for only the front half. When the compressor would kick on for the coolers in the bar above it felt as if there was a separate presence down there. Halfway through the basement, the door with the creaking hinges would have to be opened. Then eerie darkness and strong, slithery grabs by creatures had to be negotiated to make the journey past the gas boiler to enter yet another back room with the back wall that had to be reached to win tests of bravery. Opening the door midway through the basement was bad enough, but what lay beyond had all the promise of a place of torture imagined only by children. Lights could force the demons back into corners, but I knew they were always waiting there. Leaving the lights off and making the journey many times by myself seemed the best way to fight them.

The outside steps at the rear of the misplaced home over the bar faced the back alley, with the landing at the top offering a view of several city streets laid out below a long bench of a hill. That hill then rose to the local airstrip that was set in the upper flats adjacent to the Rodeo Grounds. Beyond the Rodeo Grounds the upward climb continued through a large ranch to the mountains beyond. Those mountains would one day reveal the cut slopes of a ski run developed to draw tourists. On a clear day the ski run is visible from Billings, Montana, some sixty miles away. Montana is in fact the Big Sky Country—just as the license plates have proclaimed in the past. Others may be puzzled or amused at the grand claim, until they visit and see for themselves.

Jeremiah Johnson, who in real life was John "Liver-Eating" Johnston, was the first constable of Red Lodge, or so local history claims. The 1972 movie based loosely on Johnston and starring Robert Redford as Jeremiah Johnson was filmed in Utah, but John Johnston had traversed the Montana wilderness. It was a time when you had to be rugged. Where fiction and fact might now collide is hard to determine, but that sense of a wild frontier was not far from us as children. That feeling is now gone forever unless one might venture deeper into the mountains to leave mankind behind a retreating horizon. Still, as children we could escape the world shortly past the city limits. Sometimes the world needed to be left behind. Solitary hikes and mountain climbing pitted me against those basement demons in a cleaner world. Somehow out there away from home it seemed a fairer fight, but of course it wasn't.

The second-story windows in our living room faced Main Street and gave a commanding view of the center of town as the street corridor could be scanned to the left and right until it veered out of sight in either direction. As with the view from the back of the home, the corresponding hill on the opposite side of the narrow valley climbed up to leave Red Lodge nestled in its private basin situated below the eastern slopes of the Rocky Mountains, just sixty-five miles from the northeast entrance to Yellowstone National Park. It would not be for many years that my friends and I would come to appreciate that we were growing up in a special pocket of nature that gave us a private playground with animals, mountains, hills, woods, creeks, ponds, lakes, and trails unknown by most children. It was strange that the bar could compete so effectively against so much of the natural beauty.

Red Lodge, Montana
Photo by Tom Egenes -- Flash's Photography -- Used with permission
(www.flashs.com)

Formerly the Beartooth Bar

Dad & Larry behind Beartooth Bar

Kathy & Larry

In 1954 when my friend and I were six years old, we sat one day at the top of the stairs at the rear of the bar. Randy was one of several good friends that I had, and the one who I thought might understand some of the troubling feelings that I was having. These were thoughts that a six-year-old ought not to have. I felt older than I should have, and I saw a sure defeat waiting for me. I picked my moment to tell Randy what I understood at the time to be my future: "I am going to kill myself before I am eighteen years old."

I don't know what I expected my friend to say or think when he heard these words. Children should not be part of such discussions. I don't think that Randy was able to say anything; for I recall nothing in response. I do remember looking into his eyes and realizing that he had no understanding of what I was saying. It is difficult now to put this in precise terms of what a six-year-old might be thinking. All I know is that my friend did not and could not know what I meant. I felt awkward at what I had said, and I wanted to take my words back. I had revealed too much. It would be several years before I ever again attempted such a discussion with a like-minded friend, and sadly he would eventually die in a hospital for the criminally insane. He won our pitiful bet as to who would lose at life first. Frank, I'm sorry. I wish I had known enough to reach you and help you in time.

Self-destructive thoughts enjoyed an unrestrained private playground in my mind. Laughing and horseplay with friends never erased the self-loathing, the deep desire for complete annihilation, and the far greater desire to have never known life. The distractions of Erector Sets, Chemistry Sets, Kool-Aid stands, water balloons, and rubber-band guns never broke the hold on me. Building forts and tree houses in the woods could not guard against the internal assault. Forays deep into a partially collapsed coalmine tunnel never outpaced the thoughts of death. Fishing trips to the Willow Creek ponds had us walking or bicycling past the cemetery, and I knew where I belonged. I never thought that it would be my parents who would someday lie there rather than me.

The opposing worlds that I recognized were too clear to me, and no one understood—except for maybe my friend Frank. He had been a transplant to Red lodge for our junior high years. My parents had sold or leased the bar by then, although it would later be reclaimed once more when the buyer failed to meet his obligations. I was glad that Frank never visited that basement, but I do clearly recall his absolute terror when we saw Alfred Hitchcock's 1960 movie *Psycho* at the Roman Theater in Red Lodge. Frank came and left with troubles that were far too intense. In certain ways I now feel responsible.

The home above the bar had two skylights that allowed sunlight to filter into the internal rooms that had no windows. Spring thaws would invariably produce a leaking ceiling for the flat roof as the snows slowly disappeared. Water-stained plaster buckling off strips of lath seemed fitting for the home—it had always been that way. When the jukebox in the bar below would play country western songs into the late night hours and I would lie in my bed looking up, the cutout in the ceiling that allowed me to share the light from the back skylight always revealed a peculiar shadow. It could be somewhat comforting even though I didn't trust it; for in ways it was too other-worldly. The translucent glass itself showed the shadow of a boy praying. It was a boy because of the shape of his rounded head and the folded hands—the shadow was of someone almost like me. Ventures up the wooden ladder outside in the back to the second-story roof never gave me a satisfactory explanation as to where that shadow came from. Its reality was in many ways no different than the reality in the basement. This was simply the other world—the one that I often found more real than the world before me.

Nights above the bar were usually not the best of times. The loud talk and laughter that too many beers or too much whiskey brings on punctuated the dark nights as the sounds drifted upward, and the crack of pool balls colliding as the players shot games of rotation or eight-ball confirmed that there were still enough patrons to keep my folks working late. I didn't mind that part, and neither did my sister. If we ever really needed our parents, we could rap on the radiator pipes to get their attention. The sound would carry down the plumbing into the bar. This was to be their signal to come upstairs to see what was wrong. I don't recall ever having to do this for an emergency or for any real need. My needs or my sister's never reached that level. Our parents were more comfortable in the bar than they were with us, and consequently we all retreated to our separate and private worlds.

I allowed my own mind to torture me, assuming that one has the control to prevent or allow this. Many times I would lie in bed and put my hands out before me. Staring at them or sensing their presence in the dark, I would turn them back onto myself and imagine that I no longer had control over them. I would start opening and closing my fingers as if I was forming grasping claws, and I would advance my hands toward my face and throat. I wasn't sure who was trying to wrestle the control from me, but whoever it was knew an evil and power that left me having to force my hands under my body to hide them from me. Struggling within one's self with different forces had me of course wondering if I was crazy, but this seemed too simple an explanation and didn't address the power in the darkness that I knew was really there. Perhaps this was all the overactive imagination of an intense child. After all, some parents spend a great deal of time trying to convince children that monsters are not real.

Closets with clothes that once draped over bodies presented a special nighttime challenge for me. Those clothes packed tightly together took on personalities that I did not trust. I knew, or dared to think, that there was really nothing living within or behind those clothes hanging there as if from a small gallows. There was only one way for me to handle the teasing anxiety and chilling fear, and that was to repeatedly rush into the clothes and grab at the imagined presence. Adrenalin fueled my charges into the darkness, and time after time I came up empty-handed except for the clothes in my hands. Eventually, I came to realize who had the upper hand. If I could push through my fear, I would prevail. In ways this became a model for my life. Fear could be acknowledged, but it could be overcome. It was the slower erosion of hope that was more insidious and harder to take.

There was a growing wall of separation within my mind that I knew as a child, and one that eventually in my teen years I would attempt in vain to describe to three different counselors in brief encounters, including perhaps six visits in all. The wall wasn't as simple as something dividing good and evil, or light and darkness, or even sanity and insanity. The wall was real, that much I knew; and it was black. I was on one side of the wall, and I wasn't at all sure what was on the other side. It might be bad; it might be good; but for sure what was on the other side was significant. The last of my counselors, a minister, had been the one to ask me to give the wall a color. Thinking that he would assume a black wall to be symbolic of evil alone, I lied to him and told him that the wall was something like a dark purple. This seemed to me to convey the intensity of deep thought while yet claiming a higher ground that may or may not have been justified. I wonder if I had fooled him—I think not.

Our few sessions ended as did the other visits with the previous two counselors with the recommendation that I move up the professional ladder to seek other help. The minister had been the third step up, and after him help was not sought even though it was recommended. The next step was to have been a team of two doctors in Billings, Montana, sixty miles away. After the third so-called counselor I knew then that they all were ill-equipped to deal with the thoughts that I was having. It was futile. When you realize as a teenager that adults are incapable of understanding you, it makes you feel very different from everyone else in an unwelcome and disturbing way.

The minister did request a separate session with my mother though to discuss things. All I recall from this was that she came away from the visit offended and bitterly angry, and nothing good was ever said about the minister again. Clearly, he hadn't respected the boundaries that my sister and I knew were not to be crossed, and somehow he had dared to hurt my mother's feelings. Following their visit, the subject of any further counseling for me was dropped, and I was on my own as I had been before. For me it was a confirmation of futility, and this only served to confirm my confession to Randy years prior regarding taking my own life. Time was running out, and my understood deadline of age eighteen was approaching.

I can't recall when a particular reoccurring dream started or when it finally ended. My best guess is that it visited me off and on for about three or four years as a child and perhaps even until the bar was sold or leased when I was about twelve. Dreams would start with different unrelated scenarios with the typically peculiar sequences of events that somehow make sense during dreams but afterwards seem strangely bizarre and disjointed. It was the common ending that so many of the dreams had that was unsettling and caused me to awaken breathing rapidly, sweating, and fighting the panic that wanted to overtake me. As the dreams would begin to conclude, I would find myself at the top of the basement stairs in the bar. I don't remember if I would turn on the lights or not, but the switch was the third from the right at the top. Strange, the vivid things that you remember. I would start walking down the stairs—it wasn't a choice or a challenge; it just happened. Two or three steps from the bottom there was always the same cat. It was not a typical cat, but something insidious with no definitive shape. The cat was intelligent, and it wanted to torture me. It would start with a rough, teasing and humiliating tickling, getting more controlling and more violent as the seconds passed. The tickling wasn't funny—it hurt, and I hated it. I could only move ineffectively in slow motion to try to protect myself, and my only real defense was in finally waking up in nightmarish dread.

Perhaps it was to fight this dream that I so often in real life went down into that basement alone, lights on or lights off to face whatever was there. There were other reasons though, and these reasons no one knew when I was a child. This was my secret, and part of what I knew that others could not understand.

It was not uncommon for boys in Montana in the 1950's to be familiar with guns. Although I never had a successful hunt until I was perhaps sixteen when my friend Mike guided me to a deer, I had my Montana-issued Certificate of Competency from the Fish & Game Department qualifying me for a big game license when I was eleven years old. I think that I had a license that same year for deer and elk, but I cannot now be sure of this. Nevertheless, at age eleven I was handling a Husqvarna .270 rifle skillfully, and this followed years of practice with a Marlin .22 rifle. At six years old I could load and shoot the .22. I still have both of these weapons from my childhood, passed from my dad's generation to my own.

I enjoyed the trust of my dad when I was a young boy. He had a confidence in me when it came to things like tools, work, weapons, and personal responsibility—or at least the hopeful part in me considered this to be trust and confidence and not simply a lack of interest. Extra efforts to gain attention did too often seem to go unnoticed. My mother was especially disappointed when it came to my failure in basketball, and for years much of her attention remained focused on this with many reminders for me of how much this meant to her. How much I had hurt her was revealed when she said more than once, "Why can't you be good in sports like Tommy and Ricky?" There was not the slightest doubt regarding whom she would have preferred to have as a son. Still, no one ever questioned my work ethic or my other skills—although these traits were not worthy of the same kind of praise that sports could provide for a needy parent.

There was that one time as a young boy when I finally convinced my parents to come to the swimming pool to see how far I could swim underwater while holding my breath. They had watched when I dove in, but when I finally surfaced to gasp for air they were talking and looking at the other kids. Their smiles for them were more genuine than their smiles for me—I wasn't blind. I remember wishing that I would have drowned so they might have had something worth watching.

The locked room in the basement held our weapons, and I was given the key whenever I wanted it. In those days, accidents from boys playing with guns were preempted by one main factor—those of us who were trained knew that we had to be careful. You didn't draw a bead on something with a real rifle to shoot it unless you intended to—we knew and respected guns. Accidents were of course possible though, and later a high school hunting tragedy did occur involving others when someone mistook another person for a deer. It was very hard for those of us who were trained to understand how such a mistake could be made. You always made sure of your target before firing. As children, we did not point real weapons at each other and pull the trigger in a game. We knew which were toys and which were not. Saying this, I must admit to one time when two of us shared somewhat close shots aimed near each other, but we still had trusted our aim and our intentions.

The room with the rifles, fishing equipment, and other personal belongings within was built for security with partitioned walls in the basement. In it was better lighting, and this area did not have the same ominous feeling as the rest of the basement. When inside this room with the door closed, a certain sense of privacy, relief, and safety was felt. Yet it was this very room that saw many hours of my tears and struggles. To this day I do not understand the paradox, but I now believe that I was not alone in there. During especially troubling times, I would enter the room, load the .22 rifle, secure it in place, and then rig string onto the trigger through a pulley type of system so that I could sit with the muzzle resting on my temple for extended periods. One tug on the string would have ended it all, and that thought was comforting. Beyond a much larger unseen hand restraining mine, there was a favorite aunt and uncle whom I did not want to hurt; and it was these gentle restraints that kept me from pulling the trigger. I cannot now imagine the grief the extended family would have felt at the suicide of one so young, but I can still understand the child.

The timing of events is now impossible to piece together, but a separate event at a family reunion in North Dakota fits somewhere into this same timeframe. Our road trips to North Dakota were not pleasant. These six hundred and fifty mile trips on two lane roads before the interstate highway system was completed were started at daybreak and ended well after dark. We forget that trips for children seem to take forever. Making things worse, both of my parents smoked. I had asthma, and I would often open a window slightly to try to capture fresh air, but the smoke still found its way into my lungs. I can still hear the lonesome sound of wind whistling past the window, and I can still smell that wretched foul smoke. It was a silent reminder that I was breathing the same air as my mother, and I hated this. I earned praise from my parents for begging them not to smoke, but there was no personal sacrifice from them on this point. Their promise to me was that if I didn't smoke or drink by the time I was eighteen that they would buy me a car. I expected that would be too late for me, and I didn't really believe them anyway.

There was one reason to look forward to going to North Dakota, and that was to spend time with Aunt Jennie and Uncle Harold in Buffalo when they otherwise would not be heading our way for these precious awaited visits. I'm not sure that two finer people ever walked the earth, and my sister would be the first to agree. This particular visit though was marred by a reunion that stole their time from my sister and me. We wanted to be with them at their house, not visiting and competing with relatives for attention or being kissed and hugged even if you didn't want this other affection. Wet kisses on the cheek from aunts with too much lipstick were not high on a little boy's list of favorite things. There were seven of those aunts at this reunion; nine if you count the two married to my two uncles. Grandma and

Grandpa and lots of cousins were gathered, and we were all to meet at the café in Litchville owned by one of my aunts.

Cousins who were near my age and I were playing in the kitchen area. In those days the excess food from cooking and the remnants left over from customers' plates were kept in a barrel for later transfer and feeding to pigs. This would have been the equivalent of a 55-gallon drum—the common industrial size for bulk chemicals. We had a narrow board set up over the slop barrel, and dares were made to see who would venture across. Regretfully, I took the challenge. I lost my balance and fell into the barrel and was covered with the filth and the shame. This was shortly before the family reunion photo was to be taken. Poorly fitting bib overalls of an older cousin were soon located for me, and I was changed in time to be part of the photo that probably still exists in some old albums. My desperate begging pleas to my mother and my tears to not to be part of the photo were to no avail. During later visits with relatives when the photo albums were opened, more than once I heard, "Wasn't that the time when Larry fell into the slop bucket?" The chuckling was always one-sided. There was one very sad little boy in that photo whom I remember quite well—one nobody else knew.

Humiliation lasts long, and it sometimes becomes one of the sources for deep-seated anger and hatred. There were many other far more serious humiliations, perversions that were psychological and sexual in nature, that I knew as a child at the hands of one who should have been trusted the most, but that story need not now be told in detail. That story would take on an unhealthy life of its own and clamor for the spotlight, and I cannot allow that. That door opens back in time to another with its own history of abuse. I have no monopoly on hard times, and others have suffered far more than I have. This writing is not a competition for recognition in that sad realm—that is a contest I would not want to win.

The dare to walk out over the slop barrel resulted in tearful sadness and shame, but not in a learned lesson. I was not the sort of child you would dare to do anything dangerous if you expected to win. When I was ten years old and in the fifth grade, our teacher was giving a lesson on the three states of matter: solids, liquids, and gases. Dry ice (solidified carbon dioxide) is a curiosity for children because it changes directly from a solid state to gaseous state, unlike regular ice from water that first melts into a liquid and then evaporates. Dry ice is cold: -109°F (-78.5°C). Touching it can rapidly result in frostbite, with severe injury following longer contact.

Our venturesome teacher carefully placed the dry ice that he had obtained from the grocery store into a towel that served as an insulator. The baseball-sized chunk of dry ice was then passed around the classroom for students to touch quickly to feel the immediate burning sensation if they dared. I think everyone gave it a quick touch, realizing that one touch was enough to learn the lesson. I noted the timidity of my classmates, particularly that of one of the toughest boys in the class. I sensed an opportunity, and it soon came.

The teacher presented a challenge. He said that he would give anyone ten dollars if they held the dry ice for ten minutes. I knew that holding the dry ice would hurt, but I didn't know that it would cause serious injury. Ten-year-olds tend to trust their teachers, and this first male teacher of ours had made science interesting. I raised my hand to accept the challenge. As he approached my desk, I held out my right hand. He placed the dry ice in my hand, and I held it, palm up, gripping the dry ice like a baseball. The pain during the first minute was intense; for dry ice strangely enough creates a burn-type of injury as it rapidly begins to destroy tissue. Destructive frostbite follows in seconds. I am sure that the teacher expected me to quit, but we had entered a test of stubborn wills.

As the second minute progressed slowly, the harsh surface burning pain was changing into a much deeper aching pain of a higher magnitude. I was already sweating under my arms from the ongoing trauma, but I knew that I could do this. At two and a half minutes the teacher came to his senses and said: "I think that's enough." He then removed the dry ice from my hand. As he gently grabbed my fingers to open my grip further, my fingers would not move. They were frozen approximately one-third of the way through the flesh, as was my palm. The rigid whiteness looked ominous. He took me into the hall where there was a water fountain, and he ran water over my hand until my fingers could move. We then went on a tour of three of the other six classrooms in the Roosevelt School where he pointed out to the other teachers what I had done. Their returned looks were not that of favor for either of us.

By lunch time when the pain was still intense and tissue damage was becoming evident, a trip to the doctor became necessary. Doctor Coutu was outraged, not at me but at the teacher. His best estimate was that if I had held the dry ice for another thirty seconds I would have lost all of my fingers, and at sixty more seconds I would have lost my hand. The huge blisters that were slowly beginning to form would eventually burst a week or so later, soaking the large bandage that fully encased my hand. In subsequent examinations Dr. Coutu snipped away much dead tissue with surgical scissors. My hand was bandaged for a full three and a half weeks, during which time I completed my class lessons as best I could by writing with my left hand. It was months before I recovered full use. My hand continued to bother me somewhat even into my high school years, but there was no permanent damage.

The teacher's father later approached my dad to apologize for the poor judgment and actions of his son. Nothing was ever said to me by way of apology. One can only imagine what a stunt like that would result in now—probably national headlines and for sure a substantial lawsuit if not criminal charges. There were no repercussions for the teacher. I still feel that he owes me $2.50 for the two and a half minutes. He had stopped the test, not me. Neither my father nor my mother ever confronted him; it was just one of those things that happen as a boy is growing up.

The physical challenge of something like the dry ice episode while intense and difficult paled in significance compared to the silent and hidden battles within. That ill-defined struggle doesn't lend itself to understanding or explanation, and recognizing that in comparison the one is worse than the other may begin to convey the relentless intensity of battles within the soul and spirit.

The minister who had attempted to counsel me in high school was unable to help me, and he had thought it best that I travel up the counseling ladder further, which was never done. Coincidentally, his wife taught English at our high school. One assignment that she gave the class involved writing a short story about our idea of Utopia—that mythical place of perfection ideally suited for each of us. That assignment was one of the few in high school where I applied myself. I allowed myself to consider what I might really want; for although I was selfish, my needs and my wants were strangely out of focus. The selfishness that I knew was too shallow, too unfulfilling, too irrelevant.

For the assignment I tried to tap into something with greater meaning. I wrote an involved story about being a living, disembodied presence where infinity and eternity, though each by definition without limits, nevertheless were expanding with my consciousness being part of and grasping the entirety of it all. It was a journey into limitless knowledge and understanding, and my ability to receive this knowledge and understanding expanded exponentially as with light coming from a source that was not hampered even by the restrictive speed of light itself. I received a C for what was the spiritual equivalent of the opposite of the theory of celestial black holes before any of us had even heard of black holes. Classmates who (literally) wrote of tropical islands with limitless quantities of ice cream or equivalent stories received the better grades. Admittedly, this puzzled me.

I had first shown the writing to the minister, and he had told me to let him know if his wife didn't give me a good grade for the paper. He and I had smiled at our mutual understanding. Nevertheless, it was probably better for all of us that I never raised the issue. There was something about that woman that I didn't trust. I couldn't say that she disliked me, but something wasn't right. Malicious or cleverly controlling people raised my defenses, and often those who struck me this way could also sense my inner disapproval of them—making me both a threat and a challenge to them.

I don't know if it was weeks or months later, but there came a day when I first realized how potentially dangerous I was. In some ways I had certainly already known this about myself, but the feelings of rage soon rose to match the potential within. Others should have been frightened. Although I had developed somewhat of a reputation as a borderline renegade, I could fit in with the most popular and most accomplished kids in school. I could also head the other direction and look for trouble, which too many times I did, sometimes encouraging unwitting participants to cross the line and join me. High school was not a time of rejection for me—I was not a social outcast. Some people were not sure how to take me, but school had never been a place of complete dread for me apart from a few times when life and other circumstances combined to overwhelm me. Yet publicly, I was very shy in many ways, and I despised my frequent blushing. My face refused to let me hide even the smallest embarrassment.

For our enlightenment, the teacher had decided to show our class her pictures of some of the great works of art. She opened a large book of her own that she had brought to class with a picture of Michelangelo's statue of David in his naked splendor with his genitals displayed. Perhaps I blushed slightly, I don't recall. Then she held the book open, singled me out, walked right up to my desk, forced the book inches from my face, and demanded my agreement by asking, "Isn't this beautiful, Larry?" I was crippled with embarrassment and turned a bright red. She had unwittingly ventured into a parallel hidden world where my secret history of shame and helplessness ran deep. To their wonderful credit, my kind classmates never said anything about this to me, never teased me. But I can say with absolute certainty that if they had tried to compound the shame and if God had not intervened in my thinking and protected that woman, her life would have hung in the balance. I knew what the ultimate revenge was, and eliminating her was not far from my heart. This is a troubling and ugly revelation to admit, but it is essential to understanding that there are trip points for troubled individuals. Toying with the dignity of another person can be a dangerous sport. Our headlines all too often tell us this today.

A separate situation in a different teacher's class the year prior had also nearly produced a dangerous confrontation, but this one was markedly different since the personally malicious element was absent on his part. I was one of the last students to speak a word out of turn as the teacher was trying to bring order to the slightly disruptive class. It must have already been a day of frustration for him. The man was not noted for his patience, and in his mind I obviously had not obeyed soon enough. I cannot argue that no discipline was deserved, but for me deliberate humiliation was unacceptable. The punishment that he chose was unfitting for any boy of fifteen, especially for one who had worked the previous two full summers doing jobs normally performed by men. I was told to come to the front of the class and sit down in the corner. While this may seem an insignificant punishment or a fitting command by a stern disciplinarian, it was not acceptable for me. Twenty push-ups or an extra assignment I could accept, but not being shamed like a kindergarten child in front of my peers. I was not disrespectful or rude, but I answered carefully and firmly, "No, you are not going to make a fool out of me."

He became enraged, and very nearly lost control. In those days, teachers were sometimes physical with students, and I half-expected him to try to physically force me into compliance. He could have beaten me to death, and I would not have submitted. My decision was final, and I regretted the impasse. I can't remember what followed after that—this may have been the time that I was assigned to my own private study hall for the remainder of the school year. At any rate, there was no physical confrontation. I never held that situation against the man. He had acted out of understandable frustration and not sadistic malice. I regretted the embarrassment that I had caused him in front of the other students. I do not know if he was ever able to forgive me for not submitting to his authority.

One more confrontation with a teacher deserves mention. Miss Rigler was a fine teacher and one who was exceptionally interested in the progress and well-being of her students. One day she overheard me say something rude to another student in a joke gone awry. I was out of line, and I knew it as soon as the words escaped my mouth. She addressed the situation properly in class, giving me the appropriate rebuke for my insensitivity, and then she returned to the subject being studied and resumed teaching. I respected this lady, and after class was dismissed I stayed to apologize personally to her for my behavior. Tears were in my eyes, and then in hers as I spoke. She was a great teacher. I was not continually bent on evil as a kid, I just needed some understanding.

At the end of the day this was the child and the young man seen by most people, and perhaps this was the young boy my grandmother had seen years prior when she thought that her grandson might even someday become a minister—a sensitive child, wanting to do right, conflicted, troubled when he disappointed others, and spiritually responsible. I had an expectation of perfection for myself, and I fell woefully short of that impossible goal. I believed that perfection would bring acceptance and understanding. Without it I was doomed, and I might as well head the other direction.

Chapter Two

Rivers of Darkness

The tugboat charged up the Harvey Canal toward me that summer in 1973. The canal had been built to provide access to industrial and inland areas across the Mississippi River from New Orleans, Louisiana, but this night it was my escape route back to the river. The tug had seemed to come out of nowhere, and the race was on.

Things were happening fast that dark night. Having never drawn my .357 magnum revolver against the search team that had quickly scrambled to the riverbank, I had instead found myself racing against the tugboat that was bearing down on me as it clearly wanted my part of the approach to the river. I narrowly avoided being overrun as I swam on my back holding the package that promised to hold the extorted money. With the tug then passing between me and the riverbank, I knew that I was at least temporarily on the other side of the action and briefly in a safe zone as the flashlights from the search team began to bob in and through the bushes and trees along the riverbank. Seeing no boat participating in the extortion pick-up, they had assumed that I was on foot, which had been my intended diversion. My growing concern was that a small search boat might be my next challenge, but for now the search team's operational focus was away from me.

I continued swimming and ripping open the plastic wrap to thoroughly flood the contents of the package in the event that explosives or electronic tracking devices had been implanted by the law enforcement personnel involved. I doubted there were any explosives inside because of the complicated legalities and liabilities, but regardless it was something that I had considered. I had fully expected an electronic device, and in fact it was now obvious that by removing the package I had somehow triggered the search team's race to the scene.

That night Old Man River was my friend. The tugboat's searchlight scanned the west side of the canal bank near the area where I had made the pick-up. The scanning was either coincidentally part of the tug's normal navigation procedure or it was deliberately assisting the team that had been deployed to catch me. She was moving fast. As the tug left the Harvey Canal and then headed upriver, its searchlight continued to scan the riverbank along with the ground team. The noise from the throbbing diesels began to diminish as the tug continued its course upriver.

I never learned if the tugboat's presence was a coincidence in timing or part of a coordinated plan to catch me. At any rate, the tug very nearly did get me. The large propellers would have shredded me as if I were in a giant blender if the timing had been only seconds different. But that had not been the first close call within the previous few minutes.

The decision to proceed with the crime had been made with calculation and deliberation. I was not filled with a particular overwhelming malice at the time, but rather I was fed up with a general sense of continuing frustration with life. It was a poor excuse, but there were other reasons—though none worthy—that were nevertheless more driving. The element of danger was appealing, but as a commercial deep sea diver I was already satisfying to some degree the need to be close to the edge of life. I also needed the money, but my demands relative to the risk were minor. I had hoped that the seemingly modest sum of a $30,000 demand would dissuade South Central Bell and the legal authorities from mounting an extensive operation to catch me. (As hard as this is to believe, this amount would be almost $150,000 in today's equivalent dollars adjusted for inflation.) My concern was that it was so small a demand that they would dismiss my threats as an ill-conceived prank. They hadn't.

On another front, my reestablished fragile relationship with Beth, a young woman whom I had first met in Cleveland in 1970, had left me feeling as a poor provider with the slow start of my diving career. A financial boost would have helped with the ongoing house renovation and her mounting medical bills. Furthermore, because of recent legal events that were rapidly coming into play, perhaps it was simply seeing that trying to play by the rules was not proving promising. Also, while somewhat embarrassing to admit for implications regarding the male ego, the James Bond movies of the 1960's and early 1970's likely had some part in contributing to my daring escapade. As I said, there were no good reasons.

Root issues were there though that had continued to gnaw at me from within, and these presented a greater motivation than some of the frivolous reasoning above. I had completed high school in three and a half years, having enough credits to graduate halfway through my senior year. I had lacked only second semester English—four full years of English were required at our school, so during the first half of my senior year I had taken a supplemental correspondence course in English to satisfy what would be the last outstanding curriculum requirements for graduation. I had wanted to quit school and join the Air Force, but the recruiter was a strong advocate persuading me to see things through to early completion.

I enlisted at seventeen and completed basic training at Lackland Air Force Base in Texas well before my classmates had graduated from high school. When they had their graduation ceremony I was already at Lowry Air Force Base in Denver, Colorado, being trained in electronics having passed the security clearance requirements for the Top Secret classification for my field. Even a high school classmate who had his honesty challenged by me when I thought that he had overcharged me for a bottle of whiskey had spoken well of me to the investigators. Sometimes you enjoy far more grace than you deserve.

I had selected the Air Force because I was quite certain that I would be unable to meet the physical requirements for the Army or Marines. My strength and general toughness were okay, but my asthma prevented me from being able to perform extended runs. I honestly didn't think that I could run with a pack on my back for five miles—I was good for about a mile, and then shortness of breath began to take its toll. This never seemed to be something that I could overcome with any measure of success.

While others in 1965 during the Vietnam era fretted over the draft, at seventeen I had lied about my asthma and passed the Air Force physical. I had lied to get into the service, while some others were lying to stay out. Another positive consideration for enlisting in the Air Force was that having believed the recruiter, I thought that I might receive a better education in that branch. Somehow this took the sting out of appearing to be a failure compared to my classmates who would be going on to college as a prelude to promising careers. Our class definitely had some high achievers. A less thoughtful analysis had kept me from joining the Navy—I didn't like their uniforms.

When I entered advanced training after completing basic electronics at Lowry AFB, I finally learned the exact nature of our particular field. I was dismayed to learn that our specialty had no related wartime mission. Our field was completely separate from events taking place in Vietnam. I then attempted to transfer into the Army into their warrant officer program, hoping eventually to fly a forward observer plane scouting in Vietnam or to become involved in anything more heroic in my mind than electronic babysitting, even though if I really wanted to flatter myself I could call myself a spy in a classified electronics field. However, the Air Force had already invested enough resources in my training that transferring was not an option.

My disappointment compounded when six of us out of our class of eight students were arbitrarily selected to become instructors at Lowry. At eighteen years of age I learned that I would be teaching some men nearly twice my age who had transferred to our field—this was not what I had hoped for. For one thing, speaking in front of a group was for me more terrifying than the thought of being shot at. In hindsight, my job assignment was of course something that I should have been extremely grateful for, but young men often have their own preferred agenda.

I was able to spend my final year in the Air Force in Chiang Mai, Thailand, in an operational role. Again, we had no connection to the war that was only two countries to the east, but at least being in Thailand was an adventure. It was excellent duty, embarrassingly easy and comfortable compared to the life of a soldier serving in Vietnam on the front lines. Some of us befriended the local Thais who participated in the rough sport of Thai kick boxing. These quick fighters who were well short of my six-foot height became visitors a few times to our quarters. They eagerly provided me with a few lessons—I suspect it was fun teaching the bigger American that smaller men could be very tough. There had never been any doubt in my mind after having watched some of their bouts. I remember my shins being mighty sore after our sessions. Fortunately, they were not there to win, but to share friendship and teach their sport to the curious foreigner. They appreciated the genuine good will and the respect that I had for them. Although I did not know it at the time, their lessons would later prove invaluable to me.

I was discharged from the Air Force two months prior to the completion of my four years. Several of us had been offered what was called an "early out", and I accepted this so that I might take a job waiting for me in Cleveland, Ohio. It was December, 1968, and I had returned to Billings, Montana, where my parents had moved after I had joined the Air Force. Other than stopping for a few naps along the way, I had made the first leg of the journey driving 2,400 miles non-stop from Travis AFB forty-five miles outside of San Francisco to Cleveland for the job interview. My future was on course. I now had only to spend a few days visiting my parents, pack my stored belongings, and head back to Cleveland to begin my civilian career working as an electronics technician for the Warner & Swasey Company at their research center based in Solon, Ohio. My plan was to simultaneously attend night school in Cleveland to begin studying toward a degree in electrical engineering.

It was good to finally be twenty-one years old and be able to enter bars legally and enjoy the nightlife. Denver had had a drinking age of eighteen for 3.2% beer, and Thailand had no restrictions for us, but being twenty-one was the last completed hurdle for leaving my youth behind me. This was a time of transition, and opportunities awaited me as my brief stay in Billings was drawing to a close.

The Midway Nightclub in Billings was known for its bands, dancing, and good times. I went there one evening, proud of having completed my military service. The last thing I wanted was trouble, and I had only intended on having a drink or two at the bar, listening to the band, and perhaps even dancing with someone if the opportunity arose. Having completed my enlistment was a cause for solemn reflection and subdued celebration.

It was a time when racial tensions were high among some people—for me this had never been an issue of consequence. Montana was new to an influx of black people, and it was likely that the colleges and the medical community in Billings were the main draws for this new diversity. Although Billings was a city that was progressing in this sense, on its fringes in some areas it was still a rough cowboy town where weekend barroom fights were not uncommon. Any excuse—even race—was enough to start things rolling. This night proved to be no different. A black man was shooting pool with one or two other people. He was quiet, polite, and creating no conflicts. Three men singled him out—I had seen this coming, and I didn't like where I knew it was heading.

I had already taken off my watch and was weighing the odds; they were not good. Of the three men, one was my size: about six foot tall and about one hundred and seventy pounds—he was the one I was the least concerned about. The second man was perhaps three or four inches shorter, stocky as a bull, and the sleeves of his T-shirt were swollen out with muscled biceps. The third man was exceptionally large. He stood almost a full head taller than anyone in the crowded bar, and I am sure that he weighed well over two hundred and fifty pounds—and it wasn't fat. His head was large—compared to many in the bar he was a Goliath. The two larger men were not simply ornery boys; I estimated that they were between 30 and 35 years of age. Their wives were with them. I learned later that they had served as strong-arm men for a local union. They were serious trouble.

They approached the black man and told him to leave. He gave a disappointed sigh and shrug of his shoulders, slowly laid down his pool cue, and was clearly intending to leave while perhaps trying to delay his departure. I could tell that he wanted to move at his own pace to maintain a trace of dignity. Unfortunately, he didn't move fast enough for the three thugs. They began working him over, and it quickly was turning ugly. Although the bar was full and all attention had turned to the fight, no one was stepping in to even the odds. The man went down, and kicking was started. Decency would not allow me to ignore the brutality. I did not want a fight, so I stepped in and said politely, "Look, it doesn't take three of you guys."

Their attention was immediately diverted from the man on the floor and now focused on this clean-cut young man who dared interrupt their fun. Somehow the black man made it outside during the distraction that I had provided. I was to be the sport for them now. There was one brief moment when I considered going on the offensive. My mind was working at lightning speed. I might have been able to kick the stocky man in the groin, almost simultaneously roll to the left and punch the large man in the groin, and then take out the man who was my size, hopefully being swift enough to return to the others before they recovered. It might have worked, but if it didn't, I knew that I would be in serious trouble. Prudence seemed the better part of valor, and I elected to use the minimal resistance necessary to survive rather than give them cause to seriously hurt me.

A few punches were thrown, and I blocked some and was hit with others. The stocky man then began to take me on by himself. He attempted a choking headlock type of maneuver, leaving me no choice but to increase my level of resistance. I peeled away from him and managed to get him pinned under the extended bar countertop. I let loose a barrage of punches, oblivious to the other two men who had allowed me a moment of one-on-one action with their partner. He wasn't doing well, so they stepped back in.

I then caught a punch or two in the back of the head from the others, which halted my attack on the stocky man. From then on the fight continued its slower, more deliberate cruel pace. I began to catch a few more punches as I slowly backed out the door. Running away had never even occurred to me. The wives of the two larger men were pleading with them to stop, but they were having fun. It was the big man who enjoyed it the most. He was a bully—a coward reveling in his glory. As the fight moved outside, I continued to block some punches, continued to get hit with others. One punch completely took out one of my two buck teeth, root and all. My other front tooth was left pointing in a new direction, and it would eventually be lost also as a consequence of the fight.

It was the lessons from the Thai boxers though that had proven the most valuable for my defense. I successfully blocked several kicks, and I never went down. I have always wondered if I should have given 100% in that fight and tried for the early offensive that I had first contemplated. . .to this day I have such thoughts. This wasn't Hollywood though. I have relived that fight far too many times.

The fight finally ended outside after they had had enough fun. About that same time a man came out from the bar with a club. I assumed that he was going to start on me next. I said with a lisp from my missing front tooth and the damages to my mouth, "Hey, man, I'm leaving," hoping that he would let me go without further fighting.

It was the bartender, and he said, "I came to help you." It was too late, but at least someone had finally found some courage that night. I left, continuing to believe in the system and not wanting to take justice into my own hands. I had served my country well in the Air Force, and words like duty and honor meant something to me.

I went to my parent's house and stepped into the kitchen from the side door. I called out to my dad that I needed to see him, and I told my mother to stay in the living room. Instead, they both approached, and there were sad groans as they saw my face. I asked what hospital I should go to, and my dad and I made a brief visit there.

We then went to the police station; for I was going to follow the rules and press charges. From the Billings police we heard that the Midway Nightclub was not in their jurisdiction. I was more than a little skeptical of their claim. We then went to the Yellowstone County Sheriff's Office, where again I was essentially ignored. My dad and I pressed harder, and it was finally agreed that they would investigate. Two sheriff's deputies drove to the bar, while at the same time my dad and I drove there.

When all of us entered the bar it was what you would expect for a packed nightclub on a weekend. People were mingling, drinking, laughing, talking, dancing. Across the crowd I saw the largest of the men involved as he towered over others—the one who had enjoyed beating me the most. I pointed him out, and he was escorted over. When questioned, he denied there had been a fight. He was rubbing his hand at the same time and my dad spotted the blood on his knuckles: "What's that blood if there was no fight?"

He smiled a sickening smirk and answered, "Oh, that's nothing." The deputies had no further questions of anyone beyond asking the large man if there had been a fight. My beaten face and missing/rearranged teeth failed to be sufficient evidence.

Out of the full nightclub, not one person would come forward to assist in the so-called investigation. The deputies themselves were not interested in pursuing the matter further. In fact, I later learned that there was some fear locally of the two main bullies. And so the books were closed on the case, never really having been opened. This now was what I saw when I saw the world: cowards could intimidate others and get their way, people who tried to do what was right were punished or ignored for their efforts, and nobody cared. I had served four years in the military, and this was my welcome back to civilian life.

That night a former rage returned, and this time it was there to stay. Revenge might take years, but it would be mine when I wanted it. I learned the names of the two larger men, but it was only the biggest man whom I wanted—I had already proven myself with the stocky one, and he knew this. The third man who was my size was essentially irrelevant. It was the big man who would be mine—he had been the one who had most enjoyed giving me the beating.

Before the extortion attempt I made two secret trips to Montana from Louisiana to try to even the score. On the first trip I found the man I wanted, waited until he got off work, followed him and his wife to a restaurant, and then followed him home. In the early hours of the morning I then put several well-placed shots into his parked pickup. I was not ready to take him out yet—it was still too close to the time of the fight, and I could well become a suspect. I simply wanted to give him something to think about.

About another year later I was ready to make my move. Initial checks had indicated to me that he was still in Billings. I had grown a beard as an unconvincing disguise for the occasion. After completion I would immediately shave. I went to another bar that he supposedly still routinely visited to start my surveillance. My intention initially was only to find him, check him out, and then later pick my opportunity. I was now confident that after the elapsed time there was no way that he would recognize or remember me. I walked into the bar and saw him sitting there. Years of unbridled hatred started to erupt within and my intended plans were forgotten. I walked slowly and deliberately toward him. He was unaware of me. Although he was sitting at the bar, his stool was turned around and his back was to the bar. He was looking to the left of me at others. That large head was my target—for my fists, not for the .357 magnum pistol I had in my car that had been my intended weapon of choice to use later when I would have the element of surprise and overwhelming force on my side. Confronting him in the bar was not my plan, but I was driven to attack.

As I got within the last few steps the curtains of blinding hatred were raised, and I saw to my shock that this was not the man. He had the same type of head and general appearance, but this man was closer to my size; he was not the Goliath. It was clearly a case of mistaken identity, and I had very nearly attacked an innocent man.

Shaken by my incompetence and error but still determined, I continued on for a day or two in my search. I learned that my intended victim had moved to Alaska and that my information that he was still in Billings was wrong. That was the end of my second and final attempt to even the score. Something would later happen to remove the hatred before I acted again, but that would not be for another seven years. In all that time the burning hatred for him had never dissipated. I had still intended at some point to set out to find him again. Whether I would have or not I do not know for certain—all it would have taken would have been for the right trip-point to push me over the edge. I wanted this to happen.

When I decided to proceed with the extortion plan five years after the bar fight, my opinion of law enforcement was not the highest. I respected individual officers of merit, but I despised the injustices of the system at large. Hatred burned within me. In the months preceding the extortion attempt, another poor excuse encouraged me to resort to crime. I had been arrested on January 28, 1973. A used appliance dealer in Covington, Louisiana, had filed false charges against me after I had angrily confronted him following the failure of all three appliances that I had purchased from him. One by one the units that I purchased with my very limited funds all failed, and his verbal guarantee had proven as untrustworthy as the washer, dryer, and refrigerator. I had anticipated and accepted that perhaps one of the three might prove faulty, but two failures had sorely tested me and led me to file a small claims suit when he refused to make repairs as promised. When the third appliance failed, my fuse had been lit.

It was a Saturday afternoon. I drove to the dealer's home out of which he was operating his business and knocked loudly and angrily on his door. A child of a visiting friend of his came to the door. I asked the boy through the screen door, "Is Mr. Crawford here?" Three men started to come forward from a back room in response to the commotion; the first was Crawford.

Seeing him, I asked heatedly, "Are you going to come and fix the refrigerator now, or am I going to have to file another small claims suit for that piece of s___?" He knew that I meant business.

His response was immediate. He turned to the other two men behind him and said excitedly, "Come here! Come here! I want you to see this man. I want you to see his face."

I knew exactly what he was doing. I should have known better than to deal with him in the first place when two months prior he had proudly told me of a scam that he had been part of in Texas. Someone was involved in a legal dispute with him and filed a lawsuit against him. He had boasted to me how he countered with a phony lawsuit, and that eventually both were dropped in a negotiated agreement giving him the dishonest victory. His plan now was obvious. He wanted these men in his legal corner, as well as perhaps to fight with me if it was now going to come to that.

The screen door was never opened. I backed away, but I wasn't finished. Wanting the fight, wanting to let loose my anger, I put out my challenge:

"If you want trouble, you know where I live. I'll be there in five minutes." I hoped they would come. If anything was going happen, it was going to be on my property, not his. He would gain no legal advantage over me.

I raced home the two miles to Abita Springs to prepare. I burst through the front door. I rapidly loaded my pistol and my rifle. Beth was terrified at my anger and the pending danger. I told her exactly what to do. She was not to come outside under any circumstances. If she heard shots, she was to call the police.

Fully armed, I ran halfway up my wooded driveway to pick the spot for my ambush in the heavy cover. This fight with three men would this time be on my terms, not theirs. I had no doubt who would prevail. I waited for perhaps two hours. I should have known that cowards do not come forth against strength. I returned home. Although I kept my weapons loaded and handy that night, I was fairly certain there would now be no fight.

The following morning, a Sunday, a deputy from the St. Tammany Parish Sheriff's Department drove up my driveway. My first dreaded and bizarre thought was that perhaps someone had killed Crawford that previous night in a cruel coincidence, and that I was now going to be the fall guy. This wouldn't have surprised me; I wasn't keen on the fairness of life. The deputy brought no such news, and for this much I was relieved. However, I heard the words: "Mr. Whited, I have three warrants for your arrest."

The clever and unscrupulous Crawford had filed charges following my angry visit the previous afternoon. The charges included the following: (1) Simple Assault, (2) Disturbing the Peace & Using Obscene Language, and (3) Breaking & Entering. I sighed and began to explain the situation. Law enforcement officers routinely hear concocted stories as lies weave in and out of explanations, but the deputy listened patiently to my side. It was clear that he believed me as I related the entire story, including admitting to my anger and the profanity that I had used (more than admitted here). Nevertheless, the warrants had been issued and his duty was required. He kindly asked, "Do you want to ride with me, or do you want to drive yourself down?" It was an extraordinary courtesy afforded me at risk to his own position.

I tried to reassure Beth that things would be okay, but knowing that I was being arrested was terrifying to her in her fragile world. I was supposed to be her knight in shining armor who would always protect her. It was the role I had learned from my father. The setting in the woods was her fairytale retreat from reality.

I elected to drive, and I followed the deputy to the St. Tammany Parish Court House in downtown Covington. After we arrived but before we entered, the deputy came up to me. He had a troubled look on his face. He had been in radio contact with the Sheriff's office, and this was the explanation that I was given: "Larry, there is no such charge as 'Breaking and Entering' in Louisiana, so they have amended it to the next closest thing. You are being charged with Simple Burglary, which is a felony." There was no investigation, no evidence, no truth. It didn't matter. The charges had been filed, and my arrest was required.

Inside the Court House the deputy extended a further kindness to me. I was standing right beside him when on his own he called up a judge that Sunday morning and said, "Judge, I've got a real bull s___ deal here. Can you set bond for a man charged with simple burglary?" The judge did not question the deputy's judgment, and bond was set for $1,000. Since I didn't have the $1,000, a bondsman was called. I never had to be jailed, and within a few hours I was headed back home after the booking and all the paperwork was completed.

Interestingly, when the bondsman heard the story, his eyes opened wide and his mouth dropped half-open. "Is that SOB back in town?" The bondsman had entrusted Crawford to cover the payments on some property several years prior while he was overseas on an extended job. The payments were never made, and Crawford enjoyed the free housing. The bondsman lost his property when it was repossessed.

That evening when I was back at home, the events of the previous twenty-four hours took their toll on Beth. Among her other problems, not the least of which was me, she had occasional epileptic seizures. The anxiety over my arrest no doubt triggered her seizures that night. As I held her I wondered at life and all its ugliness. Here was this beautiful young woman of twenty-two, more of a child trapped in her own troubles than a woman, who was now convulsing in tortured muscle contractions as an unscrupulous man two miles away thought he was going to teach me a lesson. I didn't like what I saw when I looked at the world. I knew that I was no better and was in many ways worse, but that was hardly a point of consolation. In my mind, we all deserved to be destroyed.

I eventually proceeded with my small claims suits, losing them because there were of course no written guarantees for the appliances. His plan to drop his charges if I would drop my claims had met with my firm and uncompromising, "No deal." After paying mounting lawyer's fees related primarily to the felony charge, I was rapidly nearing the end of my willingness to play by the rules. Much to my lawyer's dismay and concern, I dismissed him. He had pleaded with me that if I was not satisfied with his counsel to please get someone else to represent me—the charges were serious. Louisiana lockup is not the kind of place where you want to do time. I instead elected to defend myself at the trial that would eventually follow—this was becoming way too personal for me.

Jail would not be an option. If I would lose, it was over; and I intended to go down fighting with a committed resolve that they could not imagine. I had felt for some time that my life was heading toward my own personal Armageddon. Rational thoughts would be followed by irrational thoughts. I wanted to lose the restrictive control that nearly always kept me in check in spite of my wanting to explode. Perhaps this was finally the time.

Case number 039141 in St. Tammany Parish ended favorably for me after all the frustrations and concerns when the reduced charges that I was finally arraigned on of Simple Assault and Simple Battery failed to produce a conviction. (The felony charge had eventually been dropped.) The prosecutor could never have seriously considered the merits of the case nor done any investigation. I had paid the price of lost wages for some diving jobs that I had been forced to turn down because of various legal appointments, and both Beth and I had endured much turmoil because of this fiasco that had lasted eight months. I had never even been interviewed beyond my first conversation with the deputy. The trial on September 25, 1973, had followed by about one month my extortion attempt. Had I died in that crime, the trial in Covington would not have been necessary. The timing was far from being a coincidence.

After the tugboat was well clear and headed upriver, I swam further out into the dark waters of the Mississippi. The swimming was largely effortless, as had been my approach to the area from four miles upstream. The current of the river moves steadily and swiftly along, and my wetsuit with its natural buoyancy allowed me to float comfortably past docked barges and other facilities. I had about another mile to go before I would swim to the riverbank where I had stowed my dry clothes to allow me to proceed with the final phase of my escape. But because of the activities that had preceded the encounter with the tugboat, I now knew that a full-scale search was underway. I decided to modify my plan and exit the river prematurely and enter an industrial area to wait for a few hours before continuing downstream.

After I crawled out of the water while maintaining a low profile, I completed opening the package that I was still carrying. Inside was an electronic device, as I had anticipated there would be. Keeping in mind that this was 1973, the device was probably not very sophisticated, although it would have been the best available to the FBI at the time. I hoped that flooding it had quickly disabled any searching and locating capabilities. I smashed the flooded unit on the riprap (rocks lining the riverbank) to completely destroy it, and then threw it back into the river. The neatly stacked and banded small bundles were not my hoped for cash. Not surprisingly they were only cut paper. I smiled and half laughed at the situation—it had been a lot of work for nothing, but at least it had been an exciting night.

I entered the industrial area that afforded some good hiding places. I settled down in my wetsuit, getting as comfortable as I could for a wait for an hour or two. I had until daylight to complete my escape. There was less than a mile to go. I had no idea of the forces committed to capturing me.

Chapter Three

No Small God

We had moved from North Dakota to Montana when Kathy was six and a half years old and I was two and a half. In a large part the move was considered necessary because our affections were being disproportionately enjoyed by our Aunt Jennie and Uncle Harold.

When my dad was in the Army in World War II and Jennie and Harold had provided a home for my mother and my sister, it had been natural for a little girl to be drawn to the man who was right there and who so loved and adored her. These early years preceded my coming into the picture, and there developed a uniquely loving and everlasting relationship between Kathy and her Uncle Harold. It was the knowledge of his love that carried her through many of her own dark hours. It was this same knowledge of Jennie and Harold that helped restrain my hand from pulling the string going to the trigger on the rifle in the basement starting four years after our move to Montana.

There had always been something exceptionally special about both Jennie and Harold, a childless couple with so much love to give. At each of their funerals which were separated by nineteen years, it was humbling to hear of all the stories of how they had helped so many people during their lives. Harold died in 1970, and it was a full fifteen years later when I finally learned from Jennie that he had spent many hours on his knees in prayer for me, sensing that I was in great trouble. I can only think of such a man with tears in my eyes.

After the war in which my dad had been shot in the arm during a tough mission outside of Manila in the Philippines, he and my mother restarted their lives together in North Dakota where they bought their first bar and built their home. They knew success in those early years. When the disturbing realization that the love of their children was being enjoyed by the aunt and uncle who lived directly across the driveway from them began to take its toll, the move to Montana followed. Kathy, being so close to Uncle Harold, was devastated emotionally when the move came. Her pain extended into the following years when the void was not filled except during the infrequent visits with Harold and Jennie on the 4th of July and Christmas. Six months between visits can seem forever to a child. We know that it also seemed forever to Harold and Jennie.

Harold and Jennie were not the only relatives who were supposed to be kept at arm's length emotionally. Our dad's sister, Auntie Florence, also came under direct fire if we dared show her too much affection. Florence, having never married, found her close-by niece and nephew to be in some ways the children that she too never had. Coincidentally, the adult daughter of a highly respected schoolteacher in Red Lodge had said concerning my sister and me: "If ever I could adopt two children, it would be Kathy and Larry." It was interesting that others would see us in such light and want to take us as their own. We were either especially wonderful children, or children seen in need. We didn't feel all that great about ourselves, so the vote comes down firmly on the side of recognized need.

Seemingly misplaced love was a source for a lifetime of bitter conflicts within our family. The tension from this deep resentment constantly hung in the air like an ill-defined cloud of swamp gas; there was no escaping it, and it permeated everything. While in some respect there was recognition of the undeniable kindness of Jennie and Harold, there was also something very unhealthy conveyed in the tone of our mother's willingness to share us with them. The real message that far too often found its way into both words and actions spoke not of shared love but of stolen affections and the unfair obligations involved with sharing. Jennie and Harold knew both the spoken and unspoken boundaries, but they would not abandon their love for us. They carefully navigated these constantly troublesome emotional waters, whenever possible deferring to our parents while yet giving us their unselfish and steadfast love.

Our dad was not in the least mean, cold, or abusive; and in fact he regularly earned praise and recognition for being a good man, a man of integrity. Running a bar did not tarnish his reputation—everyone knew that if a man forgot a twenty-dollar bill on the bar he would get it back. People liked my dad, and he liked people. However, he did not have a personality that allowed him to connect with his two emotionally needy children. He was an exceptionally loyal and devoted husband, and it was this trait that others saw in abundance. We were often told of how much our father was respected. Strangely, this praise at times could hurt, for there was no place for us in this equation, and it amplified the distance and the void that we felt. Nevertheless, it was good having a dad who was respected.

Mom was also quick to praise Dad. Although she lived in the shadow of his respect and received no such recognition for herself, she was the driving emotional force for the family and the magnet for attention and a demanded love. She was seemingly the weaker person, but emotionally she was certainly the more powerful—and denying her of what she wanted invited her tears and resulting vindictive compulsions. As children, my sister and I were warned repeatedly: "You just wait until you have kids and they treat you the way that you treat me. Just wait, your turn is coming." The words were part of an emotional arsenal used against us to punish us for various offenses often linked in some imaginative way to our affections for Jennie and Harold or for anything not directly supportive of her needs. She wanted and intended for us to pay for this betrayal. Any love or attention shared elsewhere robbed her of her due.

The intended and timeless message struck deep within our hearts: "You are going to be hated someday, and you deserve it." We had failed to give her the love that she needed, and for this there would be no forgiveness. The often repeated words: "Just wait, your turn is coming," have hung like a curse over us; much more so for Kathy because they were words against the motherhood that she herself would someday have and which she would desperately try to perform perfectly. Kathy could write her own book on how these words have ripped into her heart.

When Kathy and her husband Ken were in college being helped financially through those lean years by Harold and Jennie, my mother would not allow Harold and Jennie to give a used car to their struggling niece and her husband as a much needed gift. Instead, when they had wanted to drive from North Dakota to Montana to visit Kathy and Ken and their baby to surprise them with the car, my mother demanded instead that she meet them halfway and that she would be the one to hand over the car—there would be no need for Harold and Jennie to make the entire trip themselves.

Jennie and Harold complied, and hearts were broken. Jennie's plea that: "Allie, do you think that Harold is the only uncle who has ever helped his niece?" met with no surrender. My mother delivered the car as she had planned, proudly handing over the keys. Dad understood.

Stepping back in time, it was totally out of character that I would receive the unexpected gift from my dad. He was not a religious man. Nevertheless, he respected religion, had no animosity against churches or faith, would attend Christmas services when sufficiently prodded, and he humbly called preachers "holy men" or "men of God". He did have a shrewd eye for charlatans, but he and my mother listened carefully and respectfully to many television sermons by Billy Graham in their later years.

There had been an occasion for my dad to make a trip by himself—the reason for which I now have no recollection. I would probably have been eight or nine years old at the time. When he returned he brought me the gift, which was unusual since we didn't expect to be rewarded at unscheduled occasions. Birthdays and Christmas yes, but not out of the blue. Perhaps my regular attendance at Sunday School had led my dad to think that this gift would be special for me, but the answer will forever remain a mystery. If he had shopped for it on his own as a special gift for me, all my speculation regarding him would now swirl in humble and grateful appreciation. I never thought to ask him while there was still time.

My dad handed me what appeared to be a single block of wood, about one foot square and one inch thick. I was thrilled. The rich wood promised to be something that I could work with. I already had tools of my own, plus there were the assorted tools typically collected by dads that I could now use to make something special. I had been one to make trips to the Thompson Lumberyard in Red Lodge to buy small assortments of scrap lumber when my allowance or money earned from chores would give me enough for such purchases. The Coast-to-Coast store regularly sold me nails and incidental items for my various projects—I had already earned an endearing reputation as a little worker, shoveling what had seemed to be vast quantities of snow in winter months. Local store owners treated me well and always had smiles for me.

As I received the gift I realized that it was not what I thought it was. It was not a block of wood as such, but a thin cardboard box with a paper overlay that made it look like it was wood. I hesitated, being careful not to show my disappointment, and I simultaneously wondered what might be inside. Opening the box, I found a religious plaque. Now I really was disappointed, but again I did not show this. The plaque had on the left side the historically popular (since 1941) picture of Jesus as envisioned by Warner Sallman. On the right side of the plaque was a quote from the gospel of John, verse 14:1 (KJV), in gold-colored raised letters: "Let not your heart be troubled: ye believe in God, believe also in Me." At the bottom was an inscription by the creator of the plaque: "Jesus Never Fails."

Religious plaque with verse from John 14:1

I was by no means anti-religious at the time or not interested in God. In fact, it was not uncommon for me to pour out my heart to God in lonely agony. However, I had no affection for religious objects as if they had a magical power. This is hard to describe without giving a child more credit than he deserves, but for me God was just too big and too powerful to be thought of in this way. The Ten Commandments, which I had memorized, had also made it pretty clear to me that God didn't like these kinds of things either. That was one side of the equation. On the other, I did get the message, and I did want to believe in God. If Jesus was to be part of that belief, that was fine with me, but I wasn't quite sure how He fit in. I knew of course of the cross—Sunday School had taught me this—but Jesus seemed like too much of a man. I really wanted to go straight to God. There was another world that I was very much aware of, and God seemed to be the only explanation for that other world.

I dutifully mounted the plaque on my bedroom wall, somewhat uncomfortable with looking at the face of what someone thought Jesus might look like. The gift created a conflicting obligation for me—I had to show respect for this Son of God who seemed to be quite comfortable ignoring me. The extra message that "Jesus Never Fails" frequently produced my private comeback of: "Well, He sure goofed with me." Little did I know that a quarter of a century later recollections of that long-forgotten plaque would come out of nowhere to change my life forever.

A pattern began to develop: when I felt good about reaching out to God or when in agony I could do no less than reach out to Him, I would then have the plaque displayed on my wall. When I felt empty or I felt that He was ignoring me to the point that this was too overwhelming or hurtful, the plaque would come down and be tucked away in my dresser drawer. By my high school years the plaque had found a permanent resting place somewhere out of sight and out of mind. I didn't like the feeling that someone who had seemed to let me down was still watching me. It was like discovering a hole for a surveillance camera into my mind being used by someone I wasn't sure I could trust. The saying that "Jesus Never Fails," had become a teasing jab—an invented assurance that I was obliged to agree to simply because it was expected. To me, all this spoke of a dishonest, mandated submission. I wanted to see; I wanted to touch; I wanted to believe; I wanted to experience.

I wanted God to be real. A verse from a poem that I had written when I was twelve or thirteen read, "I need to see the burning bush and view the holiness; to see my Master near by me would cure my emptiness." The plaque fell far short of giving me the assurance I needed.

Times of downward spiraling depression were increasing for me as my teens approached. I say depression, but that isn't really the best description. It was more of a desperate and lonely anguish—of the heart being too empty but at the same time filled with an invisible despair tending towards rage. My mind was turning against itself in its own hatred. There was no clear formula as to the timing of the incidents, but the times of despair that once seemed to visit me most intensely about once a year were rolling in about twice a year or more often by junior high. In high school the frequency increased further, and it was a guidance counselor who first recognized what I was otherwise able to hide from most others.

I had as much or more pride than anyone, but there was an inexplicable parallel self-loathing that stared back at me from the mirror of my own soul. I knew for certain that there was something very wrong within me, and I didn't like it. I wondered if the valleys of despair would eventually join contiguously to leave me insane with grief and anger. This had allowed me to make that pitiful wager with my friend Frank that I would be the first one to lose at life. I so regret that bet.

By the time I left my young childhood the times of sitting for extended periods with the muzzle of the loaded .22 rifle pressed against my temple were over, but now it was far more common to act on impulse and place an empty rifle—either the .22 or the larger .270 that was for deer and elk—against my head in various positions and pull the trigger to hear the relief of the tempting click. There have been times when I have trusted weapons to be empty rather than checking them; the relief was greater that way. I have shot myself multiple thousands of times. One verse from a poem I had written later in life read: "A magnum load of deadly seed—the final answer for the final need." To this day it is difficult for me to relate to people who express how much they would love to be young again. I would not want to go back into those younger years for anything.

I had reached my decision, and it was clear that my thoughts that I would kill myself before I was eighteen had been right. I wasn't racing to meet a deadline, and I would in fact gladly not have had the thoughts or feelings that plagued me, but that was not to be. For all the talk of guns, once I got beyond the times in the basement of the Beartooth Bar, the less likely it was that this would be the way that I would end my life. This was too messy, too brutal, and too ugly for those who had to live with the consequences. The often imagined bullet blasting into my brain was simply the handiest means to envision the end of all things and a desired nothingness. It was like imagining being struck by lightning, wanting to be struck by lightning, but knowing full well that that was not going to happen. Plan B, the real plan, would always be something different than a bullet unless there were no better options available.

With the Beartooth Bar now in their past, Dad was the County Assessor, having run successfully for the office. He often worked late into the evening with the lights in his corner office in the Carbon County Courthouse burning much later than those of any others. There wasn't overtime to be earned; there was work to be done. On weekends he sometimes tended bar at Richel Lodge where my mother was also working to supplement their income. Mom was then working as a waitress at this popular resort lodge nestled about twelve miles up the canyon from Red Lodge in the direction of Yellowstone Park.

My parents seldom took a real vacation. Our trips to North Dakota had always been more of an obligation for them than a vacation. Bowling trips to tournaments by one or the other might have qualified as a vacation, but the notion of going somewhere together as a couple or a family to get away and relax—unless it was a fishing trip not far from home—was not something that they considered for themselves. With Kathy and Ken attending college in Bozeman, Montana, and with four hundred dollars in dimes saved from tip change from my mother's waitressing over the years, my parents finally decided to drive to Nevada so Mom could play the slot machines. Dad would have enjoyed a game of low-stakes poker with other men given the opportunity, but this was really to let Mom have a good time. When the budgeted money was gone they would be finished with the gambling. Kathy and Ken could certainly have used some assistance, but that responsibility was considered finished by my parents when Kathy reached the age of eighteen. Friends of theirs had been making trips every once in a while to Nevada to gamble, and it was now their turn to have some fun.

I was sixteen years old when my parents took the vacation. Staying on my own was something that I was easily capable of well before I was ten, and at sixteen there wasn't the slightest concern about leaving me at home by myself. By that age my friends and I had spent many days on our own camping in the mountains, and there were times when I had camped alone. I was on my third car by then, having overhauled the first two: selling one and trading the other. I had worked the previous three summers at full-time jobs. I occasionally ran one of the service stations in Red Lodge when the owner would leave for brief trips. I had run away from home with a friend the year before using my second car, been captured in Wyoming after a four-state alert was put out for us, been returned to Montana, and had an uneasy silent understanding with my dad that we would try to respect each other until it was time that I permanently left home, which would be none too soon. Staying alone was fine; it was what I preferred.

With my parents in Nevada I had the house to myself. I cannot say for certain that this was shortly after the time that the teacher had delighted in embarrassing me in class when she had demanded that I acknowledge how beautiful the naked David was, but I do know that the timing was very close. It is a troubling coincidence as I now reflect on this.

At the time, pills seemed to be the most convenient way to end my life. A high-speed crash in my car would likely have been adequate, but there always was that terrible chance that I would survive and be paralyzed or a vegetable, trapped in the very life that I wanted to escape. A bullet could also have been effective, yet the thought of leaving a bloody mess and the mental image of splattered tissue and blood for others to remember seemed unnecessarily cruel. I was not a jumper—heights scared me, even though this fear led me to some very interesting climbs on my own. The thought of razor blades slicing into my flesh left me squirming uncomfortably. With all things considered, leaving an intact body for my family seemed more kind. While brave in some aspects, I didn't mind looking now for an easy way out. I was not keen on suffering in pain for the sake of pain, and

I saw no advantage in making my death any more miserable than it needed to be. Pills would be my choice, and I hoped this method would be quick and efficient.

My mother had asthma as I did, although for the most part I had outgrown mine by my mid-teens except for having somewhat inefficient lungs. For both her use and mine, there was always a prescription supply of pills at home. I searched for all that I could find, and I came up with eighteen tablets. Had there been fifty, I would have taken them all. I firmly believed that the eighteen would be sufficient, since often half of one of the potent pills had been all that was needed to arrest an asthma attack as a younger child. The plan was in motion.

I was impulsive in some things, yet extraordinarily methodical and deliberate in others. This was a time to be deliberate. I prepared brief letters to my parents, to Kathy, to Jennie and Harold, to my Aunt Florence, and a general letter meant for all—envisioning the audience that might need to understand the compelling lonely agony that would drive someone to do this—and hoping that they would actually even want to understand. One thing about dying—it makes you think. Although in certain cases I had considerable anger to deal with, I now sought to comfort and console everyone. Not even the love of Jennie and Harold was enough to restrain my hand this time, and with Kathy no longer at home the routine visits with them had begun to draw to a close. The games were over now—this was the time for me to act.

In the letters I explained that this was what I wanted—that this was something very well thought out, and not an act for which anyone should feel responsible. I then took small slips of paper, eighteen of them to match the number of pills, and on each slip I wrote a separate reason and then placed a pill over it on the table before me. It was a strange little ritual of indulging heartache while yet sensing coming relief. I cannot now say for sure what all those specific reasons included, but they focused on my own criticisms of myself learned from a lifetime of self-loathing, personal disappointment, assisted criticism, and simply emptiness.

As a courtesy to the undertaker, I prepared my body to the extent that I could. I had used the bathroom and taken a bath. I had clean clothes on. Everything was in order. I swallowed the pills one at a time in rapid succession. I was surprised that my heart started racing even before the last pill was taken. I then laid down on my bed to die. As the pills dissolved and entered my system, my heart began to hammer violently within my rib cage. No physical exertion in sports had ever come close to anything like this. There was absolutely no comparison.

I won't pretend to ascribe accurate times to this; I don't know the length of time that was involved. The point came when I was out of my body. I felt expanded in size and presence, being now an entity above and beyond my body. Although the room was still there visually, it presented no confines for me; things were now transpiring in a different realm. Full separation was likely only minutes away, or less. There was no fear, and there was no hope. There was only a spirit separating, no longer joined to the body below. I was given no glimpse of the other side—no tunnels with a light at the other end, no voices, no visions. There was only a solemn, prevailing awareness of the substance of my existence that was no longer within a body. This wasn't the oblivious transition into nothingness that I had expected. I was still alive, but I was approaching and beginning to enter another realm.

Then, inexplicably, there was an understanding that I must not do this. What I was doing was not right. The course was to be reversed—I was given this undeniable responsibility. This was not a time of psychological anxiety, not a time of second-guessing; it was in fact a simple yet intense understanding and mandate requiring that I comply. I began struggling to get back into my body. I concentrated on my entire presence that was then above and beyond my body and tried to draw that presence back into itself and then concentrate further and force my presence back into the physical body below. Awareness of my still throbbing heart became intense again, and I slowly completed the return back into my body. Now the physical fight ensued. The beating of my heart remained exceptionally volatile for an extended time. It was a curiosity to me that my heart had not burst.

At some point after I was fully back within my body a friend stopped by the house. I cannot recall why he entered and found me in my bedroom.

I told him what I had done. He desperately wanted to call for an ambulance, but I told him no. I tried to pace my words carefully to limit my exertion: "If I can't. . .handle this on my own. . .then I don't. . .want to make it." Although this obligation of silence placed a terrible and unfair responsibility on him, he agreed. No one was called.

With my natural curiosity and a detached objectivity, I asked him to place his hand over my heart. He was able to feel my heart hammering away. I then gently raised my arm a few inches above the bed to show him how this slight exertion greatly increased the intensity of my heartbeat. He jerked his hand away from my chest in fearful apprehension as my heart violently pounded harder. We both knew how serious this was. He didn't stay long.

Recovery would finally start to set in at some later point. I had a long and difficult night. I remained in a weakened state for three days, but I was now to reach eighteen after all. For a while at least, suicide was no longer an option. When the subject of suicide would later be mentioned by others in conversations, my disproportionately adamant stand against it caused some raised eyebrows and suspicious looks. It was almost as if I was hiding something.

The year before, when my dad and the sheriff had driven to Wyoming to escort my friend and me back to Montana after we had run away from home, meeting him was tense and awkward. I knew that I had embarrassed him in the community and brought a measure of shame to our family. I later learned that some adults had considered this a childish impulse typical of what boys sometimes do. To have viewed this as a childhood stunt was a serious miscalculation. It had been my firm intention never to return. Denver, Colorado, had been our destination for a start, and I had anticipated shoplifting or doing whatever I had to do to maintain myself until I found a situation where I could start a new life. Our plan was interrupted by an alert patrolman in Wyoming who spotted us after the call had gone out to be on the lookout for two boys from Montana in a 1950 Ford. We were pulled over, and he asked: "You boys have permission to leave home?" Shortly after that we were in a Wyoming jail awaiting an escort back to Montana.

Upon first seeing me after driving with the sheriff to Wyoming, my dad's exact words were: "Have you thought about what this would do to your mother?" That was his concern—that was all of his concern as far as I could tell. It was always all about Mom. The fact that my dad was on the verge of losing his only son forever in this committed attempt at running away had meant nothing when balanced against the needs of my mother. I knew this already, but the largely silent drive back home left me understanding this as I had never understood it before. These were the times of sacred, vaunted motherhood, and mothers were on a pedestal—especially in our family. I could not point out to my dad the things that I knew and had seen and had experienced in our home. This was his wife, the woman he loved. I was trapped in a world that demanded my respect, and I was rapidly spiraling downward as I saw too much and my mind was both imploding and exploding in self-destruction.

A year later and a week or two after my suicide attempt, my mother discovered the letters that I had not yet destroyed. Knowing that she at times searched through my belongings, I had sealed and hidden these letters well enough that I was certain that they would not be discovered. Additionally, I had thought that her searches had for the most part stopped by then. My signal traps of carefully arranged objects were no longer being moved to alert me that she was still going through my things. This was no subconscious hope for discovery—the letters were a glimpse into a special private world where no one else belonged. These reminders of my brush with death were also in their own way a fading link to the rescued life that I now had. This was as personal as it gets. The letters were within days of being destroyed, and I was very much aware that this needed to be done soon rather than risk discovery. Nevertheless, I had delayed too long.

As I entered our house after school I walked into the living room to find my mother with all of my previously addressed and sealed envelopes torn open before her. Each personal letter to others had been read. I don't recall the words that we had, but they were brief and I was exceptionally angry. It was now not unusual for me to be openly angry with her as I came to more fully realize her unhealthy impact on my life. Having my soul exposed to the one person I trusted the least in the world left me obsessed with an anger that I could do nothing with. Certainly I knew that this situation was painful for her—but I did not want this to become yet another situation where life would have to revolve around her, as it was bound to do. It was too late though, this was going to be all about her. My dad was of course told of the letters.

Later that night my dad took me for a short ride. He was sad, genuinely hurt. These were not the kinds of issues that he knew how to handle. In his sad bewilderment he managed to say: "I guess you've had it rough too." If only he could have left off the telling word "too".

The "too" spoke volumes to me. I was immediately being compared to my mother and coming in at my usual place of a far distant and irrelevant second. I really didn't want to talk about my mother right then and about her struggles and her various disappointments including her oncoming menopause that somehow in the brief conversation that followed was found to be competing against my death for attention and winning easily. I didn't want to hear this from my dad, and I didn't want any of those thoughts in my mind about my mother's sexual crisis—as if the world always had to stop for her. My dad's one half-hearted statement about me also having it rough concluded all of the counseling that I would ever receive for very nearly taking my own life.

Totally unknown to me were Kathy's parallel struggles. Neither of us knew that the other was going through similar battles alone. Though we were separated by four years, our struggles were simultaneous in childhood because mine had started in earnest at an earlier age. Her lonely agony was captured perhaps best when as a child she formed the single word "death" in the snow, not expecting anyone to link her to the inexplicable declaration. A perceptive friend had wondered though, and she had later asked Kathy if she had written the word. Kathy was embarrassed at having been caught. Later as a young teenager she confided in a friend that she wanted to commit suicide. She was serious enough to have determined the method, and it was to be carbon monoxide poisoning using automotive exhaust. The friend described what he understood would be a bloated body resulting from using this method, and the grotesque mental image in part helped her to never follow through. Additionally, there were other changes in her life including an early marriage that helped begin to lead her out of this darkness, and certainly the love of Harold and Jennie was a strong deterrent.

It was not until Kathy and I were both adults that we learned of our simultaneous struggles with this forbidden subject. Whatever it was, there was a powerful negative undercurrent and a persistent messenger of death in our lives that was aimed at our punishment and our destruction. It is not hard to imagine that if either of us had committed suicide, that the other would then have followed shortly thereafter. Not many families would have such a sad legacy regarding both of their young children.

Paradoxically, I had to carry the high hopes and expectations of my parents—I was to be a success for them. From the outside it would have appeared that life had not given me excuses for failure, but rather reasons to succeed. I was to be the one who would leave my parents cheering in the stands and the envy of their friends as I excelled above others. It was my duty; it was my responsibility; it was my obligation. The little red devil costume complete with red ears and a red tail that as a young child I wore for two consecutive years for Halloween parties and trick-or-treat adventures did not automatically have to foretell my future, but it did speak of a chilling potential. There clearly were competing interests for my soul, and I was the hapless rope being stretched in this spiritual tug-of-war.

Different worlds can be lived in at the same time. For me, there were not only the two worlds of the seen and the unseen; there were several other different worlds that I found myself in. There was success, there was achievement, there was happiness, there was hope; but there were also the pitfalls common to all, and there were the dark mirror images of failure and despair that stubbornly hung in my mind. I tended to take things to the extreme in whatever world I lived in.

From my suicide attempt one of the first real spiritual certainties I would come to understand, at least for a while, was the wrongness of taking my own life. However, this didn't provide much of a positive spiritual foundation for moving forward. I managed to continue living at home long enough to enter the Air Force when my four years of high school were condensed into three and a half years. The years were often trouble-filled:

drunken high speed drives through winding mountain roads, skipping across the railroad tracks in an S-curve sideways at ninety-five miles an hour (exactly where a classmate would tragically later die under similar circumstances), outrunning the police in high speed chases, having multiple motorcycle wrecks, and standing alongside a highway one cold Montana night tearfully screaming at God—wondering why in a lifetime of begging for His presence that He would continue to remain so silent. All I had really wanted that night and so many others was to know if He was real—it didn't seem an unreasonable request given all His promises to us. I did not have low expectations for God; I had high expectations. I wondered at those who were satisfied with a small god.

The team of two would-be mountain climbers had stopped in the turnout area far below me as I looked down on them from my lofty perch at the top of the large rock outcropping known as Point of Rocks three miles south of Red Lodge. These cliffs had provided me and some of my more adventurous friends a place to test climbing skills and courage. This was one of the times that I was alone—I would have been eleven or twelve years old at the time. This day I had made the much easier climb that involved an ascent from the backside of the cliffs rather than climbing up the main rock face. I had my .22 rifle with me, so real climbing that day was not an option. I watched curiously as the men below appeared to be gearing up to make the climb.

I had been right, they were equipped with rope and pitons and whatever else it is that mountain climbers use—for me some discarded communications wire retrieved from the garbage cans at the telephone company had worked fine for lesser climbs. I watched their ascent with interest, secretly proud that this was my territory. I positioned myself so they would not see me whenever they would glance upward. Hours later they were nearing the top. Perhaps thirty feet separated the two men as the lead climber worked his way upward. I knew that I should not do what I was going to do, but I just had to do it. I had a good vantage point, and as the lead climber looked up and the second climber was focused on securing his own position, I leaned over farther to look into the lead climber's startled face. I quietly and cheerfully said, "Hi," hoping that I wouldn't scare him enough that he would fall.

I then immediately withdrew from the edge so that he would never see me again. I heard him shout down to the other climber, "Hey, there's a damn kid up here!" I never let the other climber see me. I grabbed my rifle and made my escape. It was a good day.

I can only wonder at the lifetime of second-guessing that the lead climber would have had regarding his sighting of the mystery boy and the subsequent suspicions of his fellow climber who saw nothing. I can almost hear him say in his puzzled reasoning, "But I did see him and hear him say 'Hi'; I really did. Didn't I?"

I had climbed those same rocks previously on my own to try to work through my fear of heights, and this in part was why I was proud to know that I had accomplished what grown men had set out to do. Months before on the steep vertical face I had pushed myself into a situation that was well beyond my skill. As I tried to inch upward I slipped. I started down the rock face grasping blindly and frantically at anything to try to stop my fall. During that instantaneous moment I had that experience of one's life flashing before his eyes. It was not consecutive scenes or particular memories that passed by—it was instead a singular awareness of my life as a complete experience of all that I was. It was so definite and defined that it could be sensed, but yet it cannot be explained. A single wild bush growing out of the face of the rocks had broken my fall as my hand passed over one of its small branches and I seized it. I was hanging against the cliff wall looking down, suspended in time and space; my fall and acceleration had been mercifully halted. Had I fallen, no one would have known where I was. Yes, I needed a big God. We all do.

Chapter Four

Closed Doors & New Challenges

Entry into the Air Force in February of 1965 was a relief for me, an escape from a youth and a life that I did not like. I faced the same uneasy intimidations coupled with the welcomed challenges that any young man has when he first leaves home. At a young seventeen I was undergoing basic training at Lackland AFB outside of San Antonio, Texas, with some men who were four years my senior, and we were all treated alike—no special recognition for the sports heroes, no advanced classes for those who were excelling academically, and no knowledge of who I was. The playing field was level in all aspects. There was a strict regimen that left little time to contemplate life. This was a fresh start for the rest of my life, and I was glad to be there.

Basic training concluded with no outstanding issues except for two minor confrontations. In the first, a particularly obnoxious and overbearing fellow for some reason singled me out to try to bully and insult. He was considerably larger than I was which gave him an undeserved confidence. After about the third time he mocked me by making fun of my two buck teeth I grabbed him and slammed him up against the wall and yelled at him, "Give it to me Barrington, give it to me!" Anger fueled by adrenalin often provided me with an adequate, albeit brief, compensator for size and strength. What I wanted from him was his fists if he was so inclined, not his pathetic, childish teasing. He declined, and he and I no longer had a problem. It would be just under four years before those teeth would be lost in the defense of another man. I never much liked those teeth anyway.

The second confrontation involved several airmen singling out a relatively small recruit who was Jewish. For a couple of nights in a row they paraded around him, mocking his name in a threatening manner. I saw something then that I had never seen before, and I began to understand how a Nazi Germany could have happened. A few of us would have none of this, and we stepped in to stand with him. Again, the issue was immediately resolved. I disliked bullies even from an early age, and that trait continues to this day.

I was transferred to Lowry AFB in Denver, Colorado, after basic training. There I commenced the training in electronics that eventually led to me being selected along with five other airmen to remain at Lowry to become instructors. We were not chosen because we excelled far above others, but rather because six of the eight of us in our class were necessary to meet personnel replacement requirements as others either went to the field or completed their military service and were discharged to reenter civilian life. In this same process of rotation of personnel I was able to conclude my Air Force enlistment by spending my last year in Chiang Mai, Thailand.

One key and crucial happening marked my years in the Air Force. After basic training and after I was assigned to Lowry AFB, life began to take on a less regimented routine, and spare time left me again fighting the same psychological and spiritual battles that had plagued my life. Old demons, some perhaps literal, arose from the past to renew their assault on me. There came a Sunday when all things culminated, and I finally admitted to myself that I desperately needed help to fight this turmoil; I could not do it by myself any longer. I knew of only one place to go for help; there was only one possible source that might be able to arrest these thoughts and feelings, purge my mind, and give me some sanity and peace. Through blurry eyes I used the base directory to obtain the telephone number for the base chaplain. If ever I needed God, this was the time.

Using a pay telephone, I dialed the number and reached the chaplain who was on call for emergencies. With great difficulty I told him that I needed to talk to him. I was weeping, and putting my words together was difficult. There was no question that I was having a complete breakdown. I had always known that this was going to happen, and it was happening now.

I was shamed by my weakness, but I needed help. Life had won against me. He replied, "Our office hours are eight to five, Monday through Friday."

"Sir…no…please…I have to talk…to someone now." The tears were flowing, and my voice choked with heavy emotion. The words were coming hard.

Again came the disinterested reply: "Like I said, our office hours are…"

I slammed the phone down with a vengeance and a dangerous strength. I walked slowly toward our quarters, seeing through rapidly narrowing tunnel vision. I was bewildered and beaten as a mountain of assault poured down on me and crushed the life out of me. As I walked along, a spreading numbness began to permeate my body. I had never before felt anything like this in my life, and never have since. What was transpiring in my mind was so intense that it was literally shutting everything else down. Although I still had control over my movements, by the time I reached my room I could feel nothing but a tingling from my neck down. I lined myself up against the concrete cinderblock wall, and I repeatedly slammed my fists into the wall. I then fell back onto my bunk. I let the numbness have me, and a cold cynicism went to work to unravel the feelings that had plagued me. Much died that night, and overnight I became an atheist. I had no doubt that God was an illusion, a fabrication perpetrated on humanity. There was no such being; it was all a corrupt lie. In a sense this was a relief; for I finally knew truth.

A few months later I became acquainted with the writings of Ayn Rand, herself an avowed atheist. Atheism was not her primary message, but it was very much integral to her philosophy. Related works by Nathaniel Branden who published a newsletter entitled *The Objectivist* would also eventually become a mainstay of my reading. Books such as *Atlas Shrugged, Anthem,* and *The Fountainhead* became meat for my soul as rugged individualism, objective reasoning, and a deep distrust of supposed altruistic motivations became bedrock to build on rather than the shifting and untrustworthy sands of religion. This was a welcomed liberation from religion, and my mind became engaged in learning. I was no longer vulnerable, no longer weak. I was in control.

The mysterious and ominous wall in my mind that had left me on one side and something else on the other vanished; I was free. I alone had the responsibility for my life. Yet I was not a god unto myself, for there were no gods. I had a life on this earth as a result of a cosmic accident where matter and energy combined in some inexplicable and unpredictable way; and life, strange as it was, developed and evolved from some primeval sludge apart from any concocted divine intervention. Science was the best way that we could search out the answers to the questions and mysteries of life; for religion was a dangerous and ludicrous abandonment of reason and an embracing of superstition. Pity those souls duped by the puppet masters. It was certainly no harder for me to believe that matter and energy had always existed than it was to believe in a far more complicated and contrived god who was the primary cause for everything, that for all practical purposes reeked of chaos.

Many self-proclaimed atheists are in truth agnostics—those who straddle the intellectual fence and say that you can't know for certain either way, and so they don't seriously commit. Instead, I was a genuine, even militant atheist proving it at every turn in my own mind for I finally did know that God did not exist. This was not an inherited shallow knowledge fed to me in a book or classroom by a pseudo-intellectual that had prompted my pride to agree; this was learned and tested experience and an awakening to reality. My mind was fully engaged. I correspondingly became exceptionally angry at religion in general; the credibility given it had blinded me to truth. I had an inner knowing with an intensity and commitment equivalent to that of faith; but this was not a contrived faith—it was a sure confidence in objective reality, in matter and energy, in truth and reason. Too many years had been wasted beating my head against the wall to think otherwise. I now was better equipped to handle life. I had a new confidence in myself and in an objective reality that was independent of man's consciousness. Finally, I had a measure of control over my life. I was only eighteen years old when I had it all figured out, which may invite the criticism of the more mature, but to me it had felt like a long and difficult eighteen years.

My Air Force days concluded, and after the subsequent barroom fight in Billings I did proceed with what was expected to be a career in electronics in Cleveland, Ohio. I had a dental bridge installed to replace my missing teeth, with the work unfortunately being performed by an incompetent dentist who happened also not to believe in Novocain. When a new partial bridge was installed in Louisiana a few years later, I then had the new misfortune of finding a dentist who found in me a willing participant for experimentation with his unique patented removable dental bridge. The downside of it was that it would fall out of my mouth at inopportune times or break, leaving me with a rather frightening smile with a band of metal where my two front teeth were supposed to be. These irritating reminders of the past never left me until an excellent dentist in Boise, Idaho, replaced all of the former work some twenty years later. Barroom fights can be expensive and pack with them a long memory.

Cleveland proved to be an eighteen-month pit stop in my life. I was working directly for some exceptionally bright and dedicated engineers at the Warner & Swasey Research Division in neighboring Solon, Ohio. I began night school classes at Cleveland State University, and my performance was in line with my expectations. What was disturbing was that when I measured my own potential against the high achievers in the Research Department for the machine tool division, I came up short. I was out of my league, even allowing for the fact that nearly all of my schooling still lay ahead of me. This was not a lack of confidence or an underestimation of my ability; it was simply as I saw things based on a reasonably good understanding of my skills and potential. On the other hand, I had no doubt that I could push through my reservations and do well, but striving hard to reach the position of those above me was not where my heart was. I was engaged in a game of mental ping-pong, and I didn't like games.

Additionally, as I drove around the streets of Cleveland and the surrounding suburbs, I realized that many of the homes looked no different than the adjacent ones, and that this was the best that I could hope to achieve if I stayed on my present course. It wasn't enough for me. I was restless, and I wanted something else—not at all sure what that might be. Beth, the girl who lived with her mother in an apartment on the second floor above mine, had caught my eye; and after nearly a year of both of us trying to meet the other we finally did. A relationship then quickly developed, although there was not enough between us to result in commitment. It was time for me to pull up stakes and look for something else.

With a trailer rented for my motorcycle, I drove back to Montana to drop off my car and belongings at my parents' house in Billings. I had no specific plans beyond that, except to hit the highways on my motorcycle and just be free for a while. At twenty-two I had already worked a fair amount in my life, and this was to be my first real extended vacation. I longed for that romantic sense of the open road similar to that depicted in the then popular TV program called *Then Came Bronson* with Michael Parks as the lead actor. Bronson was a free spirit, full of life and experiences, and he traveled the country on his motorcycle helping people and relaxing in who he was. It sounded good to me.

Passing through North Dakota, I of course stopped to visit Uncle Harold and Aunt Jennie in Buffalo. I didn't feel the joy there that I had always previously experienced during my visits with them. I knew they wanted to see me, but something wasn't right. Harold had seemed unusually sad when I left. I knew that he didn't like what he saw happening with me; yet he offered not a single word of criticism—that was not Harold's way. His eyes and his voice conveyed a hidden grief for me, a love and an agony that I could not grasp. I learned later from Jennie that it was at this time that more prayer began in earnest for me as Harold went to his knees daily. It was three months later when Harold died unexpectedly after a brief illness. He was only sixty-three years old—an emotional giant of a man.

My severely strained but not broken relationship with my parents had continued in spite of occasional setbacks. Our family turmoil was never discussed in a constructive forum other than privately between Kathy and me, when as adults we tried to reconcile our feelings and situations with our difficult childhoods. Nevertheless, we all tried to remain a family, and to that end we always remained open.

I was welcome at my parents' house, but generally a three-day visit was the limit before tensions began to build unless remodeling or other helpful projects for them kept me busy and focused. I often found it best to excuse myself and retire to privacy as the evenings progressed in front of the television. There virtually always was an evening ritual of one or two drinks by my parents, with my dad revealing no effects from the alcohol but my mother rapidly becoming overly emotional after only one drink. This was their daily routine of relaxing, but for me the times could be especially difficult and awkward. I never drank in their presence, which earned me criticism from my mother as she wondered aloud if I thought I was too good to have a "social" drink with them. I wasn't too good for that—but I did know that no one really wanted to see my other side that alcohol sometimes revealed.

After the visit with my parents was completed and my car and belongings were stored that mid-summer of 1970, I mounted my 1969 BSA motorcycle that was loaded with a duffle bag and a sleeping bag. I pulled out of their driveway in Billings for my adventure that was to take me across the western states. Accelerating up the on-ramp connecting to Interstate 90 heading west toward the Rocky Mountains felt good. Accelerating on a motorcycle heading anywhere always felt good when I could forget what was behind me. It was a clean, refreshing, and invigorating feeling; those who ride, know.

I had left Montana without pursuing my target for revenge from the barroom fight in December of 1968. Retaliation could not then be achieved against the big man. I had considered setting him up for a phony drug bust by obtaining and hiding narcotics in his vehicle, but my known presence in Billings and the possibility that this might link me to him prevented me from proceeding with any such operations. All was not forgotten, and the near disaster with mistaken identity was still a couple of years away.

My first destination after a few detours of whim was to be my sister and brother-in-law's home in La Habra in southern California. As I drove along the open highways with both a welcomed sense of freedom and a corresponding concern that I needed some real direction in my life, I tried to reduce things in my mind to the essential minimums of what I wanted out of life and what was necessary to achieve this. Four simple yet clear guidelines for my future eventually came to me as the miles began to drift by.

Recognizing that I had been uncomfortable with the schooling that I had been taking in Cleveland and with the corresponding mental requirements for the work in electronics, I realized that the more I thought, the more that I used and demanded of my mind, the more it was that troubling confusion took over. This produced my first guideline requirement: I did not want to have to think excessively. Second, I had always liked to build things, so a construction-related trade of some kind provided my second requirement—I wanted to work with my hands. Third, I wanted to make money, the more the better. Given the first two stipulations, this third one seemed to present a problem regarding feasibility. Fourth, the old death wish still lingered in the background. Danger would be good. Or, at the least I might as well take advantage of not having an obsessive fear of dying. I saw nothing wrong with turning this attitude into a marketable resource, and it might help with the third requirement with respect to earning money. It wasn't much of a plan at this stage, but it was a start.

Simplified, my four guidelines for my future were therefore: (I) to not have to think excessively, (2) to work with my hands, (3) to make a lot of money, and (4) to have an element of danger. That was all fine, but I didn't have a clue as to how to put this together into any kind of a workable plan. For now though, the vacation was to be my main focus. Unfortunately, beautiful damsels in distress were not to be found flagging me down, and no heroics were required with high speed runs to obtain help for someone in desperate need. Making things worse, sleeping out under a bridge in Idaho that first night resulted in a rather hungry (or ornery) rat eating a significant portion of the lining out of my imitation leather jacket. The thought of his return the following night led me to move on sooner than I had planned. The dust and the ants were not much fun either.

Sleeping out under the stars proved to be more of a challenge than I had expected. As vast as the west was, unless you went to a designated campground to find a suitable place to bed down for the night you were left exploring too many side roads that offered poor alternatives. This wasn't at all like the areas around my hometown of Red Lodge that I knew so well. All in all, this was not proving to be as delightful an adventure as I had hoped for. Bronson in the television series never seemed to have these issues. Motels soon became my preferred choice for how to spend an evening. With limited finances and with not having the same kind of luck as Michael Parks in his role of Bronson, this vacation of mine was fast beginning to lose its appeal. My sister's home now became my primary destination rather than one of many possible leisurely stops.

Kathy and Ken were playing by the rules in their lives. Both had graduated from college, and they had just had their third child. They were a family; whereas I was a loner. Not long after I arrived I could not help but realize that my life was not on course as theirs was. My wonderful adventure on the open road had me realizing that I needed to get my life together sooner rather than later. Fortunately, sooner was to become a reality.

As I watched their television, a commercial for deep sea diving caught my eye and jarred my memory. When I was a young boy we had one of the inexpensive 3D viewers that came with several discs with assorted slides. A lever on the side of the viewer would allow you to advance through the various slides, and the three-dimensional effect provided an intriguing sense of visual depth that placed you within the scene being viewed. One of those discs had several views of a helmeted deep sea diver as he was working adjacent to and climbing onto a small craft. He was wearing the Navy's heavy gear, the large Mark V diving helmet made of spun copper with its brass attachments and the bulky canvas suit. I remembered often looking at that diver and wondering with all the interest that a child could muster what being a real diver would be like. It suggested to me a secret world where one explored alone.

Walt Disney's 1954 movie based on Jules Verne's classic *Twenty Thousand Leagues Under the Sea* had further sparked my curiosity, yet all this spoke of a world that was a thousand miles away for a Montana schoolboy and far beyond reach. Reading the novel later in my youth had continued to perk my interest, but this was all science fiction writing and only meant for dreams and movies. Jules Verne's brilliance in envisioning the future had always left me in awe of one with such a mind; for in the 1800's he was writing of submarines and space travel with considerable insight for one trying to peer into the distant future. But the thought of open doors for such adventure had never been considered a possibility for me; that is, until I saw the commercial for a career in deep sea diving.

The mental list of my four requirements leapt into my mind. First, was not having to think excessively. Certainly a man had better not elect to be willfully stupid in this field, but neither did he have to comprehend quantum physics to be successful as a working diver. Second, was to work with my hands. Perfect: underwater construction. Third, was to make a lot of money. Commercial diving appeared to promise this, and my first two requirements did not present limitations in this field. Fourth, was having an element of high risk. Again, perfect. Diving was inherently dangerous. My new career was set before me as a possibility—it was almost as if a bluff had been called. But I was presenting no bluff, and I began to study the commercial diving industry. I contacted the Coastal School of Deep Sea Diving in Oakland, California, and I registered for the next available three-month class. This was not the same school advertised in the commercial that I had seen on television, but after review of the different schools Coastal had been the one that I had selected. It has now gone the way of history.

The day of graduation had been a day of celebration initiating some of us into what was an accepted tradition for divers: heavy partying and questionably raucous behavior. In the brief interim since I had last visited Kathy and Ken, they had moved from southern California to Contra Costa County southeast of Oakland. With the day's and evening's partying completed, I telephoned her. I asked about seeing her and her family for a final visit before I left for the oilfields in the Gulf of Mexico where I hoped to find diving work. I had been drinking excessively, which it was my nature to do when it came time to party hard. I was not a habitual drinker, but I definitely was an infrequent binge drinker. While on the phone I tried to sound sober, not wanting to embarrass either of us. "Yes," I could head their way to visit. "No," it was not too late. I was convinced that by the time I got there I would be sober enough. She had never seen me drunk, and I didn't want her to.

I drove my car out onto the Nimitz Freeway heading south. Heavy rains began, and visibility was limited. No matter, I was used to driving fast under difficult circumstances such as icy roads in Montana where I had pulled off some foolish but successful stunts. As I sped along, the traffic did not appear to be heavy. I was pumped with enthusiasm. Life was mine.

The collision was a total surprise. I had no idea of what I had made contact with or why this had happened. My hood popped straight up and slammed against the windshield, shattering it. All forward vision was lost immediately as I worked to maintain control. I was driving blind in the pouring rain at night, still at a high rate of speed. I looked directly out to my left and I could see the guardrail next to me racing past. I fixed my eyes on it and used it as a reference to guide my car to a stop, hoping that nothing else was in front. I was alone on the freeway except for a few passing vehicles. No one stopped. I quickly got out and used my flashlight to wave any oncoming traffic around my stalled and destroyed vehicle. The rain slowly brought home the reality of the crash.

By the time the California Highway Patrol arrived at the scene I had sobered up considerably. I had stood in the cool night rain for at least thirty minutes and waved traffic around me. A wrecker was dispatched, and my totaled car was towed away. I had cancelled my insurance collision coverage two months prior. The irony was not lost on me.

As I sat in the back of the patrolman's car, I started talking to the other passenger in the back seat. It took me a while to realize that he had been the driver of the car that I had rear-ended—that car or what was left of it was somewhere behind us. In my stupor I had not even thought of another vehicle or of anyone being injured. The other driver was unhurt even though he had rolled, and his vehicle was totaled as well. I was not convinced whose fault it was. I tried to piece the events together, and I surmised that I had been traveling in the high-speed lane with nothing ahead of me and that someone must have veered sharply into my lane, but his story did not match mine. Points of impact would later reveal inconsistencies in his story and support mine, but I was hardly in a position that night to argue. With alcohol-impaired judgment, I definitely held the weaker hand and by far the greater responsibility. Realizing that a drunken driver might receive little mercy, I decided that I had better keep my mouth shut.

I was charged only with careless driving resulting in an accident. Keeping track of car and motorcycle accidents was becoming a bit of a challenge. I was running out of fingers for the tally. Wrecks and near wrecks had begun as early as age fifteen, and they were beginning to add up. This now meant that I would have to travel back to Montana and get my motorcycle and use it to drive to Louisiana to start my diving career. My now-wrecked 1967 Pontiac Tempest had been purchased in part for me by Harold and Jennie when I was still in the Air Force. Now that very special car was destroyed. That was a sad realization, but the far greater concern and the one that I was genuinely grateful for is that no one was killed or injured that night as a result of my drunken driving.

The criminal indifference of my behavior had nearly cost another man his life. If he had been seriously injured or had been killed, I would not have wanted to live with that on my curiously selective conscience. I was not that strong. That big God who had supposedly abandoned me had watched silently and protected others and me again from afar, and I wasn't even aware of this.

During the three months of dive school I had worked hard to achieve a good standing in class as we had been told that there would be job offers for the top graduates. There were none for us, not a single offer. We were soon to learn that graduating from diving school simply meant that you had a chance of getting a job interview to become a diver tender, essentially an apprentice, for one of the commercial diving contractors located along the Texas and Louisiana Gulf Coast. Contrary to what we had been told in dive school, being a graduate did not guarantee that you would find work. Doors eventually opened though, and I was able to start what would become a successful diving career for nine years. I was made for diving, for pipeline construction. I was like a kid with a giant industrial-grade Erector Set.

The start for me and for a few of my fellow classmates did not come with us being sent at first out into the Gulf of Mexico to work pipeline construction, which was the main focus of commercial oilfield diving. Instead, we were hired to do an inland job: a piling maintenance project along the Mississippi River just upstream from the Greater New Orleans Bridge. Perry Street Wharf, which was situated on the Westbank across from New Orleans, required that protective wraps be installed around the deteriorating support pilings. Some of us who were new arrivals and eager to find work had met the installation qualification requirements when our test wraps were completed during trials and subsequently recovered for inspection. A few of the intended divers for the project had failed to achieve satisfactory results, presenting an unexpected opportunity for those of us who had qualified.

Perry Street Wharf was about two and a half miles downstream from the Harvey Canal, the area that I would eventually select for the drop-off location for the extortion. There is something to be said for criminal profiles—comfort zones are definitely the preferred territory. After three months of daily diving in the Mississippi River with its murky waters and swift current, I had grown to feel confident in the river, knowing it in ways that others did not. I would later use this experience to my advantage.

While divers did receive relatively large paychecks compared to most other workers in the construction trades, there nevertheless were lean times for many of us as we worked through seasonal careers. As the reality of life and financial responsibilities began to set in for me, money soon became a primary motivator. Still, a close second was always the nature of diving work itself. Using a crane line from a barge anchored two hundred feet overhead and coordinating this with directing two air tuggers (pneumatic winches) simultaneously rigged to maneuver a pipeline subsea tie-in assembly into position, or installing a clamp onto the leg of an offshore platform for a new riser (vertical section of a pipeline), or setting a multi-ton pipeline burial sled with it suspended and surging over you because of rough seas, or aligning and bolting up two pipeline flanges in zero visibility with limited bottom time and a personal demand for high performance was the work that I was made for. Divers worked alone for these projects, and eventually confidence was earned. Work later moved into deeper waters as the search for oil led in this direction, but the work essentially remained the same: challenging and rewarding.

I had a typical lean start with diving. I lived in a series of less than desirable, comically pathetic, rental situations. After a year and a half I located a dilapidated house in Abita Springs, Louisiana, situated on two heavily wooded acres, some thirty-five miles north of New Orleans. I was able to purchase this property at a sheriff's sale for unpaid taxes as well as covering what remained of the previous owners' defaulted loan. In 1972 I had paid eight thousand dollars for that property that no one else wanted and that nearly anyone would have considered uninhabitable. Any city inspector would have condemned it. The house's flat roof was a source of many leaks, termites were actively at work, vandals had set fires inside, mold was throughout, and yet I saw promise there. I could fix it, given enough time and money.

But in the background all the time working against me in my thoughts was constantly remembering people like the barroom thugs, dealing with people like the used appliance salesman, and seeing boastful divers too often getting chosen for jobs on the merit of their talk and not their performance. These were among some of the things that tended to discourage me from within, and the obsession with always trying to get even was a defensive stand that was doing me far more harm than my opponents. I began to think that there had to be another way.

Additionally, I was trying to establish a life with Beth, the young woman from Cleveland whom I had asked to join me shortly after I purchased the property. Three weeks after I completed moving her to the house in the woods her mother died from a drug overdose. I had known the lady, and she had before overdosed on prescription drugs more than once, including at least one time while I was still living in the Cleveland area. Beth had been the one to find her that time, and she had been the one to call the ambulance. Directed by Beth, I had met the ambulance outside the apartment and led the team inside. I had been solidly impressed with her suddenly mature and authoritative handling of the situation.

But now this last time her mother's latest overdose had finally proven fatal, and alcohol was also likely involved. There was hushed speculation that the overdose was deliberate, but this was never confirmed. With no one there this time to rescue her, she had died alone. Starting a life together under such circumstances with Beth was difficult at best; for other related problems were also beginning to surface in her life. I was starting to stare into a bottomless pit. I was not familiar with dealing with addictions, but I soon would be.

Rescuing others wasn't working out too well for me, and neither had standing up for what I thought was morally right a few other times worked out very well either. Morality seemed to have few rewards other than finding yourself spitting out shattered teeth, and life seemed to be a chance roll of the dice—and not everyone was lucky. Many of my poor choices in life had come to feel like inevitable outcomes as I drifted along, almost as if I was watching my life unfold from a distance. Being falsely arrested in the confrontation with the appliance dealer tended to be the final straw for me, and seeing Beth helpless in her subsequent epileptic seizure following the turmoil of my arrest would eventually help give me the excuse to act in the extortion—inexplicably against innocent others. When the helpless suffered, something aggressive and dangerous clicked inside of me and wanted to explode and take everything with it to wipe the slate clean. The injustices of life seemed to mock all existence.

In my mind the blindfolded lady holding the scales of justice—the Roman Goddess of Justice—needed to take the blindfold off for a while and purge this miserable earth; but then there were no gods, so this wasn't going to happen. The circumstances that I was faced with were not a recipe for a happy life, and soon all options were on the table. I was thinking hard, and I began looking hard in the wrong direction, knowing full well the implications. I had some reasons to be discouraged and disgruntled, but I also knew that I had no legitimate excuses. Such reasoning no longer mattered enough to stop me.

Chapter Five

Decisions

A burglary was to be my first challenge in committing calculated, premeditated crime. This was not an ill-conceived youthful stunt or an outburst of pent-up anger; this was a conscious choice to break the law. Selecting the sporting goods store followed some other options that I had considered. The thought of free access to a gun case was tempting, plus it was possible that there would still be the day's proceeds in the cash register. Initial checks had revealed to me that it was unlikely that there was an alarm system installed. The back door of the store was constructed with tongue-in-groove 2x4's secured with additional bracing to make it a strong, yet nevertheless easily surmountable obstacle with the proper tools and approach.

It was April, 1964, and I was sixteen years old. I certainly did not need a handgun or even especially want one that I could not carry legally, and the idea of stealing a small amount of cash was not the motivation. I knew that if I were caught that this would change my life forever and be something from which I might never recover. I also knew that if I were caught that this would bring unbearable open humiliation to my parents and to Jennie and Harold. Even my friends and classmates would look down on me, and there would be some sadly disappointed teachers who had stood by me. There would be a lot of people truly disappointed that I would do such a thing. Consequently, I would never have proceeded if I had thought that I might get caught. That was not going to happen, and I would plan accordingly. I had not yet determined that I would be enlisting in the Air Force, so I was not knowingly jeopardizing that future decision.

An oftentimes difficult and contentious home life; psychological, spiritual, and emotional turmoil; running away from home followed by an awkward and heartbreaking return; an incident with a teacher deliberately humiliating me; multiple failed counselors; a nearly successful suicide attempt; motorcycle wrecks and near wrecks; and an assortment of other happenings now present a confusing flurry of kaleidoscopic activity that when I look back on I cannot properly sort out as to the exact timing of events. I could manipulate those events now in an attempt to produce a convincing timeline explaining how I might have chosen to deliberately ignore my conscience, but I honestly cannot point to an identifiable, circumstantial, "cause and effect" for my actions; it is not that simple. I only know that I was in turmoil, and I was determined to act. Also, there was by now simply selfish meanness at work in my life.

With my plan established I was ready to proceed. The back door of the sporting goods store was hidden from the view of any potential watchful eyes at night. Any car proceeding through the alley would first cast its headlights ahead of the vehicle, thereby alerting me and allow for my quick retreat to a place of hiding. I would wear boots not matching my own, leaving no potential evidence in my tracks. I would use a brace & bit, a traditional crank-type of tool with an attached auger bit for hand-drilling holes in wood. This would be quiet and efficient. I would drill a series of consecutive holes, each touching the other, to make a perimeter around a central plug of wood that I could then easily knock out after the holes were drilled. With a suitable hole in the back door for my arm to reach through, it would then be a simple matter of reaching inside, with a gloved hand of course, to release the otherwise substantial and sturdy door locks. I anticipated that this could be accomplished in perhaps twenty minutes, thirty at the most.

The real issue for me was not the crime itself, not the stealing—I could not be proud of this—but rather the accomplishment of a successful mission. Yet if I were to be the only one who knew that I had engineered the break-in and pulled it off, then in a certain sense it was all pointless. As a sixteen-year-old, in some ways it was still all about identity, about recognition, but more importantly it was about being someone to be seriously reckoned with. I decided to get an accomplice to join in the action, and preferably more than one like-minded individual who could enjoy the adventure itself and find satisfaction in getting away with it. However, I never lost sight of the fact that this was about adult criminal activity, which in part was what made it appealing.

Mike, my closest friend at the time, could not be considered for this venture in spite of our occasional wild escapades of drinking and driving together, as he was not inclined to the criminal side of life. Instead, I confided in two individuals who I suspected would be willing to participate, and who I believed could keep this a secret. It would have to be just the three of us who knew, but that was enough.

On April 25th, 1964, the burglary went precisely according to plan. Two handguns, assorted ammunition, and the money remaining in the cash drawer were taken without incident. The stolen items were immediately hidden, and they purposely would not be recovered until several months had passed. If for any reason I might be suspected, no search would produce the stolen items. The next step was to lay low, show no interest in the break-in, and simply enjoy having successfully pulled it off.

Identifying and understanding all the motivations is difficult from the perspective of well over four decades later, but I do know that I felt so dead inside that I had to get closer to the edge of life to feel something of consequence. I was a "life" junky and a "death" junky, and owning neither presented a frustration that I handled poorly. There were reasons why I raced along mountain highways skidding through curves at high speeds, why I rode a motorcycle and pushed it to the limit, why I entered collapsed coal mine tunnels where methane gas sometimes prevented any entry at all, why I climbed rock cliffs even though heights scared me, why I had twice successfully outrun pursuing patrolmen in high speed car chases, and why I would break into a store to steal something when I didn't approve of stealing. My mind could not handle the pieces of life that I was obliged to try to put together. My conscience made me guilty; my mind made me responsible; my pride and anger pushed me on; and my inner emotions teetered between nothing and full speed ahead. And, as I now know, there were powerful and determined forces that were competing for my soul.

The only flaw in the plan proved to be one of my accomplices. He was younger, and he was just as proud of the successful break-in as I was. When the Carbon County News that was published every Thursday had an article on the burglary that had taken place the previous weekend, my partner-in-crime was eager to point out the article to me at school. A later related article stated that it was believed that "outside professionals" had committed the burglary. Had one alert bystander seen the excited attention that he had given the articles, we would have been compromised. Seeing that his enthusiasm could undo everything, it was then that I realized that I was in more jeopardy from him than from performing the actual crime. I encouraged him to stay silent and to be more careful, and I am assuming that he did. The incident rapidly faded from attention and was forgotten in the minds of most.

The stolen weapons and the ammunition were eventually disposed of, and the small amount of cash was incidental. Stealing was not intended to be a way of life for me, and I had no respect for those who chose that path, including myself when that line was crossed. My regrets were never translated into an apology though until sixteen years later when a renewed conscience led me to make amends. My confession and letter of apology in 1980 were sent to the former storeowner along with restitution. The storeowner replied with an exceptionally gracious and kind letter. Sometimes kindness received hurts more than you think it would. That is the curious thing about grace; it sometimes hurts as it heals.

In fast-forwarding ahead from the burglary to my decision to proceed with the extortion in 1973 there were no other deliberate criminal activities performed after the burglary that might suggest I was inclined toward a life of crime, revenge intentions and occasional drunken driving aside. My conscience was tugging just as strongly in the direction to do what was right, and more than once this was done at considerable personal cost and sacrifice. When it came to committing crime, my decisions necessarily had to be cold decisions, knowingly made for strictly selfish reasons. With having soundly determined seven years prior that there was no God to whom I was ultimately accountable, those decisions were becoming easier to make. A personal fading conscience is no match for a God-enlightened conscience.

The burglary of the sporting goods store nearly ten years prior had always remained in my mind as assurance that I could plan and execute an operation. The observation that "there is no such thing as a perfect crime" conveniently seemed to ignore the fact that many crimes are never solved, so in their own right they were perfect enough. I viewed the hypothetical argument that no crime is perfect as an intellectual indulgence that ignored the practical limitations regarding law enforcement resources that could be reasonably employed to catch a criminal. Therefore, as I contemplated a new criminal venture my first thought was to control the likelihood and the circumstances of any possible confrontations with law enforcement. Typical crimes such as bank robberies were too violent, too unpredictable, and too unmanageable unless extreme and ruthless violence were to be employed. Additionally, a team assault would provide the best attack on a bank or on any substantial physical target, and I wanted to work alone to minimize any possible potential confrontations and to maintain control and secrecy. I remained extremely concerned about physically hurting anyone. I had not fallen that far yet, although I knew that such action was possible if not likely if I continued down a criminal path.

After mentally running through a list of different options including various financial schemes and ruses, one crime stood out to me as the most feasible and the most suited to my skills and purposes, and that crime was extortion. A corporation would be my target, alleviating the moral dilemma of inflicting injustices on any particular innocent individual. The victim would be faceless and anonymous. I knew that this was rationalization and did not justify my actions, but it helped mitigate the guilt factor. No one ever really hated Robin Hood. Even the infamous D.B. (Dan) Cooper who had extorted $200,000 from Northwest Airlines in 1971 and bailed out over the skies of southeast Washington to complete a unique escape from the hijacked airliner had become more of a folk hero than the uncommon criminal that he was. Extortion was a crime I could live with.

Cooper's escape was a nearly perfect plan, save for his precarious parachute descent into unknown territory. In his crime were the same elements involved as in my own. A demand for money was made. He knew full well that law enforcement would be involved whether or not threats intended to restrict their involvement were made. His plan therefore included an escape whereby following him would be either impossible or impractical, and his plan stretched the limited resources that could be used to pursue him. I do not recall how much of an inspiration his crime of two years prior had been to me, but I know that I had followed with interest his originality if nothing else. His was a popular story of the time, and that case remains as the only officially unsolved case of hijacking of a United States plane. Speculation abounds about his real identity and ultimate fate. My intention was not to perform a copycat crime, but neither did I care about being original in every aspect—I just didn't want to get caught, and the factors that pertained to his crime and escape were also relevant for mine.

I went through a variety of potential targets for the extortion attempt, and I quickly determined that public utilities presented equipment vulnerabilities that I could exploit. Bombings, poisonings, arson, hijackings and other acts of violence all presented unacceptable consequences for others because of the initial acts that would be required to prove my serious intent. The promise of personal harm to others was a bluff that I was not prepared to turn into a reality. However, I was willing to cause property damage, and this would be required to step past what would likely be typical occasional threats by would-be extortionists that never advanced beyond the hoax stage. These were not yet the times of reoccurring terrorist scares where nothing is now taken for granted. Instead, these were still the times of common and uncommon criminals, and I needed to rise to the level of the uncommon to be taken seriously. I could accomplish this by disrupting service. With no particular target in mind, I started looking and thinking.

Certain unguarded facilities of South Central Bell, the telephone company then servicing Louisiana and other southern states, satisfied my requirements for soft and vulnerable targets. With minimal effort I could cause significant disruption to service. The greatest drawback was the very real possibility that my actions would prevent necessary fast response teams such as fire, police, and ambulance from reaching victims of emergencies; and this was where my greatest reluctance rested. I hoped that service could be restored rapidly or that backup systems would automatically be employed so that no harm came to another person, but I had no assurance that this would be the situation. A cold and selfish decision would be required with complete disregard for possible consequences to others. My plan now lost any semblance of being a romantic Robin Hood adventure; real lives could be placed at great risk by my actions. Conscience was overruled, and my plan would proceed.

Escape then became the next problem to solve. The extortion would involve damage to facilities with a subsequent demand for a payoff to prevent additional and greater damage. The payoff would involve a physical encounter whereby I would be exposed and vulnerable during the recovery of the money. Meeting a person for a handoff was out of the question. I could be identified later; I would not have absolute control of the situation; and I would have to be willing to subdue or in an out-of-control situation even kill the messenger if necessary—which was not acceptable. Instead, I asked myself the question: "What do I have, what is it about me, that I can take advantage of to achieve what I want?" The answer was death, and although this sounds melodramatic, it was true. I was willing to place myself in a situation where others would be unlikely to follow. Obviously, I was not thinking of certain death, but of calculated danger—of circumstances that would be unanticipated by those who would be pursuing me so that I would have the element of surprise coupled with enough time to escape.

There was something else unique to my situation besides my willingness to take risks—and this was my experience with diving and specifically with the Mississippi River. If somehow I could weave this experience into my plan then I could be at a significant advantage. I had a hard time envisioning any law enforcement personnel following me into the Mississippi River at night. River currents, vessel traffic, speed of emergency response teams, and the exact locations for entering and exiting the river would all have to be matters carefully worked out, but I did like the thought of using the Mississippi River to my advantage. This made sense to me.

Deception and trickery offered some possibilities that seemed promising. Elaborate plans such as those depicted in movies came into consideration, but each involved complicated circumstances and related personal exposure in one way or another that left me unconvinced that success could be had this way. I might have been intrigued by the James Bond movies and fantastic schemes acted out on the big screen, but I was a little more grounded when it came to expectations regarding my own means and ability. It was also a forgone conclusion that law enforcement personnel would be involved one way or another, and I needed to minimize the duration of my exposure as well as the concentration and efficiency of the resources that would be employed to capture me. Risk was further amplified by the high probability of a tracking device that would be deployed within the package. I would be dealing with people who had made a career out of anticipating the moves of people like me. I had no illusions that I was smarter than they were, but I also had considerable confidence that if I planned things well enough that my chances of getting away were high. They would be waiting—that much I had to assume.

I had to make the waiting difficult for them. To reveal that I would make the pick-up at a set time allowed law enforcement a great advantage. Keeping in mind that this was 1973, exceptional measures of surveillance and monitoring were not the common practice that they are today. The number of personnel necessary to ensure my capture would likely have to be tripled if the time of the pick-up were open-ended. In one easy move I could therefore greatly reduce the efficiency of the resources available to capture me—I would simply allow them to place the drop-off, and then I would wait. They would be informed that the time of my arrival would be unknown—pick-up would be anytime within thirty days. It would now also become a question of practicality: would they want to, would they be able to, justify spending money and resources for what might far exceed the cost of the original demand? I had arbitrarily determined that I would ask for the relatively small amount of $30,000. While that amount in today's dollars adjusted for inflation would be in the $150,000 range, the cost that the operation would represent for authorities to achieve an adequate concentration of law enforcement resources might be prohibitive.

The plan was slowly coming together. I had my main target identified; I had the specific limited acts of equipment destruction determined; I had certain elements of the pick-up figured out; and a slow tilting of the odds in my favor was beginning to evolve. This was doable. My weakness was in my reluctance to put others at risk; my strength was in my willingness to put myself at risk. Taking advantage of this second fact still represented my best chance for success, and accordingly the Mississippi River continued to draw my focus.

A boat speeding away from a pick-up location would likely share the same quick fate as a vehicle attempting to escape. One well-stationed U.S. Coast Guard vessel or equivalent with more horsepower than a small boat ought to have would undoubtedly result in my rapid capture. Consequently, I gave no serious consideration to using any kind of a boat for my escape.

The question then became whether or not to utilize scuba equipment whereby I could immediately go underwater; or should I simply wear a wetsuit with its natural buoyancy, be essentially invisible at night, and rely instead on stealth and swimming? The black water of the Mississippi River made any thought of using a compass and swimming along the river bottom out of the question. In daylight there was usually approximately six inches of poor visibility for the first ten feet of descent, after which visibility was then completely lost as you descended further and looked into the blackest black that you could imagine. My work of two years prior for three months at the Perry Street Wharf had left me well acquainted with the river and the hazards that it presented. Additionally, any unplanned necessary ascent to the surface would result in a visual disturbance that could well be sighted by anyone responding to the scene after the pick-up. The only underwater option that seemed reasonably feasible would be for me to submerge adjacent to the drop-off site and remain there waiting for an extended time, hoping that the crime scene would be abandoned when I would later resurface. But then there would be those revealing bubbles that might be spotted. The weak links with using scuba equipment were too many. Attempting to disappear underwater was never a good option.

Rather than attempting a disappearing act in the sense just described, pairing speed and deliberately introduced confusion seemed to offer a better alternative. Dividing the waiting law enforcement resources also ranked high as a priority for me. If I selected the right drop-off location, I could steer the thinking of those waiting for me into two primary directions: by land or by water. By land then offered two more likely possibilities: escape by means of a vehicle, or escape by running along the riverbank. Escape by water offered only one likely possibility: speeding off in a small powerboat. What fool would attempt to swim the Mississippi River at night? Logic would help steer the search teams away from me into at least three different directions. My remote hope still remained that the high cost of surveillance and capture teams deployed for an extended time would be cost prohibitive, but I also knew that giving in to an extortionist was extremely unlikely and would go against everything that the agencies involved stood for. I had to expect that they would be waiting.

River Road snakes its way along the Mississippi River heading upstream from Harvey, and then through Marrero and on into Westwego. These small cities that merge together comprise in part what is called the Westbank, although the area in question is actually on the south side of the river from New Orleans. New Orleans itself is known as the Crescent City because of its curved layout along the winding river. Downstream from Harvey also on the Westbank is Gretna, although River Road ends before the 4th Street Bridge over the Harvey Canal takes you further east into Gretna and then into Algiers. River Road passes through industrial areas and along the adjacent riverbank levee. Levees are the raised portions of land designed to help prevent flooding from hurricanes and high water that had been largely successful until the 2005 hurricane season when Katrina overpowered the city. Trees and heavy brush lined much of the riverbank levee along River Road in 1973, making it ideal for my purposes.

The escape plan had come down to this: I would enter the river about four miles upstream, let the current carry me downstream to the drop-off point where the Harvey Canal met the Mississippi River, exit the water and make the pick-up as fast as possible, reenter the water at the canal, swim back to the main river, and then continue downstream another mile to where I would have my vehicle pre-staged for the final phase of the getaway. I would also use the water to my advantage by immediately submerging the package, which I anticipated would help disable and neutralize any electronic devices that might have been placed within. I had also considered it a remote possibility that light explosives might be implanted, although this would have presented legal complexities and liabilities for the authorities that likely would make such action unacceptable. Nevertheless, I had no way of knowing what might await me.

The drop-off package itself would have to be in a protected enclosure staged to look as if it belonged there so that weeks could pass with no one interfering with it. For this I decided to have the telephone company install a typical pedestal-type service junction box, a type that once was commonplace in neighborhoods and along roadways. This served two purposes. First, seeing the box installed exactly where I had directed them to place it would tell me that they had responded to my demands so that I would not be making a potential wasted run to see if there had been action taken, plus I could make this observation by driving along with other traffic while drawing no attention to myself. Second, with the box being well away from any buildings, any surveillance teams would have to be stationed at least 200 yards away giving me enough time to get back into the water once I opened the box and grabbed the package. I would be highly compromised and vulnerable for perhaps one minute. Given two minutes I could be well into my escape with the package flooded and submerged. A trial run would of course first be required, and the outcome of this would determine if I had a workable plan.

One problem with my reliance on the Mississippi River involved the very nature of my occupation. New Orleans was a known staging area for oilfield construction diving. If there were any suspicions that a diver had been involved with the extortion, then the investigation could rapidly be narrowed to a few hundred possible suspects. With divers working offshore, it would then be an easy matter to narrow the field of potential suspects further to those not accounted for offshore on the involved critical days. Good detective work could land the authorities right on my doorstep in weeks if not days. I didn't like where this was heading, and I considered this to be a major weak point in my plan. I didn't want my strength to become my weakness, and therefore my undoing.

To help counter the possible speculation that a diver might be involved, I would introduce some deliberate deception. In my threatening extortion letters to South Central Bell I would provide a few subtle hints—almost Freudian slips—that would suggest I was a very determined current or former employee or other knowledgeable individual who had access to major installations. I hoped that this would steer investigative interest to a more likely suspect who was or had been involved within their own organization, help divert possible attention from anyone in the diving business, and also raise their level of concern that far more serious damage would be forthcoming from an insider if the relatively modest extortion demand was not met.

As other divers were getting the breaks that I felt I deserved, as financial pressures were pushing me into the corner of failure, as I realized that I was a poor provider for the woman I had asked to join me, as I considered her difficulties, as the courts entertained false criminal charges against me from an unscrupulous appliance dealer, as a poorly fitting dental bridge reminded me daily that others had gotten the better of me, and as anger and frustration churned within; I deliberately chose to try to convince myself that morality was a fool's game. My conscience was a handicap that had left me at a disadvantage and a loser compared to others, and I was ready for a change. If the extortion plan worked, I would win. If it failed, I would be free in death. My capture was highly unlikely given my predisposition to self-destruction.

And so in a not-so-unique fashion I found the excuses that I needed to allow me to proceed. Deceit has many faces, and I have seen most of them in the mirror. I was no different than any other common or uncommon criminal who tries to justify taking out his failures and frustrations on the rest of society. I would give up the only thing that I really had control over and something that did matter to me—my own integrity—to try to attain a temporary and hollow satisfaction. The troubling thing was that through all this I knew that my excuses and reasoning had no legitimate merit. I had never been able to fool myself, and that was forever the maddening thing about having a conscience. It was stubborn evidence of the God who I was determined to believe did not exist.

Harvey Canal and the Mississippi River / The actual escape route
(Photo location shown on map below at bottom arrow)

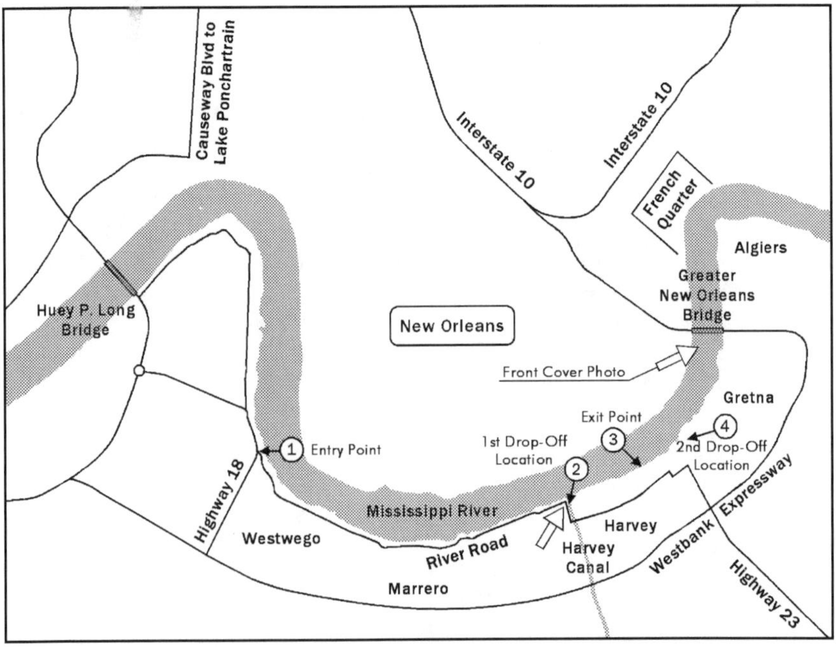

Map of New Orleans showing crime scene locations

Chapter Six

Test Run

In June of 1973 with the extortion plans firmed up, I knew that I needed to perform a test run to confirm the feasibility of the pick-up and escape. I would have to perform a combination of floating and swimming down the Mississippi River under closely simulated circumstances for what I could expect when the time came to act. There would be the physical risk of doing this alone with no one to come to my rescue if I got myself into trouble, and there would be the legal risk of having some mighty difficult explaining to do if I were found entering or leaving the river in the late night or early morning hours after slipping through private property either dressed in a wetsuit or with it in hand. The line was going to be crossed from having adventurous plans to performing actions with potentially serious consequences.

Consulting my old dive records reveals that I had only twenty-four days of diving work in the first half of 1973. Having had to turn down some of the scarce oilfield work that was available at the time to attend to the false legal charges filed against me and also to proceed with what would become the failed small claims suits for the three defective appliances had left a bitter taste in my mouth. Then, to have to pay a lawyer to represent me for the contrived felony charge when he may well have been sharing evening drinks or weekend barbecues with the District Attorney had compounded my anger. Whether or not there was in fact this small-town collusion and rubbing of shoulders within the legal profession that I suspected, in a very real sense didn't matter to me—psychologically it was enough that I felt that there was this nodding and winking among those whose responsibility it was to guard against injustices. My thoughts had been that if society wanted a world of injustices, then I could oblige, more than they ever anticipated.

When I dismissed my attorney after deciding that I would defend myself when the trial came, I did sense a genuine concern from him that I was making a dangerous and foolish decision. He reminded me that the charges were serious, and he recommended that I obtain other counsel if I was not satisfied with his. Louisiana prisons never have enjoyed a good reputation. What he did not know was that a conviction, if it ever came to that, would have been the trigger that I was looking for to unleash pent up rage. We are tragically more familiar with things like random mass killings now than we were in the 1970's, but Charles Whitman was in the back of my mind. It was highly unlikely that I would ever go to that extreme, but I was willing and wanting to release my mind to whatever anger it wanted to work out if I was going to be sentenced to prison because of a used appliance dealer's false charges.

For those unfamiliar with Charles Whitman, his was the first most shocking event of campus mass killings that would come to rock our nation over the years. Whitman had been a student at the University of Texas in Austin in 1966. Following an inexplicable decision to take innocent life, he had shot and killed fourteen people and wounded another thirty-one in a campus shooting spree before he was himself shot. I had never wondered that he had shot so many, but so few if his intent had been to take as many lives as he could. I had no anticipation or intention of inflicting that kind of hell on others, but I nevertheless knew that I was dangerous. I likely would have staged a spectacular shootout in which I would be shot (suicide by cop), but when the bullet holes would have been examined later in my carefully selected targets it would have been obvious after the fact that had I ever intended there would have been scores of others killed. I felt there was more than one way to make a point.

New Orleans itself was not new to sensational shootings. On January 7, 1973, Mark Essex had turned the downtown Howard Johnson hotel on Loyola Avenue into a vantage point to shoot seven people and place the downtown area under siege for several hours. Anger had again driven a man to take lives. Essex's violence had been racially based, as he purposely was after only white people who represented to him the source of the injustices that he believed he had suffered. January 7th was exactly three weeks before my arrest. In hindsight there were some frightening pieces of a potentially tragic puzzle beginning to fall together. I cannot recall all of the imaginations that I was entertaining throughout 1973, but I do recall the intensity of anger and the feelings of futility and frustration. . .these are dangerous ingredients to mix together.

As for my upcoming test run, an accomplice would have been helpful for the transportation issues involved, but an accomplice—assuming that I could even find a suitable one—would leave me forever vulnerable to the indiscretions that might follow as they had for the burglary that I had performed in high school. One word, one boastful comment, one slip to the wrong person, one conscience touched, and I could find myself as a suspect. Nevertheless, I had earlier tested these waters one time by mentioning a possible unrelated criminal scenario to a man and his wife who were my trusted friends. Their reaction was a firm but seemingly non-judgmental refusal. My respect for them was consequently higher than that for myself. As my plans firmed up, it became essential that I act alone. The reality of the severity of possible consequences for anyone involved with me also required that I put no others at risk.

The Mississippi River flows along at approximately 2 ½ to 3 knots in the mid-to-late summer months through the New Orleans area. Therefore, calling the current of the river in this area approximately 3 miles per hour would be a reasonable average. During periods of high water runoff associated with the spring thaws for the Mississippi River Basin in the upper mid-west, the current increases because of the increased volume of water having to make its way to the Gulf of Mexico. Additionally, the current is affected by the course of the river with its various bends, the width at any given location, and the water depth. Closer to the riverbank where I would be doing my combination of floating and swimming, the current would be the equivalent of a moderate walking pace, making it both manageable and ideal for my purposes.

Current is misleading, as too many people have tragically discovered when attempting to drive across a flooding roadway. Heavy vehicles can be moved as children's toys when the threshold is reached where the rush of water takes over. The force of water moving in high volume is often underestimated, even by those who are experienced. There is a certain sense of helplessness when the water assumes control and you find yourself going along for the ride. I already had a strong sense of this from my months of diving in the river, yet it was this very aspect of being carried along that would be to my advantage. I was not a strong enough swimmer to even begin to think about a demanding five-mile swim. Instead, I would let the river do most of the work.

Logistics required that I enter upriver and exit downriver at locations approximately five miles apart. I would stow my wetsuit at the upstream location where I would be entering the river. Dry clothes would be hidden near the area where I would be exiting the river. A taxi ride would be required to get from the downstream location to the upstream location to initiate the pick-up sequence, but there were suitable options for this.

The best location that I could determine for exiting the river was in Gretna, one mile downstream from the Harvey Canal and immediately upstream from the Jackson Avenue & Gretna Ferry that provided another transportation link to New Orleans. This was a few hundred yards from the Gretna Police Station that was located in the Gretna City Hall building, which had formerly been the old Jefferson Parish Courthouse. The area now looks to be an unlikely place to choose for these escape operations, but in 1973 the area was significantly less developed. Although this might sound bizarre, I very much liked the thought of parking near the police station not only for the test run but also for the eventual extortion.

If the situation ever deteriorated to where police activity was heavy, perhaps the best place to be would be the most unlikely place. The police would be dispatched from the police station, not to the police station. Also, parking along some dark side-street where I didn't belong and approaching my vehicle would draw more attention than walking confidently to a car parked in a secure area not far from the Gretna ferry. There were also a few businesses in the immediate area, as well as a bar that I could use for an unsuspicious pick-up point at night for the taxi that would be necessary to transport me to the upstream location. Although the five mile walk would have been easy to accomplish, unless a lengthy diversion were taken most of the walk would have to be along River Road, which was precisely the area where I wanted minimal exposure. I was satisfied that I had selected the best downstream location coupled with the best transportation option available to me for my planned escape.

The location that I had selected for entering the river was four miles upstream from the Harvey Canal where River Road and Louisiana Highway 18 intersect in Westwego. This was where the Mississippi River transitioned in one of its many bends from a southerly flow to an easterly flow. Between this location and the Harvey Canal, the area was and still is an industrial area. There were few other good places for me to enter the river while maintaining a low profile. The last thing that I wanted to do was draw attention to myself. Conveniently for me, at this intersection was another bar—which fell perfectly into place making it a likely destination for the taxi ride from the Gretna bar. This would not raise suspicions or be memorable in any way to the driver. Nothing about my appearance or the ride would be extraordinary; I would simply be a man in his mid-twenties going from one local bar to another. Exceptional detective work following the extortion might result in a check of taxi records for the night of the crime, but what is the likelihood that an extortionist would have taken a cab hours before the crime to a location four miles away? A nameless fare who paid cash would be a hard lead to follow.

The name of the old bar in Westwego has changed a few times over the years, but it still sits on that same corner looking out of place. You can't help but wonder where their customers have come from for so many years, but it survived while many other businesses have come and gone. The building remains essentially timeless—it still reminds me of the 1950's. The parking lot is paved now and no doubt there are other changes, but revisiting the location for this writing reminded me that some things are very slow to change.

In late June of 1973 it had become time to proceed with the necessary test run. The operation was to be as described with the exception that I would not have my dry clothes pre-staged at the downstream location. Because my swimming efficiency in the water was not critical for the test run, I would place my clothes in a waterproof bag and tie them to my diving harness to allow me to float down the river with my hands free. If for some reason I was unable to exit the river where I had planned, I could then float as far downstream as necessary and still have my dry clothes with me regardless of where my journey might end. I really didn't want to be found walking along some road wearing only my wetsuit. Additionally, the bagged clothes would simulate the extorted package of money that I hoped to recover, and this consequently helped serve to create a more realistic test situation.

As the many different aspects of the escape plan began to fall into place, I began experiencing a momentum of confidence. It was that same sure confidence that I had when I held the dry ice when I was in the fifth grade or when I planned the burglary in high school. I was recognizing a frame of mind whereby I knew that I could do this. The planned extortion was fast becoming much less a chance for self-destruction and much more a clear challenge that I was being drawn to accept. I was by no means over-confident in a reckless way, but I definitely was aware that I could succeed if I maintained my resolve and focus. I was beginning to feel in control.

The one-hour drive from Abita Springs to Gretna allowed me to review the elements of the escape plan and thoroughly reevaluate whether or not I really wanted to set everything in motion. I think I knew that if the escape proved possible and likely to succeed, that I would then be so psychologically caught up in the momentum that there would be no turning back. Stopping at any point was of course always an option, but mentally on that drive certain doors were opening while other doors were closing. In much the same way that current can carry a person along for the ride, I found myself beginning to be carried along with a plan that was starting to develop a life of its own. Control seemed to be mine, but it may have been the illusion of control.

Passing through Gretna I drove to the upstream location in Westwego that night and parked near the bar. When traffic permitted me to walk across River Road toward the river without being seen, I took my wetsuit, fins, and the bag to be used for my clothes and headed out. I found a suitable place near the water's edge to leave everything. When the sparse traffic again permitted, I returned to my car and headed back east along River Road toward Gretna. At the Harvey Canal, River Road makes a hard right turn toward the south. As I approached the turn I slowed down and pulled off the left side of the road where there was a small turnout area for cars to park. My headlights passed directly over the area that I soon hoped to be checking out from a different angle of approach following my swim down the Mississippi River. I stopped and got out of my car for one last look at what I would be encountering.

I recall that the view from there almost always seemed peaceful with New Orleans spread out along the opposite bank of the Mississippi River. The Greater New Orleans Bridge was silhouetted off to the right against the night sky, and the city lights would shimmer and reflect off the water's surface. You might hear the low throaty blast of a cargo ship's horn in the distance or the drone of a small push tug chugging along with a string of barges. There was a personality of the city present there; the good side of what New Orleans represented. It was the kind of nostalgic feeling that you could attribute to something like Mark Twain recollections of old river days. Snapping reluctantly back to reality, I returned to my car and continued into Gretna after turning left and crossing over the 4th Street Bridge.

Parking near the Gretna Police Station gave me a confident sense that this was another part of the plan that was exactly what I wanted it to be. I left my car and walked to the old neighborhood bar that was close by. I was not after the liquid courage that alcohol can deceptively provide, but I did need to blend in as much as possible to become an invisible patron. The one beer that I slowly drank was not something that I wanted in my system that night. Still, it was part of the plan. I called a taxi after a short while to head to the bar in Westwego that was five miles upstream. All was proceeding as expected.

After arriving at the other bar, I paid the cab driver and watched him pull out of the parking lot. As hoped for, at the time no one at the second bar was coming out or going in. I walked across River Road and then up and over the riverbank levee to my stowed gear near the water's edge. It was starting.

As I dressed into my wetsuit, I felt alone in a good sense. There were not the distractions of a mad world with its many jabbering voices; there was only a wide, strong, and quiet river with distant city lights on the other shore and a simple focus for me on this shore. I bagged my clothes and shoes to ensure that they would remain dry, and I secured the bag to my diving harness with a quick-release. Although I rarely used swim fins during diving construction work, they now were necessary for efficient swimming in the river. With putting on a neoprene hood and dark gloves, all that remained light-colored in the darkness was my face. I saw no reason to pretend that I was a Navy Seal and go to the extreme of blackening my face—that would have been like putting on camouflage gear to go target practicing. This was not a role-playing adventure; this was my life. In spite of enjoying the movies, I knew that I was no James Bond.

I slipped into the water with no special sense of apprehension beyond what I had expected there would be. My neoprene wetsuit with its natural buoyancy was effectively the best equivalent lifejacket that a person could wear, so drowning was not a concern. In fact, wetsuits are why a diver must wear a weight belt as it is necessary to compensate for the buoyancy to allow a diver to submerge more easily. For much of the swim I was enjoying floating on my back and paddling gently with my fins to increase my speed as I moved along with a current that seemed minimal. Nevertheless, I was making surprisingly good time. There was nothing that was raising my concerns that I might be on a fool's deadly mission. I was looking for the weak links in the plan and so far finding none. I did find myself farther out into the river than I had expected, but this was a controlled move and not a result of me being swept out into danger. I preferred this course because it kept me well clear of moored barges along the riverbank at the various docking facilities.

As I approached the entry to the Harvey Canal I could see that there was no vessel traffic. Even so, I swam to the riverbank upstream of the canal entrance rather than attempting to swim into the canal itself. I was not sure what the current would do right there, and I initially preferred to sneak up on what would eventually become the pick-up site rather than swim boldly to it the first time. I left the river, removed my fins to carry them along with my clothes, and walked to where I intended to have South Central Bell install the pedestal-type service junction box that was to hold the money package. I wore neoprene boots to provide adequate foot protection for the short distance required along the riprap, which consisted of rocks that lined the riverbank to prevent erosion to help ensure levee integrity. The junction box would be installed a few yards from the roadway in an ideal location for a car to stop next to just long enough to make a quick grab and getaway, or for a person sneaking along the riverbank next to River Road to do the same and be on his way back up the riverbank, which was precisely what I was not going to do.

I needed no additional time at the pick-up location. I was satisfied with what I had discovered. I now decided to return to the water's edge within the Harvey Canal itself rather than head back to the main riverbank. When the time came for me to make the pick-up, I would absolutely have to get back to the water as fast as possible in the event that law enforcement personnel would be alerted. I would also want to flood the package immediately to neutralize any enclosed tracking devices. Moving quickly now to better simulate the escape, I put my fins back on and reentered the water. Nothing regarding the current was raising any concerns where the Harvey Canal and the Mississippi River met. I would in fact be able to swim directly to the pick-up location as I had planned, as well as reenter the water at the same location. This meant that I could stow my fins at the water's edge and move unimpeded during the pick-up.

This now was the final leg of my test run: the one-mile swim to the downstream location. As had been encountered along the upstream areas, a few barges were moored along the riverbank. With time now to spare during this uneventful test run, rather than again heading farther out into the river to go around the barges, I instead elected to go through the relatively narrow area between the barges and the riverbank with its pilings for securing barges and boats. In the event that search boats would be summoned to the location after the pick-up, this would be my alternate escape route rather than heading back out into the main body of the river where searchlights might spot me. I didn't particularly like the feeling of being wedged into uncertain close surroundings that could well become a trap, but this was after all a test run to determine the best options available to me if I was being pursued.

I carefully approached the first barge, staying close to the riverbank. It looked like I would be able to follow along the length of the barge and move downstream, while at the same time move safely around the docking pilings. I preferred the open water, but this could be a good and necessary alternative. Being next to the barge, I quickly had a better appreciation for the current, for it definitely wanted to carry me down along the side of the barge. In the main body of the river there were no good points of reference, so it was more difficult in open water to realize the effect of the current other than noting the ease with which distances could be traveled.

I was in an exploring mode, checking circumstances and options. I had not yet started my move down alongside the barge, but I was instead holding onto the barge's barnacled port bow corner, being the front left leading edge of the rectangular barge where the current was pushing up against it with subtle full force. For the first time I felt somewhat uneasy with what I was experiencing. Recognizing this discomfort, I knew that I needed some more answers before completing the test run. The night of the actual extortion would not be a good time to try to figure things out.

At the corner of the barge I turned to my right to look down along its side and to my left to look out across the sloped bow that descended down into the water. I wondered if I could move across the bow at this point and reach the open water if I ever needed to do this. I could feel the current trying to pull me downstream, but with the buoyancy of my wetsuit and with being able to swim with my fins I thought that I had the ability to swim safely across the bow. The suspicious small ripples that were evident even at night that were backing up and breaking around the bow of the barge should have been a warning to me as to what was about to happen. I started my move across the bow and was almost immediately sucked under the barge by the strong current. If this happened it would be a hundred feet or more to the opposite end where another barge would then be waiting to pull me under it next. I knew immediately that if I was pulled under the first barge that it was over. I barely managed to keep one hand at the corner of the barge—the few barnacles helped provide a rough surface to maintain my grip. Only with full effort was I able to pull myself back from the leading edge of the barge and escape the current's strong undertow.

I had thought that I had respected the current well enough, but I then realized that I could easily have been killed because of it. If I had gone one foot farther out along the bow or if I had not been wearing my wetsuit, I am certain that I would have been pulled under the barge and drowned. In an instant I knew how children swimming in the river can easily die. The leading, downward-sloping, upstream edge of a moored barge is not a place that you want to try to negotiate. I should have known this; it had been a poor judgment call; and this was painfully obvious in hindsight. As bad as this was though, I had learned the lesson well. This would not be a mistake that I would ever repeat. Simultaneously, I had the assuring realization that, yes, the river was dangerous, and that it would almost certainly be considered an unlikely choice for an escape. I had no way of knowing then that I had just received the first of what would later prove to be several undeserved breaks throughout the extortion.

I continued downriver along the side of the barge. At one point I had to take the inboard side around some pilings and climb through some wooden braces. None of this proved to be a major obstacle. Only the current would require a greater respect, and it now had that. As I left the industrial area with the barges and drifted closer to where I was going to exit the river, the Gretna ferry appeared ready to depart for a routine run to Jackson Avenue on the New Orleans side of the river. Because the ferry's docking facilities were less than two hundred yards downstream from where I would be leaving the river, I swam to the bank to wait for the ferry to get underway. My concern was that its lights might catch me in the river, and if that happened there would likely be emergency personnel dispatched with the intention of either rescuing me or arresting me, and I wanted neither.

The ferry pulled away, and after completing its course adjustment to traverse the river it soon was far enough away not to be a concern. I then resumed my downstream journey. I did not have a precisely targeted location for where I would exit the river except for about a 50-yard stretch, and the test run was in part to help identify such a location under the cover of night. I cannot now recall if in 1973 there were still some homes located there or if it was more of a fringe commercial area. I did find a suitable place to leave the river, and I made the necessary observations and references to be able to find that same location again.

I stripped out of my wetsuit and in short order I was dressed in my clothes and shoes that had remained dry in their bundle throughout the five-mile swim. I used the same bag for my wetsuit and fins, and crossed up and over the riverbank levee. There I found a wooden stand with garbage cans in an area that had minimal exposure to lights and traffic. Walking back to my car that was parked not far from the front of the Gretna Police Station at two o'clock in the morning with a bulging plastic bag would not have been wise. Instead, I simply placed the bag inside one of the garbage cans and continued on.

Reaching my car and unlocking the door was a moment of victory—it was mission accomplished. Granted, it was only a test run, but it had definitely been something above and beyond the norm of daily life. If anything, it felt like the time when as a young boy I had peered over the top edge of the rock cliffs that the two mountain climbers were ascending and where I had startled the lead climber with my cheery greeting. This time though, I was sensing something much darker than a mischievous and comical pride—this was from the other side of life; it was over the line.

After taking a brief ride to ensure that I was not being followed, I drove back to the rack of garbage cans. I quickly recovered my wetsuit from the can where I had placed it, making a mental note that this would be an ideal place to store my dry clothes when the actual extortion would be committed. Garbage would not be added to or picked up in the late night or very early morning hours, and if for some reason my plan fell apart and I had to head farther downstream, my dry clothes would disappear with the next trash pick up, thus allowing the evidence to conveniently disappear rather than having it hidden near the water's edge. Again, the plan continued to firm up with every step along the way. I had no specific plans for what I would do if I did have to head farther downstream, but if that had been the case I would have been forced to resort to stealing a car or making some other hasty plan. In actuality, I did not anticipate having to rely on any further options. What I needed was already planned for and determined.

I returned to Abita Springs and to Beth who was sleeping soundly and not concerned. She was loosely aware of some of my plans, but she seemed strangely removed from the concept of actions and consequences.

She trusted me, of that there was no doubt, and for her that was enough. How I provided for her never seemed to be a concern for her. She had her hideaway in the Louisiana woods with her four pet geese that had their own clawfoot bathtub with an approach ramp. Gustav, Toodles, Tillie, and Pecan were a happy bunch; often all fitting into the tub at the same time. Plants grew as if they were in a magic kingdom; and azaleas, gardenias, huge elephant ears, and unstoppable green ivy camouflaged much hidden turmoil. Beth found her imagined world more inviting than the real world, and this was reflected perhaps best one time when I returned home and found her outside asleep in the pen with the geese. That photo has been lost over the years, and it is probably best that it has been. Captured in it was a doomed hope and impossible future for her. She was with the wrong man in the wrong world. She needed a private Shangri-la, and only that could work for her. It was not to be found with me.

Chapter Seven

Last Chance

With the test run a success and the upcoming trial drawing closer for the charges that had been filed against me by the appliance dealer, I wanted to proceed with the extortion. In spite of the fact that I knew that there could be no legitimate evidence presented against me at the trial, I had absolutely no confidence and no assurance regarding the outcome. Too many unfair things were teasing my mind, and a growing negativity had resumed to convince me that life was futile. I was unable to appreciate what I had, and I could only see what I didn't have. A friend once commented that sometimes people can see only the dead birds—meaning that negativity can blind us to the good things in life, and the blessings that we are enjoying can be strangely invisible. In fact, a heavy blindness was upon me. Even worse, it had become a willful blindness.

The success of the test run became a road sign to me that in the area of criminal behavior I was more fortunate than when I bridled myself and subjected myself to society's rules. There of course remained the very real possibility that I would ultimately fail with the extortion, but failing in a spectacular way was much easier for me to accept than failing by being pulled or pushed into an ignoble downward spiral of anger, defeat, and frustration—or on the other hand, failing by being sent to prison on false charges. Would-be cowboys and make-believe soldiers don't do well with road rage of the soul.

The time had now come to bring South Central Bell directly into the equation and set everything in motion with the extortion. To avoid possibly inspiring anyone else to commit acts of extortion or sabotage, I will refrain from telling what specific types of facilities that I chose to damage, and exactly how that damage was performed. This may be an overly cautious consideration, but my actions in 1973 inflicted damage and trouble that I do not want to see repeated. Facilities were targeted that allowed me to cause damage across different segments of the New Orleans area. By having different targets there were no geographical patterns that could yield clues, and therefore no anticipation of my subsequent actions was possible. My destructive actions required no elaborate planning, and security and surveillance were largely ineffective at the time for the type of activities that were involved.

I was not necessarily restricted to nighttime operations for the damage that I would cause. At the time I was able to exploit a vulnerability, and I used this to my advantage. When performing this damage, I did recognize a lingering and sickening dread within me—there was a distasteful ugliness associated with my actions that I could not deny. This was definitely one of those times when I had to choose to override my conscience. It was bad enough to wantonly destroy someone else's property, but also at stake was the real possibility that disrupting telephone service could well have unintended consequences for anyone who might be relying on the rapid dispatch of emergency services. There was absolutely no justification for what I was doing. This was nothing but selfish criminal behavior. The test run in the Mississippi River had been exciting, adventurous, and even enjoyable in some aspects apart from the criminal implications. This was none of that. This was a time when I was an embarrassment to myself. I was a hundred times more accountable than someone who was oblivious to all of the considerations of which I was acutely aware, and I was far more accountable than someone who simply did not care.

After I targeted three facilities on July 7th and July 8th of 1973 and the results revealed the level of damage that I could inflict, I was then better prepared to compose the extortion letter that I had been contemplating in my mind for several weeks. The method in which I was going to approach this was as much a part of my decision as the specific words that I would choose. I could type the extortion demand using proper grammar and punctuation, doing so on an untraceable typewriter to try to convey at least some level of professional sophistication; or I could hand-write the message, risk the direct link to my handwriting, and express myself in such a way as to seem criminally amateur and somewhat irrational. There were advantages and disadvantages to both approaches.

If I could come across as smart, knowledgeable, and calculating, then there might be a measure of reluctant respect given me in the sense that this might be an appropriate time for a cautious company to compromise with a criminal who was focused and deliberate, rather than risk the significant damages that he was promising and appeared capable of inflicting. I would have wanted to convey a sense of the absolute futility of attempting to capture me to fulfill the profile of being a clever person. The glaring inconsistency with this approach was that genuinely smart and knowledgeable people do not commit extortion—or if they did, they would not do so for a paltry $30,000. Also, any thought of the authorities conceding premature defeat by acknowledging the futility of attempting the capture of a determined criminal would be completely foreign to law enforcement professionals. I felt that the bluff would be far too transparent, and the hollow promise of damage to major facilities would therefore not be believable when balanced against the type of relatively crude damage that I was currently performing. The profile would be inconsistent and seriously flawed.

On the other hand, if I could come across as a believable threat from someone who was behaving as if he perceived that he had been treated unjustly by management within the South Central Bell organization, which might therefore account for his actions, then typical investigative procedures might be followed to try to identify a suspect. The investigation would probably not focus on the public at large, but rather it would become primarily an internal one for SCB. I could present this profile in a more believable fashion than the former, especially if more than one letter would be required. This would explain my choice of the extortion target in the first place (a company deeply resented by an employee); it would allow for the fact that I might have access to more sensitive areas, thus plausibly being the greater threat that I wanted them to believe that I was; and it might lower the level of resources thought necessary to capture me during the phase when the pick-up would later be made if they thought they were after a more common criminal. I wanted them to think they were after someone technically savvy but criminally naive.

Common sense strongly favored trying to present myself as a current or former employee with a pre-established grudge against SCB, since such a person would be more inclined to act irrationally. This would also account for someone taking such an incredible and foolish risk for only the $30,000 being demanded. Therefore, this would be the path that I would choose. It was in many ways an appropriate joke on my own irrational self, and I knew this. Nevertheless, it just might work. Who would suspect a deep sea diver originally from Montana with no ties to the telephone company and absolutely no grudges against it?

Whether or not these elaborate mental gymnastics and my resulting conclusions had any merit I wasn't sure at the time, but this revealed the extent to which I was trying to anticipate countless different aspects of the crime. In short, I intended to succeed. Years later I would come to learn just how effective the ruse had been.

I was convinced that I would need to come across as an angry malcontent familiar with the telephone company's equipment and internal operations. Before I began composing my extortion letter, I became someone else. I literally imagined myself as an employee filled with measured rage against the company. I became a marginalized worker who had been overlooked for promotions and one who had been unfairly demoted. I became the person who had to watch others succeed—the grumbling outcast who hated his supervisors. I tried to think, speak, and write like this angry person and therefore present myself as someone who felt justified in his actions and consequently committed to his cause. I had to become a separate personality to write the letter effectively, and I was able to tap into the anger that I felt with the upcoming trial, the old barroom fight, and other aggravating instances in my life to do this.

The risk of writing the letter by hand rather than typing it was a calculated one. I knew that if the investigators ever set their sights on me that the handwriting experts would be able to link the letter to me regardless of any style changes that I would try to force. However, I also knew that if it ever reached the point where I was a suspect, then this likely meant that I was finished anyway. I continued to think that taking the bold, illogical, and dangerous step of handwriting the extortion demands might help point the investigation to someone incapable of elaborate planning and therefore perhaps keep the investigation aimed at someone who might be blinded by a specific grudge against the telephone company. I of course would guard meticulously against leaving fingerprints or other traceable physical evidence. Beyond my handwriting itself, the evidence would be negligible. Still, it was an incredible risk.

In spite of the many considerations given the letter, the first message had to be straightforward and relatively unemotional, yet with the suggestion that anger was barely restrained. I felt it necessary to convey this frame of mind in order to get South Central Bell to treat this as something far different than a hoax. This would be beyond something that they could ignore and hope would go away.

The letter was composed with specific references to the facilities that I had damaged, and my demands for the payoff were presented. To ensure that no clues would point to me or my location, on July 10, 1973, I drove from Abita Springs into New Orleans to mail the letter. I had now driven several hundred miles to complete the pre-planning, a test run, the damage to the facilities, and now the mailing. This was becoming a significant commitment of time, thought, and energy for me. Now the wait would begin to see if they would respond. If South Central Bell installed the service junction box that was to hold the money package at the Harvey Canal location as I had demanded, I would then know that it was time to prepare for the actual pick-up. I would have the choice of when to proceed since they had been instructed that it might be thirty days before I would act.

I was not sure when would be the best time to make the pick-up. If I acted soon, those waiting for me would likely be more alert and focused—yet an anticipated long wait might also lower their immediate expectations. If I acted later, they might be getting lax, bored, or doubtful that I would show—but by then they also might have ramped up their resources and fine-tuned their search procedures if they thought that the countdown to the pick-up was drawing to a close. I concluded that it probably didn't matter when I acted—I was unable to come to any firm conclusions regarding the advantages and disadvantages of acting soon or delaying. I had no plan to follow for selecting the time of the pick-up other than not being too eager, and perhaps having no logical time to act was in itself as good a way to proceed as any. If I could not figure out when the best time was, then neither could they. It was precisely that open-ended sense of timing that I wanted there to be.

My decision was made easier by being called out for a diving job. It was long-awaited work in the 140 ft to 200 ft depth range. I would be the lead diver and the diving supervisor on the Main Pass 293A platform where we were installing newly designed flexible flowlines. It was a good job, and the timing was perfect. The extortion letter had just been mailed, and I was able to let everything run its course. Even if I was tempted to drive by the location right away, being offshore would prevent me from making such a move. It was a good way for me to wait while at the same time the hypothetical extortionist from the telephone company also waited for his payoff. I was temporarily distanced from the activities, and this was ideal.

The eleven day diving job concluded on July 23rd, and we demobilized to Venice, Louisiana. With my diving gear loaded in my vehicle, I then began the drive back to the northwest to New Orleans from this southeastern tip of the boot that Louisiana forms as the Mississippi River Delta joins the Gulf of Mexico. Here the Mississippi River has created channels flowing into the Gulf like the branches of a tree spreading out. Venice was the last town on Louisiana Highway 23 before all roads stopped and all waterways began. The disastrous BP oil spill in 2010 would finally put Venice on the map for the rest of the nation.

It was seventy-five miles from Venice to the drop-off location for the extortion money, and heading to Harvey was an easy detour for me to make on my way home to Abita Springs. On the drive I would be running parallel to the Mississippi River where I expected that I soon would be involved in the challenge of my life.

The small towns of Venice, Boothville, Buras, Empire, and Port Sulfur passed by as I considered all that was before and behind me. Except for the upcoming trial and some deep uncomfortable feelings that I had with my developing relationship with Beth, things were slowly starting to come together for me. It was amazing how one good diving job could give me a fresh perspective and a feeling of accomplishment. This was my last warning, my last opportunity to reconsider what I was about to do.

When I drove by the drop-off location on River Road in Harvey I was exceptionally careful not to look around to try to spot any surveillance teams. I would not likely be able to see them anyway, and they might well see me looking around in a suspicious manner. Instead, I was just a diver returning home from offshore, headed home this time by way of the Huey P. Long Bridge instead of the Greater New Orleans Bridge. I had to consider that every vehicle's license plate number was being recorded, but I was comfortable knowing that the number of vehicles involved would be high—plus I had a legitimate reason to be there when I was. My presence on River Road would not raise any red flags if I were ever questioned.

Glancing carefully to my right as I rounded the sharp corner to the left where River Road heads west after leaving the Harvey Canal area, I saw that to date everything that I had planned was in vain. No junction box had been installed. South Central Bell had elected to ignore me. It was yet another opportunity for me to turn my back on the extortion plan. But now the pride factor was also beginning to kick in, and selfish determination was further taking root. I continued my drive up River Road heading toward the Huey P. Long Bridge. After four miles on River Road, I passed the old bar in Westwego where River Road and Louisiana Highway 18 intersect. This was where I was to have been dropped off by a taxi for the start of the pick-up and escape run. Now, this would have to be delayed.

Even though the telephone company had not responded, things now had more of a stubborn sense of the inevitable, yet at the same time I wondered if it was all going to come to nothing. I respected them for not complying, but I stubbornly wished they would. The choices that were always there for me still remained, but as the current was to carry me downstream, so too the plan was now carrying me. I had released myself to the driving forces, and they would not be denied. I completed the drive home and began preparing for the next step.

On July 27th in the early morning hours I struck again, this time inflicting heavier damage than in my first assault. Four separate facilities were hit this time, with one of the locations being exactly where I had struck before to better make the case that I could inflict damage at will. A second extortion letter was written later that day, with the transposed anger factor ratcheted up for having been ignored. The fact that there had been no response to my first set of demands had not surprised me, but in maintaining the profile of the disgruntled employee I opened the floodgates of rage a little wider. The wording now changed to being crude and laced with profanity to the point of being exceptionally vulgar; it had to be ugly to the point of reflecting near murderous rage to be believable. Being ignored was not something that the extortionist I was envisioning could tolerate.

On July 30th the telephone company received my second extortion letter. This time I would not be ignored. Had I been, I expect that I would have given up in spite of my growing determination; but now the authorities were fully committed. I also expect that it had become personal for them, especially considering some of the terrible things that I had written.

On the same day that the telephone company received the second letter I was headed out to another diving job—this time it was for a salvage project in what was designated as the West Cameron area. This job involved one week of diving to remove debris around a platform where an overhang had been cut off and allowed to drop in sections to the seabed. It was clean-up work in only 50 feet of water and not new construction, but it was diving work nonetheless. Having completed the salvage job, on the following day I then was called to perform a one-day diving job at Avondale Shipyards, finishing it at midnight on August 6th. I should have been content with the good fortune beginning to come my way.

On the very same day of the job at Avondale—August 6, 1973—unknown to me there were security personnel from South Central Bell installing a pedestal-type junction box precisely where I had demanded that it be placed. Coincidentally, the Avondale location where I was working that day was only eight miles away. It would be many years before I would learn that this was the very same day that the box was being installed. My second letter had included no deadline for when this was to occur, and I had assumed that if they were going to respond they would do so within a couple of days after receiving the letter. Instead, it had been seven days. I had not wanted to drive by the area until at least several days had passed. However, by driving by when I did in the early morning hours of August 7th I had unwittingly chosen a time when the surveillance was likely to be the most intense. I had driven right into and through the lion's den while he was watching.

As before, when I drove past the area I did so in such a manner as to draw no special attention to myself, although just being there at this time equated to taking a tremendous risk. This time the service junction box had been installed exactly as I had directed. There was a slight twinge of adrenalin release as all the ramifications of what this meant came upon me. This was the big league now; this was a major company paired up with law enforcement agencies agreeing to take me on. It was a profound realization. They were here, and they were waiting—that much I knew. Because the crime was the extortion of a public utility company following the disruption of services, I had to assume that federal agencies would also be involved—and this meant the Federal Bureau of Investigation.

I made the trip home to Abita Springs after first crossing the Greater New Orleans Bridge over the Mississippi River and then completing the final leg over the twenty-four mile long Lake Pontchartrain Causeway north of New Orleans. Even though it was in the early morning hours before daybreak, when I reached home I unpacked my diving gear and cleaned it as a matter of routine. It would be less than twenty-four hours before I would be using the same wetsuit for the extortion since I had decided not to delay further. Everything would be neatly prepared for the crime. Only a few remaining steps had to be completed before I could proceed.

The service junction box that I had directed to be installed was no different than the one a few hundred yards from my house on Kustenmacher Road in Abita Springs. These ground-mounted pedestal enclosures that were used for the routing of telephone lines to nearby homes were approximately eight inches square and two feet high. No one but telephone technicians would have occasion to open these, and given their low priority from a security and safety standpoint there were no locks preventing entry. These now outdated boxes had a single bolt securing a hinged door panel that opened to allow technicians access for testing lines and for making local field connections.

Opening the box would not take an excessively long time using a standard open-end or box-end wrench, but I knew that seconds could well be critical. The most efficient tool that I had for this was a speedwrench. A speedwrench has the same general shape as a brace & bit used for woodworking applications—and coincidentally a brace & bit was the crank-type of tool I had used for drilling the holes in the door for the burglary that I had committed in high school. This curious coincidence was not lost on me. A speedwrench accepts sockets of various sizes in the same way that a ratchet wrench does. It had been a simple matter to size the bolt in the nearby junction box and then select the socket that would be required. Having done so, I opened and closed this convenient private test box numerous times to ensure my efficiency and speed. I wanted no surprises. Opening the box at the Harvey Canal would be quick—perhaps three seconds at the most once the socket engaged the head of the bolt. I considered this acceptable.

Because the operation would be performed at night, the reflective surface of the speedwrench was unacceptable. I certainly did not want any shiny surfaces catching the rays of a searchlight. Painting the wrench black would have been a simple matter, but I chose to wrap it with black friction tape—a cloth-type of electrical tape now seldom used. The tape provided two functions: first, it would not reflect light; second, if I bumped the wrench against the rocks lining the riverbank or anything else, the sound would be muffled: a soft thud was preferable to a sharp metallic clink that might be heard by people or listening devices. I wanted to leave the minimal number of things to chance. I wanted to succeed. This was no enactment of a death wish. If I failed and I was killed, then that was fine; but I did intend to succeed.

The big decision that I had intentionally been delaying was now before me: would I carry a firearm the night of the extortion run? I had the weapon of my choice—it was a .357 magnum revolver. The reason that I had first purchased this weapon had its own troubling history. I had wanted such a weapon for when the time would come to exact my revenge on the barroom bully from the Montana fight in 1968 in which I had lost my front teeth defending another man. But what had led me to purchase the weapon when I did was something that had happened in 1972 to a friend of mine from diving school.

Smitty was older than most of us who had attended diving school in 1971 in Oakland, California. He was a fairly large man, wiser than the rest of us, and gentle in nature. He was more prone to sitting at a bar for longer stretches than many of us, but he was never rude or rowdy. Probably the one word that best described him would be mature. Late one night after several hours in a bar in the New Orleans French Quarter, Smitty began his walk back to his apartment. Just outside the northeast perimeter of the French Quarter on Esplanade Avenue, a man approached him with a knife and demanded his money. Smitty intended to oblige, and fumbled to produce his wallet. The thug was impatient, and he slashed Smitty. Fortunately, the wounds were not lethal and Smitty survived—disappointed, but not even bitter over the unprovoked assault. He took it in stride.

I had taken it in a different way. After hearing about this, I immediately went to a sporting goods store and purchased a .357 magnum revolver. The injustice done to Smitty enraged me. In the following weeks I would occasionally drive to Esplanade Avenue and walk the area late at night. I was bait for anyone wanting to take me on. With any luck, it would be the same man who had assaulted my friend Smitty. He would learn the old lesson that it was not wise to bring a knife to a gun fight. I told no one at the time of this potentially lethal vigilantism—it was far better that no one knew in the event that there was a shooting. I had not intended on waiting for the police to show up to question me. It would be two years later when Charles Bronson would star in the disturbing movie *Death Wish* in which he took to the streets of New York as a vigilante. They say that life imitates art—but life can have its own script.

My anger over this situation dissipated much faster than my anger over the confrontation in the Montana barroom. I intended that the weapon I had purchased would someday bring a much deserved justice to the oversized coward who had delighted in beating people in Billings. It was only a matter of time—all I needed was the right opportunity and the slight push that would be necessary to cause me to act. I cannot recall now for certain, but it is highly probable that the incident with Smitty may in fact have been the psychological trigger that prompted me to make one of my secret trips to Montana to attempt the revenge that I had wanted so obsessively.

But now before me I had a crucial decision to make. I had to consider all the implications of bringing a firearm with me for the extortion. I had to know ahead of time if I intended to use it or not to defend myself if my escape depended on a final desperate act. I would not be shooting a corporation or a government agency; I would be shooting a person, and I knew this.

I could feel the awful gnawing ugliness that accompanied the thought of taking an innocent person's life: likely a father with a daughter enrolled in dance lessons and a son starting Little League practice—a man with a wife, parents, brothers, and sisters. The overwhelming hypocrisy of me wanting justice on one hand and what I was considering doing on the other left me knowing who and what I was becoming. It was an irreconcilable conflict. The weapon therefore could not be used to take an innocent man's life—that much I knew. But there was more to consider, including some deceptively compromising shades of gray that were beginning to emerge.

I had to consider that having the weapon allowed me the option of using it as a bluff if needed. However, one's imagination does not need to be very active to almost hear: "But I didn't mean to shoot anyone." Nevertheless, proceeding completely defenseless was not an acceptable option either. There was a wrestling match going on in my mind, and I knew that control during any potential encounter could be lost in an instant when fear and adrenalin would combine in the heat of the moment. I was trained with the understanding that you never drew a weapon unless you intended to use it, and now I was approaching the uncertain ground of wanting to be able to bluff someone who would have his own weapon and would be fearing for his own life. Furthermore, if shots were fired at me, then I was assuming that I would stick to my resolve of not returning fire. This was probably a fair assumption knowing myself as well as I did, but it did present an uncertainty and a loose end that I did not like.

Simultaneously, there were other thoughts competing for attention: one was desperate but perhaps understandable; while the other was foolish and embarrassing to admit. First, if my capture was imminent, having the weapon allowed for a final, personal, deadly choice. Failure of the magnitude under consideration was not acceptable for me—my death would have been required. Second, carrying a weapon would feed right into the pride factor. When I was sixteen years old I wanted to be someone to be reckoned with. Now, at twenty-five, I was going to be.

I decided that I would carry the weapon during the extortion. Not to have it would ensure my live capture if a confrontation ensued. The risk was too great that I might find myself handcuffed and headed to prison, and this became the primary overriding factor governing my decision. As for the immature silliness of any pride factors with carrying a weapon and wanting to be someone to be reckoned with, in this I could shake my head in amusement at myself and easily put this in its proper perspective. But it remained that while I felt that I could be certain that I would not take an innocent person's life, I could not envision myself in a prison environment forever entrapped in a larger world that I hated, and perhaps finding myself the potential sport of guards and other inmates. I would not, I could not, turn over absolute control of my life to another person or to an institution. I needed to have one last way out of life.

Knowing that the telephone company had installed the service junction box and that within it there was a reasonable chance there was $30,000 waiting for me, I decided to proceed without extending the wait longer than it had already been. Perhaps they had provided the money as a ploy to make me think they had complied, thinking all the while that they would certainly capture me and therefore not lose the money that was to be the evidence against me. There also was the very doubtful yet hopeful possibility that South Central Bell had truly acquiesced to my demands, fully complied, and had no intention of trying to capture me. For my part I was confident that I could make the pick-up and escape, being reasonably certain that the odds favored me unless I had grossly underestimated their effort to capture me.

As I was making my final preparations, Beth did not appear to comprehend the seriousness of what was about to happen. She had no concept of the fact that everything in our lives was on the line. Given her apparent disconnect with reality, it therefore seemed better to me not to provide her with any of the key details of what I was about to do. Consequently, downplaying and dismissing the danger was the approach that I took. I would be home later the following morning as I always was right after completing a job. This time it was just a different type of job... not a big deal.

There were so many things that reflected deep and growing problems in Beth's life. At the time hers was a separate world where beautiful fiction and unfolding nightmares were colliding. With her mother having died from an overdose of prescription drugs only three weeks after Beth joined me, our start was emotionally difficult. Then, within six months of her mother's death, the one significant man in her life from her family—her kind, loving, gentle, distinguished grandfather who was the perfect picture of what a grandfather should be and whom Beth adored with all her heart—had put a gun to his head and taken his life following his deteriorating health, the death of his only daughter, and the robbery of prized possessions that had taken him a lifetime to collect.

His collection was one of firearms and related items, but this was no ordinary collection. He had been a well-respected firearms dealer in exclusive Shaker Heights, Ohio, and his collection included several serial number one weapons and other firearms of considerable value. His collection had been his life in many ways, perhaps his great distraction from the deeply troubling things around him. Losing his daughter, his health, and finally his collection was too much for him. It was especially easy for me to understand his actions, but not so for Beth. Privately I had then wondered, and the thought still haunts me, if seeing his only granddaughter moving to Louisiana to live with a man to whom she was not married had impacted his mental state. It could have been a relief for him believing that she was going to be cared for, but it just as easily could have been another sad and bitter disappointment considering the circumstances. Granddaughters were supposed to have weddings. I knew of these rightfully expected considerations.

I can still remember the emotional devastation that his suicide brought Beth—hers was a life that could bear no more. And now here I was, perhaps hours away from adding to her misery with another strike against her that was straight out of hell—yet I didn't really believe that this would happen, for I did not expect to fail. Indeed, in the morally upside down world before me I must not fail. It was my responsibility to protect Beth and to provide for her—this was what a man was supposed to do. The luxury of abstract moral principles was colliding with the disintegration of her life before me. Empty wine bottles were becoming too many; truth was becoming as elusive as the shadows; and I could not understand how the vast quantities of food that were being consumed when I was not there could not add a single pound to this frail and delicate young woman.

In perspective, my own psychological battles had become insignificant compared to what was unfolding before my eyes. I had made the proverbial leap from the frying pan into the fire. At least with the extortion I had control, or I thought I did. In ways, it was an easier battlefield than the one of relationships.

Chapter Eight

Escapes & Illusions

There were no contingencies if I were to fail. There were no special provisions made for Beth, no instructions for what to do if I disappeared into the Mississippi River and was never found, and no steps to follow if I were killed or captured. I had performed the pick-up and escape numerous times in my mind, and once in practice. Mental checklists ensured that I had completed all of the necessary preparations for this final showdown. As I pulled out of my driveway the evening of August 7, 1973, I knew that I would either be back within twelve hours or that I would likely never be back. A lot of questions were soon going to be answered.

Within twenty minutes I was on the twenty-four mile Lake Pontchartrain Causeway headed toward New Orleans, and within an hour of leaving home I was in the city approaching the Greater New Orleans Bridge. As I was crossing the bridge I thought of the Mississippi River below. I realized that my dead body might soon be floating down the river, and I wondered how it would be discovered. I gave thought to the possibility that I might have greatly overrated my planning and underestimated those who would be waiting for me. I wondered if I was going to end up in the river much like a fish in a barrel—a failure about to be plucked out of the water who would instead have to accentuate his failure by shooting himself. Fear of failure was the only fear that was a concern for me.

I wondered too about marked bills and traceable money—about how to maintain a low profile with my coming financial windfall and how not to be careless in any way. I thought of what a relief it was going to be to not have to worry about money for a while and to be able to do more renovation work on the house. Then I wondered what was going to happen at the upcoming trial where I was going to defend myself against the charges filed by the appliance dealer. And then all the wondering stopped. The plan was in motion.

I drove to the upstream location that was four miles from the drop-off site, approaching the area directly from the south so that I could avoid driving along River Road—I wanted no additional exposure along that area where I had to assume traffic was being monitored in secret in the vicinity of the Harvey Canal. As during the test run, I parked near the old bar and waited for a clear opportunity to then walk over the riverbank levee to stow my gear near the water. What was different this time was that a black-taped speedwrench and a loaded .357 magnum revolver were part of my equipment. I returned to my vehicle and drove back to the south until I reached the Westbank Expressway. I followed it back to the east to where I then left the Expressway again and headed north into downtown Gretna, thus avoiding the drop-off site completely.

I drove to the garbage can rack where I would be leaving my dry clothes. As I had determined from my test run, this was one mile downstream from the drop-off site, less than two hundred yards upstream from the Gretna ferry, and in an area that I could easily relocate and access from the river. There was no activity, and I simply got out of my car, walked up to one of the garbage cans, opened the lid, and placed the bag inside that was holding my unidentifiable dry clothes and shoes. I returned to my car and drove directly to where I would park just north of the Gretna City Hall where the Gretna Police Station was located.

With the way that things were progressing, the only thing that I would have preferred would have been if there had been a hard driving rain to reduce visibility in the vicinity of the drop-off location, as I felt that would work to my advantage. I was ready though, and there would be no further delays. I parked near other vehicles, and then walked to the bar from where I would again call a taxi. As before, I ordered one beer, struck up no conversations, and tried to be as invisible as possible when it came to being someone who would be remembered.

A taxi was called after an appropriate delay, and I left the bar with a single unfinished beer remaining for the bartender to throw away to make room for the next bored patron who would be stopping by for a drink before heading home or catching the ferry. It was just another lazy, humid, southern night.

The taxi drove me to the old bar at the upstream location where another typical night of slow drinking was likely going on inside. After paying the cab driver I went directly to an outside pay phone to pretend to make a call. Although I thought that I might be taking things to an extreme, I was as careful there as I had just been in the taxi to ensure that I would leave no fingerprints. Listening to the silence on the phone and casually looking around allowed me to pick the safest time to leave the bar area with never having to enter. When satisfied that no one was observing me, I hung up the phone and crossed up and over the riverbank levee and down into my world. Any thoughts of turning back had been abandoned. It had been the successful test run and the boost in confidence from that as well as the pending trial and all that it represented that had essentially finalized the decision for me. I was now about to enter my comfort zone again even though I knew full well that this time it would be a much different run.

I changed into my wetsuit at a relaxed pace—I was on no one's schedule but my own. Over my wetsuit I buckled on an old leather belt with a conventional western-style leather holster that held the .357 magnum revolver. I then withdrew the pistol and worked the action a few times by cocking and releasing the hammer, giving the loaded cylinder a gentle spin during the process. The soft ticking sound of the cylinder whirring its way to a stop assured me of the pistol's readiness. I drew the hammer back one click to the safety position. When finished, I holstered the weapon and buttoned down the top snap on the holster to secure it in place. Everything felt fine, and seriousness set in.

I put on my diving harness and secured the quick-release from the speedwrench onto the appropriate D-ring on my harness. The harness already had my work knife attached to it—construction divers don't enter the water without a knife. This standard precaution is necessary not to fight the sharks that are much exaggerated in the movies, but rather to have a way to cut yourself free from ropes that you might get fouled in and to be prepared for unforeseen situations—for this night, I thought I might need it for the package. All that remained was to hide my clothes. I had no intention of recovering these items later; they were to be left and forgotten. If found by a search team at this unlikely location four miles upstream, the clothes would yield no clues that could steer the investigation in my direction. These were not the days of DNA and extremely sophisticated forensics. I could have weighted down the clothes and thrown them into the river, but I did not. No plan is perfect.

The familiar feel of the river met me as I sat down on the riverbank at the water's edge. I put on my fins, and in a few seconds I was entering the flow of the river. I was certain that I owned the element of surprise. If there were people waiting for me, they had missed their first opportunity to capture me. I figured that if they would have spotted me they already would have been giving chase. Instead, I had just successfully walked through a bottleneck approach to River Road without being challenged. Small milestones of victory were beginning to be clicked off one by one.

In ways remotely similar to the time in high school when I had attempted suicide or even in grade school when I had slipped while climbing and nearly fallen to my death, certain recollections and impressions of the entirety of my life were passing through my mind like some spiritual slideshow. When you are facing what may well be the end of your life, it apparently always has a way of coming into focus. God was not a consideration for me since I had not relented the least in my atheism, but there still was an overall sense of the presence of life and some hard-to-describe value that life represented. I still vaguely could recall that strange wall in my mind that I had tried to explain to the minister who had counseled me. Tinges of conscience passed by in my mind, and I was disappointed in knowing what I had become. Deliberately narrowing my focus to maintain keen alertness, I had to put these latest wonderings aside. As profound and important as they seemed in some kind of abstract sense, this was a time to concentrate on sights, sounds, and scenarios that might develop.

Nothing during the four miles of floating and swimming downriver gave me cause to think that there had been any kind of significant mobilization by law enforcement personnel in anticipation of my arrival, and likewise nothing assured me that they did not have personnel and means waiting to be deployed that could be sent into immediate action at a single command. I was thankful that I had done all the preparation that I had, and I realized more than ever how critical every aspect was. In many ways for me this was the secret and valiant military mission that I never went on or the daring and involved rescue that I had never participated in; but this mission had me instead being an instrument of evil, and that was a bitter disappointment. Being able to die for some kind of higher cause had always been my greatest dream and welcomed release, but this was a far cry from that lofty and perhaps noble thought. Again I had to tear my thoughts away from these wanderings and wonderings of the mind to focus on the urgency of the moment. As I floated the last five hundred yards the proper focus returned.

As during the test run, there was no vessel traffic approaching or departing the Harvey Canal. The waterway never had been an especially busy one during the times that I had occasion to drive through that area. I had seen the 4th Street Bridge raised only a few times when it was necessary to accommodate infrequent vessels. There also was no vessel traffic on the dark waters of the Mississippi River. The peaceful silence that night was not a foreboding sense of the calm before the storm, but neither did it lull me into a sense of complacency. I knew full well that at any time the situation could change instantly. The adrenalin factor clicked up a cautious notch. My main immediate concern was the thought of being suddenly illuminated by a giant military-type searchlight that might have been cleverly set up for this occasion. The thought of opening the junction box and this action subsequently serving like flipping on a light switch for a powerful searchlight was somewhat unnerving. However, I did not recognize anything that might have given me a clue for what was about to happen.

Swimming into the Harvey Canal from the Mississippi River went smoothly. I reached the bank of the canal near the location of the junction box. While moving quickly at the start of the run had not been a pressing issue, that all now changed in an instant. Speed and stealth. I had to move fast. No second thoughts. No hesitation. Full commitment. With my fins off and placed strategically for putting back on as fast as possible, I moved up the bank swiftly into position adjacent to the box with my speedwrench in hand ready to open the cover.

It had been only seconds since I had left the water, and I was just about to open the cover. Rapidly approaching headlights from the direction of the 4th Street Bridge then lit up the roadway and the light spilled over in the direction of the box. I was below their line of sight, so I knew that I had not yet been seen, but I was in my most vulnerable position being separated from the water. The car was coming fast—too fast I thought—and bearing down on the location. This wasn't good. It was nevertheless too amazing to me that they could already have responded with me having just left the water. I crouched down and waited to see what was going to happen next. With totally inappropriate and misplaced humor, this exact thought came to me: "Man, these guys are fast." I briefly entertained this untimely and amusing bewilderment, smiling as I realized that I might have been outfoxed. But it was deadly humor, and I knew what options might soon be before me. I was not going to be captured.

My relief was immediate when the car traveling at a higher than normal rate of speed, instead of stopping, rounded the corner and headed up River Road. I had no idea if it had been dispatched for me, or if its presence was a coincidence. Either way, my fastest action was now called for and all the mental stops were pulled out as I fit the socket from the speedwrench onto the bolt that was securing the cover for the junction box. Three seconds and the cover was open. With one click the speedwrench was again secured to my diving harness. I grabbed the plastic bag within the box and raced back down to the water. I barely had my fins on when another car came charging up from the 4th Street Bridge. The telltale roar of its engine left me with no doubt that someone was demanding all he could from that car.

Yet strangely enough, this second car didn't stop near the box either. It continued around the corner as had the first car, but at a much higher rate of speed. Given the vehicle's speed and performance, I knew that it was in pursuit with me being the intended target—they just happened to be going in the wrong direction. Removing the package had started a series of events that would now leave me in the race of my life.

With the package in hand, I slipped into the water moving as fast as I could. I rolled over onto my back to take full advantage of swimming in my most efficient style while yet maintaining visual contact with what was happening on the bank of the canal. My fingers tore into and through the numerous layers of plastic wrap, and I submerged the package to flood it while yet swimming. Removing the package had obviously triggered the chase. To ensure that they would not be able to start to track me, I knew that I needed to neutralize that function as fast as possible.

I was barely twenty feet out into the waters of the canal as a third car now came racing to the scene from the same direction. This one came to a hard and fast stop with its doors swinging open immediately. Two men with flashlights jumped out and ran to the box to confirm that the pick-up had been made. They then started shining their lights along the bank looking for some kind of indication to determine where I was. They had to consider the very real possibility that I was in the bushes only yards away from them and armed. Theirs was not an enviable position, and neither was mine. Never had seconds and fractions of seconds counted so much in my life. One of the two men started searching more intensely along the bank of the canal while the other hesitated momentarily and began sweeping his light from left to right out over the waters of the Harvey Canal—precisely where I was now trying to make my escape. By then I was perhaps fifty feet out into the canal.

Seconds before the light beam got to me I considered submerging below the surface to achieve a moment of hiding to give the light time to pass over me, hoping that its sweep would continue past me to allow me to surface unnoticed and resume swimming away. With wearing the buoyant wetsuit it would be somewhat difficult to submerge, but not impossible since I was wearing fins to assist. But I was also instantly aware that if I did this and then came back up for air while eyes were still trained in my direction, that I could then be spotted easily because of the disturbance that surfacing would create.

I had one remaining choice: I stopped swimming and tried to be as still as possible and lay as flat as possible in the water to reduce my floating profile. Incredibly, the light passed directly onto and over me. It was impossible, but he had not seen me. At that exact same time I had finally become aware of another danger as I heard the ominous sound of large diesel engines advancing up the Harvey Canal. After the searcher finished his sweep with his flashlight, he joined the other man. They then started running upriver along the bank of the Mississippi River. With no small boats spotted, they had to have assumed that I was on foot making my getaway. They were giving chase with their flashlights bobbing and weaving through the brush and trees in what was starting to appear like a frantic search. Where those first two cars had gone I had no clue.

Immediately after I realized that I had not been seen I had resumed swimming at my fastest pace. The ominous sound that I had heard was a tugboat that had seemed to come out of nowhere through the Harvey Canal. It was moving fast. If a vessel can be called determined, this one appeared to be as it was heading straight at me. I was directly in its path, and there was no assurance that I would be able to get out of its way in time. Its spotlight was concentrating on the west side of the canal, and its beam pivoted back and forth repeatedly as it charged ahead searching the bank.

I had no idea if the tugboat was associated with the search team or if its presence was a coincidence. It was possible that it was making a routine run and that it was simply using the spotlight for navigation purposes. At any rate, the captain didn't know that he was bearing down on a man in the water right before him. I maintained the fastest swimming pace that I could, managed to get the clearance distance that I needed, and the tugboat narrowly passed beside me. The large screws would not get the opportunity of slicing and dicing me into separate pieces. I continued my fast pace out into the Mississippi River. Once I was well clear of the Harvey Canal and again back into the flow of the river I was able to slow my swimming back to a more relaxed pace and begin to think about what I was now facing.

I gave the package more attention and did all that I could to ensure that it was completely flooded without losing the contents. All indications now were that I had the money in hand and that I had managed to achieve success in the first step of my escape. However, with the upriver search underway in earnest and with the uncertainty of the deployment of the tugboat and/or any smaller vessels that might soon be appearing—including for all I knew the remote possibility of a U.S. Coast Guard vessel—it made sense for me to get out of the river as quickly as I could. I also needed to inspect the contents of the package. This was not to eagerly verify the money but to determine what in the package might still be about to compromise me. Celebration was far off—I was now right in the middle of a major search by law enforcement personnel who were likely soon to be joined by all available local police and other law enforcement resources. My anticipated good odds at success were now down to about split-even. I definitely did not have victory in hand yet, and there were no guarantees.

Unknown to me at the time were many aspects of the stakeout and the initial phase of the attempted capture that would defy vain considerations such as coincidence or luck. It would be nearly seven years before a complex puzzle would come together and I would learn what happened that night. From the vantage point of that belated understanding I was to learn many humbling things. What I had attributed to skill and good planning were impacted by a far different influence than I had ever expected. While I am not so foolish or irreverent as to imply that God is in the business of aiding extortionists, I am also left with certain inescapable conclusions that transcend natural occurrence. As one of the two South Central Bell high level representatives who was a committed Christian would eventually tell me, "You never should have gotten away." I was to learn just how right he was.

The first of the three cars that had approached the area that evening—the one for which I had thought to myself: "Man, these guys are fast," was simply some hapless passerby whose timing was the same as mine when I had first approached the drop-off. He was perhaps driving a little faster than he should have been, or at least that was the way that it had appeared to me. When I immediately thereafter used the speedwrench and removed the package that simultaneously activated the electronic device, this triggered the dispatch of the second vehicle, which was actually the first of two search vehicles. Because the trip signal had occurred immediately after the first vehicle had rounded the corner, it had appeared to the search team that this vehicle had made the pick-up of the package and was then speeding away. Therefore, the first search vehicle had mistakenly set out in a high speed pursuit of the car driven by the innocent passerby. I can only imagine how that fearful encounter developed and concluded. This opportune delay for me allowed the first and fastest search vehicle to be sent after the wrong person, thus allowing me extremely precious seconds to begin to make my way out into the canal.

The third vehicle, which was the second search vehicle, arrived seconds later to check the scene, but by then I had already started slipping away into the night by swimming out into the canal. The distance that I had covered had been just enough for the searcher sweeping his flashlight out over the water to miss me even though I was quietly floating there before him. I might have looked like a piece of wood debris, but this is something that will never be known. I do not know what the man saw or how he could have missed me. Again, I am especially careful not to suggest that God blinded one man so that a lesser man might escape, but I do have to say—and I know—that I should have been spotted. God alone knows the extent to which He intervenes in our lives.

The ordeal with the tugboat was one of extraordinary timing. It was a matter of seconds by which I was spared. No skill and no planning alone can be credited with pulling off this narrow escape unless a person insists on a compulsive and obsessive crediting of luck and circumstances. But there is more.

Two men were stationed in a tower within rifle range of the drop-off location. One man worked for the telephone company; the other was an FBI Agent. Security personnel from the telephone company were legally excluded from being part of the arrest team, but the FBI had allowed them to be present for observation. After the first few hours had slipped by uneventfully, the FBI Agent assigned to the watch that night became convinced that no one was going to make the pick-up. A stakeout for twenty-four or forty-eight hours is one thing, but a stakeout for thirty days at twenty-four hours a day for what might be a mean hoax perpetrated by some demented employee who had a grudge against South Central Bell was quite another situation altogether. Convinced that I was not going to show up, the Agent had descended the tower and was asleep in his car below. The South Central Bell employee was left in the tower alone with the rifle equipped with the night vision scope.

Having one man stationed in the tower with the rifle would in fact have been sufficient, except for one amazing fact: the man left in the tower was extremely fearful of heights, apparently to the point of his fear being a near phobia. When I had grabbed the package and this had triggered the signal to alert everyone that the pick-up had been made, he was too afraid to approach the edge to try to use the rifle scope to spot me. He would not have had the authority to take a shot, but he should have been able to respond immediately to locate me through the night vision scope and thereby direct the search teams accordingly. Instead, he was reduced to the absurd indignity of crawling as close as he dared to the edge of the tower and then using assorted pocket change to throw dimes, nickels, and quarters at the vehicle below to try to awaken the soundly sleeping Agent. There were going to be some mighty unhappy people when this night was reviewed. My extortion run was to have consequences for others that I had never even remotely considered. As might be expected, that Agent was later reassigned to a lesser position. Also, there were still more events unfolding in the background as I was to learn later.

For my part that night, all I knew was that there was at least one car and maybe two that were somehow involved that had first raced past the scene; and that seconds later another car showed up with the two men who had started their search for me and had narrowly missed me. Then, I had nearly been run over by a tugboat that had seemed to appear out of nowhere. Clearly, a tugboat just doesn't appear like that, so with the distractions of the vehicles and the search team I must have had such tunnel vision and narrow focus of thought that I had missed the obvious. Nevertheless, it remains a mystery to me how the tugboat had come upon me so fast. At the time I knew nothing of the men assigned to the tower, and I had no realization that an unwitting driver had drawn away the first and fastest search team.

At the first good opportunity I made my way into an industrial area located downstream from the Harvey Canal. After passing a final barge that was moored to a docking facility, I had slipped in immediately behind the barge for this change of plans—I had remembered the lesson that I did not want to pass close to the bow of the barge on the upstream side. If I had not earlier learned that crucial lesson I might well have otherwise headed directly across the bow to get out of harm's way as soon as possible and consequently been sucked under the barge by the strong current.

Exiting the river prematurely was an unexpected diversion from my original plan, and as such I knew that things were now precarious for me at best. An uneasy tension was now building in a different way as rapid action was about to change into apprehensive waiting.

I had to hope that there would be no night watchmen stationed near this area, or if there were that I would not be spotted. My first action though was the inspection of the package to determine if I perhaps was still carrying the unwelcome guarantee of my capture in the form of a locating device that could possibly reactivate itself with now being out of the water—assuming that it had in fact been deactivated when I had flooded the package. I had no assurance regarding whether or not someone might well be zeroing in on my location right at that moment and that I would soon be found hiding in the center of a calibrated search grid. Additionally, I still had to consider the remote possibility that there might be some type of explosive device inside, even though I knew that legal and potential liability issues made this possibility highly unlikely. I basically had to trust that thoroughly flooding the package had disabled everything.

So without delay and without taking any special precautions, while still at the water's edge I rapidly cut away most of the plastic wrap and pushed aside the bundles within and located the transmitter. No explosive devices were inside. The riprap along the riverbank was then put to good use. I laid the transmitter down on a rock and picked up another rock and smashed it repeatedly to thoroughly neutralize all electronic capabilities in case the flooding had failed to do so. As a final guarantee and in the event that a search team was deployed to the downstream riverbank, I threw the remains back into the river to dispose of the secret permanently.

Without hearing any approaching search boats and with knowing that I was downstream from the present search operations, I felt for the first time that I could stop and more thoroughly examine the contents of the package—it certainly felt like the money was there, but not quite. The anticipated bundles of tens and twenties were instead separate banded bundles of cut-up paper. There would be no financial windfall for me from this night's activities. As I was able to muster humor when I first thought that a search team was racing to intercept me even before I had started to open the junction box, so too I now had to admit that they had indeed outsmarted me after all. I could smile and admire them for their legitimately tough and uncompromising stance, while at the same time I could acknowledge expected disappointment and some anger. I had just taken an incredible risk and successfully evaded capture, and I had nothing to show for it other than having survived.

I disposed of the cut-up paper and what remained of the plastic bag by using rocks to try to keep the items submerged at the water's edge. I then moved further onshore to search for a hiding place. While speed had before been my plan, I now was committed to patient, disciplined, and deliberate waiting. If the downstream riverbank was going to be searched on foot or by a passing search vessel with a spotlight, this would likely occur within the next one to two hours. I needed to wait long enough for the search teams to reach the conclusion that I was long gone from the area. I needed less than one quiet and uneventful hour to complete my escape, but that hour would have to be delayed. I still had enough of the night left to accomplish this, but I did not have a lot of time to spare.

Finding a suitable place to wait, I sat down and made myself as comfortable as one can be in a wetsuit. All things considered, I was reasonably relaxed given the precarious situation. The area that I was in suggested to me that it was unlikely that a guard was stationed there. The night's activities began to replay in my mind, and I remained amazed that I had not been spotted in the water when the flashlight had passed over me. The thought of the tugboat bearing down on me left me shaking my head in quiet wonder at what I had just escaped. I eased back further to wait and to consider what my next steps were going to be over the course of the next few hours and days.

I didn't even notice my eyelids getting heavy, didn't realize that the now quiet night was lulling me into a dangerous complacency. Months of thought and weeks of planning were about to be seriously jeopardized as I relaxed further. As inconceivable and outrageous as it may seem with the elapsing time being so critical to my success or failure, I fell sound asleep to become completely defenseless and vulnerable. It well could have been that the next sound I would hear would be the click of a hammer drawing back on a weapon inches from my head.

A sharp pang of immediate fear and dread leapt through me when I woke up. I had no idea at first of how long I had been asleep. In this blunder of blunders I had fallen asleep with daylight not far from approaching. The humor that I had managed before at my circumstances regarding the first vehicle and then with later discovering the paper rather than the money now had no audience with me. I felt just about as stupid as a person can feel. I had a strong understanding that if this all now concluded in failure that I deserved my fate. I was extraordinarily angry with myself for this unforgivable lapse. Finding myself incompetent was not what I could handle well, and I had just been grossly incompetent.

Maintaining the alert discipline now that I should have had all along, I kept a careful watch as I returned to the river. I had kept all my equipment with me so there was no relocating of anything that was required. I put on my fins and commenced a fast swim downriver for what remained of the final mile. The Gretna ferry was on the New Orleans side of the river, so I would be encountering no delays to avoid it. I aggressively negotiated the rest of the journey and exited according to plan while still being under, but barely under, the cover of darkness.

Leaving the river I removed my fins and carried them with me to the rack of garbage cans where I had earlier placed my clothes. Now keenly aware of the pressure of time I stepped back into a hidden area and changed from my wetsuit into my dry clothes. My wetsuit & fins, the diving harness with the speedwrench, and the revolver still in its holster were placed in the bag that had held my clothes. I returned to the garbage can rack and left the bag beside the rack.

I then walked openly and deliberately to my car that was parked not far from the front of the police station. Dawn was breaking. I still had some residual humor at having been outwitted; but I was also seriously considering taking everything that had happened as a new challenge of wills, for in many ways nothing in my circumstances had changed. The upcoming trial was still pending; my future was still uncertain. And although there was that thread of humor, it was a thin and dangerous humor. I didn't like losing. Where no humor existed was with myself for having fallen asleep. I was not used to making incredible mistakes like this.

There were some early activities now starting in downtown Gretna with increased traffic as the city was slowly beginning the new morning, but my timing had been okay. I started my car and drove off as during the test run to perform a brief detour to ensure that I was not being followed. I then returned to the garbage can rack and recovered my gear. I was driving a 1972 blue Ford Ranchero, which was the Ford counterpart of the Chevrolet El Camino. These vehicles were half car and half truck, meaning that the front of the vehicle had the appearance of a car but the rear portion resembled the bed of a pickup. The car was only two years old and stylish for the time, and it would draw double-takes from those interested in such cars—and interest as well from other eyes as I would also later learn. Just in case the bag with the wetsuit might draw additional attention from someone that morning—namely an observant or curious police officer—I placed it in front of the passenger seat inside instead of placing it in the back bed. Besides, I still wanted quick access to my pistol.

And then, with still being upset with myself over having fallen asleep, like some oblivious and blinded fool I half-wondered why there seemed to be so many police cars racing in different directions that morning. I did dare to consider for a while that it might have something to do with the extortion, but that seemed too arrogant a thought—I didn't warrant that much attention, and my current frame of mind didn't put my worth very high. For a short while at least, my anger at myself would cloud my thinking.

A little arrogance instead of anger at that particular moment would have served me well, and I should have erred on the side of caution and headed straight home. Instead, being reasonably satisfied that I had succeeded in spite of myself and with considering that all search efforts were probably concluded by then, I made the incomprehensible decision that I should return and pick up my discarded clothes at the upstream location. During the course of the night I had realized that I should have weighted the clothes and thrown them into the river—there had been no good reason not to do this. The clothes by themselves would not have been a direct link to me, but if they were found then there might be speculation that a diver had been involved. I was finding myself reconsidering one of my first concerns: if a diver was suspected then it would not take a great deal of investigative work to begin to narrow the field of possible suspects. I felt uncomfortable pressure as I thought more about all that was now coming into play. Regardless, I should have stayed well clear of the areas where I had been earlier—search teams could easily have still been there. But this loose end continued to trouble me.

I concluded that I would appear to be no different than any other individual driving around that morning. In spite of the heightened level of police activity with a number of cruisers speeding throughout the area, I drove to the upstream location, again approaching it from the south to stay as clear as possible of River Road near the Harvey Canal. While there was increased police activity on the Westbank Expressway, there was no activity near the old bar where my clothes were less than one hundred yards away. I took the gamble and opted to get my clothes. Walking now in broad daylight as if I had a purpose and nothing to hide, I walked straight to where my clothes were. I was relieved that they had not already been discovered in their makeshift hiding place. I picked them up and walked straight back to my car. After I was on my way and with no other loose ends troubling me, it finally really hit me that I had managed to pull off a significant escape. Granted, I had no money to show for all my efforts, but in some ways there was a distorted sense of accomplishment. This was more relief than it was smug satisfaction. I was starting to feel better about the way the night had gone.

For the better part of the next seven years I would live under the illusion that I had personally engineered a near-perfect pick-up and escape plan: that it was skill with a little luck that allowed me to escape the two men, and that it was strictly a timing coincidence that a tugboat didn't turn my body into a mutilated mess. There was the lingering curiosity of the first two cars and what had been going on with them, but without knowing why both had driven past the scene this afforded me no way of attaching any sure significance to their presence. The last of the next seven years would begin to open my eyes, but until I was interrogated in the office of the FBI in New Orleans in 1980 illusions and blindness would continue to have their way with me. But regarding the immediate future, I was still not finished pushing the limits with the extortion. Incomprehensively, I was still locked into the plan.

With the level of police activity that morning leaving me uncomfortable and with the growing realization of the carelessness of the latest untimely risk that I had just taken to recover my abandoned clothes, I continued along side roads to the Huey P. Long Bridge to take it back across the Mississippi River rather than risk exposure again along the Westbank Expressway. If a curious police officer would decide to stop me to ask a few questions, I would be short on good answers with having gear that was still wet sitting beside me and a loaded pistol in a wet holster. I needed to do one thing, and that was to get out of the area and return home without any further delay.

Chapter Nine

Blind Stubbornness

After the river run I remained locked into my plan even though I had a prevailing sense that it was now time to stop—time to go no further with a plan that appeared to have no promise of success and now a much higher probability of failure. Faced with having narrowly escaped, faced with the realization that South Central Bell had made a choice not to pay but to pursue, and faced with what would likely be a more efficient and determined effort to capture me—I nevertheless chose to ignore that I was getting in well over my head. It remained a challenge for me and a test of wills. This is not to say that I didn't seriously consider abandoning the extortion, for I did continue to study the circumstances and reevaluate my commitment that admittedly was beginning to waver. Still, I found myself giving in to what I knew was an unreasonable and dangerous stubbornness. It was almost a resignation to fail.

My next letter to the telephone company had to convey an increased determination and rage that could not reflect any of the second-guessing of my weakening resolve. Accordingly, another round of damage to company facilities was required and performed on August 13, 1973, to try to convince them that failure to comply with my new set of demands would result in significantly greater damage than had been inflicted to date. I wanted to raise their concern that a major and unacceptable disruption of service would be forthcoming if they again opted for capture rather than meeting my demands. It was beyond a long shot, but I decided that it was worth one more attempt.

My threats escalated to a level where I promised "to go downtown" with the use of explosives. This was pure bluff, but I composed the letter in such a way as to reveal nearly insane murderous rage for my demands not having been met and for the efforts in trying to capture me on August 8th. If it was their attention that I wanted, I certainly had it now. I would later learn that South Central Bell believed that this meant that an explosive device would be used at their downtown office. My intention had been to make them think that I would target equipment at a central communications hub, and the death threats that I had alluded to were to discourage further direct attempts at apprehension at the pick-up site. Instead, what I had accomplished was raising the significance of the crime to a level where all the stops were pulled out to try to capture me before I made good on my promises. Property threats were one thing; what they viewed as potential wholesale murder was another.

My demand was raised to $40,000, which would be today's approximate equivalent of nearly $200,000. One of the reasons that I had originally selected the amount of $30,000 was that this might have encouraged them to believe that I had specific reasons for this odd amount and that therefore if it was paid this would settle some imagined issue that I might have with them. The increase to $40,000 was a calculated increase to reflect anger in response to their not having met the $30,000 demand. I also knew that they would not pay if they thought that I might return at a later date to make an additional demand, but that they might pay if they had reasonable assurance that this would be a one-time occurrence to settle some imagined injustice. I knew that expecting them to pay even once was a stretch, but this was the plan upon which I was proceeding.

New planning was required for the pick-up and escape, and it was here that my confidence factor was fast eroding. Having played what was very likely my best hand, I had no completely new tricks. The fundamental objectives and priorities were still the same: making it costly, impractical, and difficult for the authorities to maintain surveillance and capture teams. My impatience was beginning to become a factor, and I knew that this could work against me. I would have to force myself not to act impulsively and instead take the necessary time to consider other options for the next encounter at the pick-up site. I had no assurance that they would respond again, so this uncertainty allowed for any elaborate planning on my part for the money transfer to be delayed until the time came when I could be sure that another drop-off had been made.

Once again I needed a way to determine if they had responded without going to all the trouble of a pick-up run only to come up empty-handed. I decided to demand that a second pedestal-type junction box be installed at another location near but not adjacent to the Mississippi River with $20,000 placed in it. This would help steer speculation away from any consideration that I was going to use the Mississippi River for my escape, but yet if it came to it I could make a wild race to the river from this second location. I was considering driving directly off a dock in a stolen vehicle and into the river, hopefully outrunning those assigned to capture me—having full confidence that they would not be inclined to enter the river the same way. I would also demand that the original junction box that had been installed along River Road at the Harvey Canal be resupplied with the same extortion demand, meaning that there now would be two separate boxes at two separate locations, each with $20,000 inside. Additionally, I extended the time to two months for when I would make the pick-up rather than my original thirty days. I could choose either location first, and from those results decide if I would continue on to the other.

This latest plan meant there would have to be a doubling of the surveillance and capture teams—and the pick-up would occur within two months rather than one month. These moves had doubled the costs and/or split the teams that might be deployed to try to capture me, and the time involved had also doubled. I figured that there was now a high probability that they would either make the payment or choose instead to completely ignore me as they had the first time. The surveillance costs would almost certainly be considered too high to justify. If they ignored me this time, I would abandon all efforts and concede defeat.

I was convinced that my best chance for success involved making a second pick-up at the Harvey Canal location, with the details to be worked out later. But first, I needed to select a suitable location for the second junction box with its package. Keeping the profile consistent meant that I would again select a location on the Westbank in one of the small cities that blended together. I drove around the area and finally settled on the intersection of two streets in Gretna. I parked at the street sign identifying the intersection of 1st Street and Industrial Parkway, briefly surveyed the area, and while still parked there I wrote down the names of the two streets. This was to be where I would demand that they install the second junction box. The street names were not written down from my memory later. They were written down as I observed them. This would later become a crucial factor.

This last extortion letter was the one in which I fully developed the psychological profile of someone with exceptional rage—of someone driven by anger who was dangerous and unwilling to stop until his demands were met. This letter was the truly ugly one: the language used was out of the gutter and the thoughts conveyed were out of hell. In it I mocked the authorities for their failed attempt at capturing me and let them know that if they attempted capture again that I would use deadly force. This threat was conveyed in patently vulgar terms. I wanted them to consider that they had narrowly escaped, and that it was not the other way around. I did have the advantage of being one up on them—I had indeed escaped, so I expected that they would reluctantly have to admit that I was not presenting pure bluff but was instead someone who was capable of doing that which he promised. The risk factor for them would have been perceived as increasing many times as a result of the failed capture and my current threats.

The potential confrontation had now escalated to a new level. Although I had not intended to imply in my letter that I was about to bomb the downtown offices of the telephone company, I had nevertheless successfully begun tightening the noose around my own neck.

The letter postmarked August 14, 1973, spelled out the terms: two locations, each with $20,000, the time of the pick-up left open for two months, and the promised deadly force if capture was again attempted. With the next round of damage completed and the letter sent, it was again time to wait.

The upcoming trial for the false charges filed by the appliance dealer was getting closer. At my arraignment on August 21, 1973, I represented myself and plead not guilty. The court had no way of knowing that they were dealing with a man whose present criminal activities were far more serious than those currently under consideration for which I was genuinely not guilty. The contrived felony charge of Simple Burglary had finally been dropped against me, and I was now facing the lesser charges of Simple Assault and Simple Battery—all this for standing on a man's porch and angrily demanding that promised repairs be performed. The trial date was set for September 25th. It was beginning to appear that even if I were found guilty, that jail time would be unlikely with fines now being a possible ruling rather than incarceration. I still was carrying a chip on my shoulder about this though, and it was uncertain how I would react to a guilty verdict, regardless of the results of the sentencing.

In spite of the lingering uncertainty, I was gaining more confidence regarding my chances of presenting a successful defense after dismissing my attorney and choosing to represent myself. I had been busy preparing for my case—which now would involve the safeguard of fabricated testimony by a willing witness of mine to support my position. I was not content to meekly submit to the court, and I was taking steps to ensure that I would not be found guilty. If the other side was going to be deceitful and manipulative, I could play that game as well. I had found a way to use lies to support truth. The futility of complete honesty had long since become a cynical conclusion for me in those situations that I could rationalize away, while that same honesty remained a mandated course of action for selected aspects of my integrity. To be sure, I practiced major moral inconsistencies at my convenience.

After allowing sufficient time for South Central Bell to respond to my new demands and then allowing enough time for the initial tense security to perhaps lessen, I made another trip to Gretna—this time to check the new location for the second junction box. I would be returning to the intersection that I had designated as the second drop-off location. I was uncomfortably aware that driving past this location would greatly compromise my secrecy since this would allow the authorities to begin a cross-referencing process for those cars that weeks ago had first passed by the Harvey Canal location compared now to the cars passing the street intersection in Gretna. This assumed of course that all license plate numbers were being recorded, which I considered was highly probable if not certain. I would learn later that in fact there had been extensive investigation performed on license plate numbers of vehicles passing the Harvey Canal location to determine possible leads in the case.

An attitude of finality came upon me as I made the drive to check the second location. As I approached the intersection that I had identified as 1st Street and Industrial Parkway, there was an expected adrenalin factor that kicked in—a contrary combination of dread and hope. Then, instead of dread and hope there was only resignation. They had called my bluff; they had not given in to my demands. Since they had not acted on this part of my demand, there could therefore be no expectation or assurance that they had acted on the other part and resupplied the first junction box at the original Harvey Canal location. At that moment the entire extortion plan came to a halt and was abandoned. As the profound sense of healthy resignation settled deeper into my soul, I then knew that it was all over.

Simultaneously, I found myself acknowledging a genuine respect for those who had refused to give in to an extortionist. I knew what honor was, and they had chosen that path. They were willing to risk extensive damage to their facilities rather than submit, and I could not help but admire them for doing this. It didn't matter that accolades from a criminal are offensive and worthless; they had done what was right, and I was able to see that. It would be almost seven more years before I would learn much more about what all had transpired throughout the time of the extortion. I would learn then that I hadn't known half the story.

Against my better judgment I continued on to the Harvey Canal location and drove by one final time. The first junction box stood there as a lonely marker. I wondered how long it would remain as a relic before being removed. At least this time I could relax knowing that no watchful eyes were there—or so I thought.

As I left the Westbank and drove back over the Greater New Orleans Bridge I knew that my criminal adventures in the Mississippi River that flowed below me were over. I had both failed and succeeded. I had failed at the extortion that summer in 1973, but I had succeeded in a daring escape.

That would be the extent of my knowledge about the extortion until I would make a full confession to the FBI in 1980, and then later in 2007 receive certain records of the investigation from the United States Department of Justice under the provisions of the Freedom of Information – Privacy Act (FOIPA).

With the extortion attempt abandoned, the next hurdle before me remained the upcoming trial in Covington, Louisiana. As September 25th approached, I concentrated on my defense. The facts of the case were simple. I had purchased three used appliances that had all failed shortly after purchase. In a fit of anger on a Saturday afternoon I confronted Crawford, yet I remained outside his closed screen door. Crawford came forward from a back room, but he never came outside and I never went inside. Crawford responded by immediately calling out to two other men who were present: "Come here! Come here! I want you to see this man. I want you to see his face."

Because Crawford was jockeying for legal position, I knew to leave. As I stepped away from his door I extended my challenge for a confrontation if that was what he wanted: "If you want trouble, you know where I live. I'll be there in five minutes." He never showed up, and he never knew that I had armed myself and waited for him from a vantage point along my driveway. The following morning I was arrested at my residence on charges including: Simple Assault, Disturbing the Peace & Using Obscene Language, and Breaking & Entering. Upon being booked on these charges, I was told that Louisiana did not have a "Breaking & Entering" charge, so without investigation this was automatically amended to Simple Burglary, which was a felony.

I had sought legal counsel because of the seriousness of the charges. Then, after months of the ordeal dragging on and after reaching the limits of my tolerance for lawyer fees, nonsense, and aggravation, I later opted to represent myself at the trial for the eventually reduced charges of Simple Assault and Simple Battery. I did not see how Crawford could prevail with the charges that he had made unless a lie was presented to the court that I had entered his residence. If he and his witnesses lied about that and said that I had entered, I could then find myself in an indefensible position against the weight of the testimony of multiple witnesses. I knew that Crawford was unscrupulous, but I knew nothing about his potential witnesses and to what extent they might go in backing him up. This represented an unacceptable risk for me, and one that I would have to counter.

A friend of mine who enjoyed pulling a good one over on scoundrels and who did not like seeing me being railroaded on false charges agreed to support my position. When I had driven to Crawford's I had parked my car in his driveway about fifty feet from his door. No one would have been able to give my car a close look at the time, and it was completely feasible that a passenger had been with me who had remained seated throughout the brief verbal exchange. I asked my friend if he would testify that he had been seated in my car and had observed everything from a distance. He would testify that he knew I was angry, that I had asked him to stay in the car, that there were in fact words, but that I never went inside. This was all true—everything except his being there to witness this. He would be committing perjury for me, but he would be telling the truth about the situation. I regretted having to make this request of him, but he seemed comfortable with this request from his friend.

Case number 039141 in St. Tammany Parish on September 25, 1973, followed a string of other brief trials primarily for traffic offenses. All the cases were being heard by a judge; there were no jury trials in the courtroom that day. The prosecutor reviewed the charges, and it was clear to me that he had not prepared well for the case. How could he have? I had never even been called in for questioning, not even once.

Crawford and I were both called to testify during the trial. I took the stand first. The questioning was brief. I openly admitted to using obscene language, repeating what I had said while purposely substituting the word "blank" for the expletives that I had used. Respect for the court was thus maintained while yet revealing truth. In context, it would have been clear what my exact words would have been. I admitted that I was in fact angry. I have to believe that Crawford was thinking that my unfolding "confession" was sealing my fate. I suspect that he had expected me to lie and say that I had never said such things—and he knew that his witness would back him up and confirm that I had been angry and vocal. If the testifying had stopped there, I might have lost.

Crawford then took the stand. If ever a man automatically came across as untrustworthy and underhanded, it was the unfortunate Crawford. If you needed someone to play the bad guy in a B movie, he would have been high on anyone's list. He did essentially tell the truth about the state of my agitation and about my harsh words for him when he was questioned by the prosecutor—I'll give him credit for that. When my turn came to question him, I maintained a serious, respectful, and professional composure. Unfortunately for him, he attempted to use the judge's courtroom for snide and mocking remarks.

The prosecutor objected when I sought clarification as to why I was at Crawford's residence in the first place, protesting that this aspect was irrelevant. The judge directed me to stay on course, but he did allow me a certain amount of latitude given that I was not a lawyer. The young prosecutor never objected again. I had felt it was important to my case to be able to present a credible reason for me being there and for why I had a reasonable right to be angry at the time, notwithstanding my foolish decision to confront Crawford directly in the first place.

With having been a fan of the Perry Mason television program in the late 1950's and 1960's in which Mason was a masterful and clever defense lawyer, I perhaps leaned a bit too much to the melodramatic. Nevertheless, I thought that I could undermine Crawford's credibility if I could show that he had sold me three defective appliances and that we had been involved in a continuing saga of his misrepresentations. When I asked one of my questions, he displayed open contempt and attempted to use sarcasm to discredit me. I listened and then replied, "Mr. Crawford, this is serious. This is not a laughing matter."

The judge then leaned over from his bench and gave Crawford a cold, steely-eyed look. His words went straight to the point as he admonished Crawford: "I'll decide what's funny in this courtroom." That ended the misplaced humor, and the chastised Crawford grew quiet.

My questioning of Crawford ended shortly thereafter, and I then had the opportunity to call my witness. I truly did deserve to get caught in this hoax perpetrated on the court, and it would later turn out that my deceit had not been necessary. My questioning of my witness was brief—I wanted it to be brief for fear that we might be found out. The trial moved on.

The prosecutor had a final witness to call—one of the other men who had actually been present. When questioned by the prosecutor, it was obvious that the man was uncomfortable but honest. In fact, the prosecution's witness was far more truthful than mine had been. I was given the opportunity to cross-examine him, and although it was clear that the man did not like me, he did answer my questions directly without having to be prodded. I asked him about my knocking on the door, and he agreed that I did. I asked him about what I had said, and like a displaced and unpolished soul out of the Ozarks of a hundred years ago he answered: "No sir, I can't say what you said. You was a whoopin' and a hollerin' and carryin' on."

I did not challenge his interpretation of the events—he was mighty close to the truth—a truth that was developing a clear consistency. I then came to the key question: "After I knocked on the door, did I ever go inside?"

His answer was clear: "No sir. You was out there carryin' on."

I was prepared to pursue this honest admission further when I was surprised by the sound of the judge's gavel slamming down. At first I wasn't even sure that I heard what I thought I heard, but the words from the bench had been: "Not guilty. Case dismissed."

It took a minute or two to grasp the significance of what had just happened. The trial was over, and I had defended myself and won. Nothing was left hanging over my head. I was free. The door was finally closed on this persistent aggravation. I had then, and still have now, strong regrets about the perjury that I had solicited. I had put my friend in jeopardy, and that was not fair to him. Regardless, it was a tremendous relief to be able to put this behind me.

Putting the situation behind me, however, did not mean ignoring my desired revenge against the man who had caused me this trouble. I didn't know exactly how I was going to do it, but with my sights set on Crawford I wanted to get even. Bitterness and vindictiveness can have deep and stubborn roots—some linked to things in the past that we really don't want to remember.

During the trial I had noticed what I thought might be an unusually high number of sheriff's deputies in attendance. I soon was shaking hands with a couple of them who came over to greet me. There were smiles and congratulations. For some reason, the case had drawn special attention within their ranks. I did not recognize the deputy who had first been obliged to arrest me—I hope that I didn't miss him. It had been his kind intervention that had led to having a judge set modest bail that Sunday morning after I was arrested. It was a good day when I heard from one of the deputies: "If I ever need a lawyer I'm going to look you up." It was a joke between us of course, but it did mean something to me. Even late justice can have its rewards.

After the trial, diving work did begin to pick up and financial pressures slowly began to ease somewhat in spite of growing medical expenses for Beth. Good fortune in the work place did come my way, although on the home front there was a steadily increasing sense of being caught in a hopeless downward spiral. There were good times to be sure, fine times, and Beth and I did have a special shared relationship in our secret world. This private world with her would have to be left in order for me to deal with the real world and its demands. At first I did not realize that she was unable to make the same transition that was required of me. Her world stopped at the juncture where hopeful fantasy and practical reality had to separate.

With having been encouraged with the justice system by the legal conclusion of my trial, and with no consideration of mercy for Crawford, I contacted an attorney to see if I could pursue charges of false arrest. What had angered me more than anything was the direct consequence of my arrest that Sunday on January 28, 1973. It was Sunday evening when Beth had experienced a grand mal epileptic seizure that I knew to be caused directly by the troubling events. Holding her as she went through many fierce convulsions because Crawford wanted to teach me a lesson had left an unforgettable impression on me. He had made an exceedingly dangerous choice in challenging me on this level. His humiliation at the trial had simply been the start of what I intended to exact from him.

Legal processes were being set in motion for retaliation, but a new lawyer who was advising me did not leave me with much confidence that I could expect to prevail. This left me in a quandary because of the now established record of Crawford's and my mutual animosity, and me not letting the matter drop. Direct physical retaliation could hardly be taken without me becoming the logical prime suspect. To ensure that he would not rest easy and to make life as uncomfortable for him as possible, for a short while I engaged in some untraceable harassment. The man knew that someone was after him, and I hoped he feared that it was me. I had already freely testified in court that I knew he was afraid of me—I now wanted him to taste that fear. Once in the grocery store when we met in an aisle I spread my legs and locked my hands on my hips with elbows outstretched to block his path, forcing his retreat.

Paradoxically, at the same time the psychological resignation that I had experienced over the failed extortion attempt and the welcomed relief that I felt over the outcome of the trial were beginning to become part of who I was—and perhaps there was simply a belated maturity that was finally beginning to settle in. I was faced with a deep animosity for Crawford, but I was also weary of living with hatred. I passed his residence and business that was less than two miles from my home every time I went into Covington from Abita Springs, which meant an almost daily reminder of his presence. I knew that I had a dangerous and unhealthy obsession, and I wished that I didn't. The weeks began to turn into months, and in spite of an underlying seething I was slowly beginning to let the matter go. I was actually relieved that I might not find myself bound to satisfy yet another round of revenge. Revenge was becoming a heavy, ugly load. One can hate his own hatred.

When I returned from an offshore job in 1974 and I drove past his place, I looked as I always did to see what activities were going on. Things had changed, and I realized that he had moved. Reminiscent of the resignation that I had submitted to when I realized that my extortion demands were not going to be met, I now realized for the most part that I would probably be letting this situation go as well. I still reserved the option of searching for him and obtaining my revenge, but it had now become a lesser compulsion and not an obsessive priority.

The situation came to a wretched and pitiful end several months later when we learned from a radio broadcast that Crawford had murdered his young adult daughter and then killed himself in northern Louisiana. Beth had been the one to first hear the news, screaming in agony when she heard what had happened. Things now made more sense to me as I recalled the daughter's awkward, nervous, and guarded behavior in his presence. His controlling manner around her in our brief encounters the previous year had left me uncomfortable and suspicious. I was able to key in on abuse, and I had drawn my own conclusions. In an awful way I seriously wondered if I had missed the one opportunity to set her free if I had only pushed through my conscience and become his judge and executioner. It was of course the unthinkable, but I was left wondering where our responsibilities lie when we suspect terrible things are going on. I felt that I had failed her.

Chapters in my life were coming to a close and new ones were being opened. With the events of the last year finalized, I was now living in a more conventional world. Legal and criminal adventures had given way to routine adult responsibilities associated with developing a career, maintaining a home, and providing for a woman whom I had asked to join me in my life. In spite of an inexcusable run of immoral and criminal behavior, I was experiencing a partial restoration of a healthy and active conscience as I reflected on how honor (someone else's in the extortion) and truth (a merciful verdict) had been achieved—both in spite of me, which I found encouraging. If I were the source of what was good in this life, then I knew that it was all for naught. This was hardly the conclusion that there was a God—I was still very bitter about that concept, but it did reinforce the point that truth and honor had their place. The soil that this seed was planted in was still far too rocky to yield a crop, but at least the seed existed.

Chapter Ten

Desperation & Failure

Diving work throughout the remainder of 1973 and through most of 1974 did pick up and welcomed paychecks began arriving, but rising medical bills and no medical insurance until 1975 because of pre-existing conditions for Beth kept finances extremely tight. Additionally, the house outside of Abita Springs that would have been condemned under virtually any city building code required a steady infusion of money and much labor from me as I proceeded with a complete renovation between diving jobs as time and money permitted.

Beth's diminishing confidence, purpose, and hope left her withdrawing further into herself and into a world that I no longer knew. Her once bubbling enthusiasm became more often a disconnected melancholy, a sad and lonely void that I could only describe as a steadily retreating tide. The death of her mother, which was thought a possible suicide, and the death of her grandfather, which was a certain suicide, had an impact on her that remained her own secret. Add to this her memories of childhood rape, a serious condition of epilepsy, a condition of anorexia nervosa that had mutated into bulimia, reoccurring dental problems, substance abuse, and now living with a man who was not emotionally connected; and you didn't exactly have a recipe for normalcy. Leaving her for days or even weeks at a time alone in the house in the woods as my job routinely required may well have magnified the problems, but she never offered one complaint about the arrangement or the living conditions. She had found a home.

My mention of anorexia nervosa and the eventual bulimia, eating disorders now often associated with young women who are suffering from self-image problems, was not a direct understanding that I or anyone else had at the time regarding Beth. It was only in retrospect that these disorders came to be understood—many trips to doctors during the better part of three years had failed to identify her condition. It would take until late 1975 when a psychiatrist finally correctly diagnosed this condition as part of what had plagued her for years. Prior to the diagnosis, at one point her weight had dropped to a mere sixty-five pounds. Her death had probably been not far off, and I was coming to expect it. I could walk down the street and hold my arm stiff, bent at the elbow, and she could hang on my arm fully suspended as I continued walking—it was a pitiful novelty. Complications associated with the bulimia had also been an unrealized contributor to her major dental problems as the acid in the frequent vomit ate away the very enamel of her teeth. Those were some difficult years.

It would take the death of the popular musician Karen Anne Carpenter in 1983 for the medical community and the public at large to first begin to appreciate the magnitude of the problem of eating disorders. Beth had no way of knowing that many others shared the same awful secret of binging and purging. When we would check out at the grocery store it was not unusual to hear someone say: "You are going to have to start feeding this girl." I wanted to reply that if they only knew how much food was being consumed they would be shocked. The situation was so extreme that the man hired to pump out our admittedly undersized septic tanks (private sewage disposal system) had quizzed me on how many people lived at the house, saying that he had never seen a system so routinely overwhelmed by such an amount of waste. It was not human waste; it was mostly regurgitated food although he and I didn't realize this at the time. Instead, I just didn't understand, and I grew angry at having to chase down the sources of the smell of vomit as containers that had been used, hidden, and forgotten routinely gave off that nauseating stench. I was at a complete loss to know what to do other than to plead with her to use the toilet if she was going to get sick. All I could grasp was that she was constantly experiencing uncontrollable nausea—I had no idea that the vomiting was being deliberately and habitually induced.

In 1974 with the trial four months behind us but with the weight of spreading despondency in our relationship becoming unbearable, and against what I knew to be my better judgment, I considered a possible step that we could take to better meet her emotional needs. I considered marriage, something that I knew was a commitment fraught with responsibility that might overwhelm me. I felt trapped in our worsening situation and obliged to try to fix it. There was nothing romantic in my decision to broach the subject; it just came up.

I asked the question in what was hardly a notable inspiration of love or devotion, "Do you think that you would feel better if we were married?"

Beth nodded a hopeful "yes", and we began the process to get married. Our finances were so limited at the time that I had to take my pistol to a pawn shop in New Orleans to be held as collateral for a loan for twenty-five dollars. The Justice of the Peace in Covington would require fifteen dollars to perform the service, and I did not then have the fifteen dollars to spare. The drive into New Orleans ate up in fuel costs a disappointing portion of the small loan, but these were the limitations upon us. We always had food; we always had a roof; Beth never had to work; and doctor's visits were made as necessary. No government assistance was ever sought or expected. But the times were not easy.

Our marriage license was issued, and in February of 1974 we were married in a brief ceremony in some now forgotten office witnessed by three people whom we had never met. One can only wonder what they thought at the time and what chances they gave us for success. I had made a private visit to the Justice of the Peace the day before to explain to him in no uncertain terms that I did not want the word "God" even mentioned in the token ceremony.

My atheism was not a mere intellectual indulgence whereby I fancied myself sophisticated or elite—it was a committed and non-compromising militant position that was the fruit of bitter experience. I would not allow such superstition to invade my world and demand my respect and submission. For my marriage there would be no God. Unfortunately, I was to have my way. And sadly, Beth was to have a brief marriage in which she would never hear those healing words that she desperately needed to hear: "I love you." Those words belonged to a language that I did not know. I knew plenty of people who would use a profession of love to get what they wanted from others—it was a cruel irony that this was an area where my honor was intact. I would not lie about such matters of the soul. I had a high expectation for what I envisioned love to be, and I knew that it was not to be found in my heart. I did not want to be less than what Beth needed, but I could not pretend that we were deeply in love.

After Beth and I were married, not surprisingly the situation failed to improve. A possible solution arose, which was another external change of circumstances that was hopefully to provide a fullness of life to counteract and reverse the continuing downward spiral. Beth's grandmother moved from Shaker Heights, Ohio, to join us. She was a sophisticated, educated woman, and had borne remarkably well the suicide of her husband. Nevertheless, her world had changed completely, and she now shared with her only granddaughter a numbing loneliness.

Although I had strongly preferred that we would live alone in the house, when I saw the spontaneous joy that returned to Beth when we first discussed having this new arrangement I set aside my reservations and extended an open welcome to her grandmother. I halted work on some aspects of the house renovation, and instead added a private bedroom and bathroom for our new and permanent guest. These were the first rooms to be fully completed in the house. They were in fact a modest oasis inside the unfinished home.

Within weeks I realized that the perfect relationship that Beth assured me she had with her grandmother was instead turning out to be something quite different. I found myself now with two women who both delighted in make-believe worlds with princesses, music boxes, and granted wishes; but those two worlds were in revolving competition with one another. Rather than seeing the joy of new companionship for Beth, I was instead seeing her rising anger at the control being forced upon her by a woman who professed nothing but kindness—and who in fact was nearly always very pleasant—but who also fully expected to get her way. I became a servant in my own home, trying to please two opposing women who were generations apart but who each shared private beliefs that their personal need to be happy was all that mattered. I was beginning to see a pattern of behavior that spanned at least three consecutive generations. An unfathomable old photograph—one that I could hardly believe was Beth—showed her as an overweight child surrounded by an excessive number of stuffed animals and yet with a sad look on her face. That photo was beginning to make more sense.

I tolerated much for months, but the day that it became clear to me that the situation was unacceptable was when the grandmother's demands to have her own way were clearly seen to be contributing to Beth's increasingly critical eating disorder. Again, I did not yet have a clear medical diagnosis upon which to base my observations, but watching Beth being encouraged to eat bakery treats to excess and then knowing that she was getting sick as a result told me that something wasn't right and changes needed to be made. She was slowly dying before my eyes. Unhealthy choices were being encouraged, and my careful explanations and respectful pleadings for change because these choices were harming Beth only caused her grandmother to more determinedly and defiantly demand to have her own way in spite of the damaging results. She was not about to be told what to do by a young man, even if he was being exceptionally polite in his asking. She never intentionally hurt Beth; she simply liked buying pretty pastries, wine, and anything else she fancied. It was her right, but there were serious consequences for others.

With the growing animosity in all branches of the three-way relationship, I explained to the grandmother that she could not continue to live with us. She had for the most part already come to this realization herself, having envisioned better living conditions. There was no pleading on her part to remain; and I think that she was more than ready to leave the humid south, the unfinished home, and the company of a granddaughter and her husband who seemed at odds with her. We had all attempted an experiment, and unfortunately it had failed decidedly. She returned to Ohio, and there she was to live out her remaining twenty years.

After her grandmother returned to Ohio, Beth and I then enjoyed a brief period of relaxation and renewal in our private togetherness; but the relief was not to last. Beth's need to be provided for in all aspects of our relationship increased, her health remained an issue, and her self-reliance dwindled as my efforts at meeting her needs increased. I was a reluctant but steady psychological enabler not knowing how to break the cycle. The more that I did the more there was that I had to do. I felt that I was becoming more like a father with a troubled child than a man with a grown woman as a wife.

Haunting memories began to revisit me of when we first began dating in Ohio some five years prior. Beth had talent as an artist—considerable talent that could vacillate between what at times appeared to be childlike attempts to capture some fancy in her imagination and at other times results that left you knowing that she truly had a gift. But with this skill there sometimes would come revelation of the weight of torment upon her soul. In Ohio she had hung a large oil painting of hers in my apartment because she realized and appreciated that I was fascinated by her artwork. After a few weeks, I reluctantly had to ask her to remove the painting. It was good, far too good. The entangled earth-tone colors, abstract swirls, and impressions conveyed something that was very unhealthy and destructive. It was an agonizing moan captured in oils. I am not one who is easily moved by artwork—I'm a nuts & bolts kind of guy and no art critic—but this painting impacted me. It truly belonged somewhere where it could be studied, but it did not belong and could not stay in my presence.

Continuing medical bills and the struggle to improve our living conditions was requiring of me more time offshore, but the situation at home was such that I could no longer trust Beth to properly care for herself. Certain situations were becoming unacceptably dangerous. A central heating and air conditioning system was still an unaffordable luxury, so winter months required the use of inherently dangerous natural gas space heaters. These gas units with open flames and the additional portable electric space heaters for supplemental heating left me fearing the possible deadly consequences of their improper operation, which could include asphyxiation, carbon monoxide poisoning, and the very real possibility of catastrophic fire. Also, new kitchen construction had not been started yet, and the gas oven in the old kitchen had to be lit manually. For me this was an easy task, but Beth would turn on the gas and in slow motion repeatedly strike matches and drop them onto and over the hissing oven burner where they would often go out before lighting occurred. The results were that the spent matches would collect below the burner as if the purpose was to create a fire. Sometimes the buildup of gas before ignition would result in a near explosion, and more than once Beth singed her long hair lighting the oven. These were not the days of fail-safe appliances. Many times I tried to show her how to light the oven properly, but she would not accept my instruction. She was certainly capable; just unwilling.

On one of my most disappointing days—and this is not an easy admission—I came in from offshore and found again a mound of matches under the oven burner that was an accident waiting to happen. Completely fed up and with no patience left, I grabbed Beth, put her over my knee as you would a defiant child, and quite literally gave her a spanking as a parent might give. I was not a man to beat a woman—that was unthinkable, but this last resort discipline was what my life had sunk to. Ignoring the dangerous situation was no longer an option, and childproofing the house was more than I could afford. To my surprise, the lesson took hold immediately.

It was a few weeks later when I had again returned from work that I entered the front door only to have Beth greet me with a fearful and very apologetic confession—she had dropped a single match accidentally and could not retrieve it from beneath the oven. She was fearful of what she thought would be certain discipline. I gently tried to reassure her that mistakes were never the problem; I just needed her to try. I don't know if she was ever able to make the distinction.

But beyond the issues of her safety that were troubling me more and more, there was a personal issue that was becoming a potential deal-breaker for us. Truth was becoming an elusive shadow. Simple questions were more often being met with fabricated answers that were what Beth imagined I wanted to hear, and I was beginning to distrust all of our conversations. Time after time I tried to tell her that I could handle truth even if it was unpleasant truth. We could work with the truth; we could even work with occasional outright and admitted lies. Instead there was a forever-morphing dark presence enveloping her and coming between us like a mythical creature rising from some spiritual swamp in our lives. Increasing alcohol abuse almost assuredly was playing a major role in our communication problems, as it had by then become an escape for her. As with the eating disorder where binge eating was the practice, so now with the alcohol another control was taking hold.

Beth was in a hopeless situation. Her health liabilities were enough to bring anyone to their knees; her psychological turmoil was taking a great toll; she had no source of spiritual strength; her family history included substance abuse, disturbing generational behavior patterns, and suicide; and she was now married to a man who although he tried to provide for her physical needs could not adequately provide for her emotional needs. . .and that man was starting to become dangerously exasperated.

My repeated attempts to communicate effectively with Beth came to be greeted more and more by what seemed to be a willful drawing of a curtain over her soul as I tried to reach out. By this time there were routine trips to a psychologist, and her descent into some hidden abyss was accelerating. I was also becoming overwhelmed at the desperation that I was personally facing in this situation, but my needs were far less urgent than hers.

After ineffective therapy and Beth's becoming more helpless, the psychologist called me into his office. He was blunt: "You have no choice; you have to have her committed." He was not offering me an option; he was telling me that Beth was at this point incapable of caring for herself. The involuntary commitment was to be for an extended observation and evaluation under trained and watchful eyes.

The commitment process required several legal steps, some of which were especially difficult. Louisiana law required among other things the concurrence of the Coroner who was a medical doctor. When I visited him with papers in hand I could tell that he was suspicious of me—why I was trying to have this pretty and apparently happy young woman sitting in his outer office committed? I tried to explain that he was seeing a façade as he observed her, but understandably he needed more than my review of the past and another doctor's current diagnosis. I brought Beth into his office at his request, and I then had to insert and turn the key that would force the display necessary to satisfy his professional need to know. I can't remember what specific subject I raised or question I asked, but Beth's demeanor changed abruptly and she slipped into her other world of make-believe where she ineffectively tried to hide her overwhelming despair. No further examination was required as the Coroner saw her now sitting on the office floor going through her purse in search of some distracting object, oblivious to the spectacle of her behavior. He signed the papers. I wanted to berate the man for making it necessary for me to force open this painful door, but this was not the time for acting out my frustrations.

In sad bewilderment, Beth was seeing her life being handed over to others. I no longer could cope with the situation unless I were to quit work and stay home twenty-four hours a day to care for her. This was not possible from a practical and financial standpoint. Plus, it was painfully obvious that my so-called help was not helping her at all, and in fact my kind of help seemed to be hurting her. I was somewhat surprised that I was not as emotionally troubled myself at the situation as I would have expected—that is, until I called my compassionate boss and explained to this man who was also a kind friend what was happening. My sudden tears and broken voice came out of somewhere within that I didn't even know still existed.

As I drove across the Lake Pontchartrain Causeway to New Orleans to the Southern Baptist Hospital where on the fifth floor there was a ward with locked doors, sitting beside me was my wife who knew that something awful was happening to her. She didn't really comprehend what this was, and she wanted to go home—she desperately wanted to go home. She offered some emotional and psychological resistance, but physical restraint or coercion was not required. She was finding herself now being carried along in the current of her own dark river, and in her helplessness she could not swim against the flow.

For these circumstances involving involuntary commitment, most of the checking in procedures had already been handled by the doctors before we arrived. After ringing the bell at the locked entry doors on the fifth floor to obtain assistance, we were met by someone on the staff. We walked through those locked doors and entered a world where no one wants to be. I had no idea of what to expect. I had hoped for better—for a more sterile type of hospital environment with private rooms and a cheery setting; yet I also knew that it could have been much worse. This was institutional care, and not a luxurious private hospital for the wealthy. I had been presented with a choice of two hospitals, and this one had been the one more highly recommended. The woman whom I had first met almost six years ago was now a forlorn soul who would be blending in with others who had varying degrees of a loosening grip on reality. She was being abandoned there by the man she had trusted to be her Prince Charming. She had to have felt betrayed.

It was a cruel coincidence that the deeply disturbing movie *One Flew Over the Cuckoo's Nest* had recently been released. I had heard of the movie, and I remembered the up and coming actor Jack Nicholson who had the lead role as previously having played an interesting bit part in the popular cult movie *Easy Rider* in 1969. I knew that the last thing I wanted to do was see a gut-wrenching movie about a mental hospital, but in my own way I still felt that the best way to face fears was head on. After completing the commitment process that evening, I then drove straight to a theater in New Orleans and watched the movie.

The movie played out before me in nightmarish dread. The indifference and cruelty of some of the staff forced me to consider that Beth might possibly be subjected to such treatment. The lost souls who were not understood and who were incapable of coping in a demanding world represented my fears for what might befall Beth. The utter desperation and the seemingly ordained tragedy for those who are compulsively different ripped into me, and I came out from the movie shattered. But I did not have the luxury of being weak; I would have to press on with no source of inner strength.

Following a two-week commitment Beth was released; I had not known in the beginning if the duration would be weeks, months, years, or permanent. I had visited her during this time, adhering to the limited schedule permitted by the doctors. It was during this time of hospitalization that a young, capable doctor finally provided names for the eating disorders that had wreaked havoc with Beth's health. For me at least, it helped to have some answers. Pieces of the puzzle rapidly began falling into place for this and other behaviors. I had also known there had been held back emotions, and I had tried unsuccessfully to get Beth to open up to me. It became obvious in short order during one of my visits that through therapy she had discovered her own anger.

The hospital had a punching bag that was a modified version of a heavy bag that boxers and martial arts devotees would use—modified in the sense that it was somewhat softer and more pillow-like. In my presence she began to strike the bag and release measured screams as years of rage erupted out of her. To this day I do not know if the rage was against me or against life. I did not feel that it was against herself—and for this I was thankful. I have personally always been one who is able to find some immediate release with striking out at inanimate objects, and seeing Beth willingly this transparent was both troubling and encouraging. Perhaps she could come out from where she had been hiding.

Routine visits with professionals were scheduled throughout the first weeks of 1976, and my work remained on hold to ensure that these appointments were kept. With each successive visit she began to grow more resistive—she didn't like the required submission to counseling that she didn't think was necessary. Regardless, she was still unable to cope on her own and medical intervention was still necessary. She was stronger now; that much I could see, but with that strength was a parallel defiance. I was finding myself trying to help her reach a healthy measure of self-sufficiency and independence from me, which seemed to be what was necessary. Yet she was fighting me and only wanting to retreat back into her world where neither I nor anyone else was welcome except on her terms rooted in fantasy.

Tension between us was rising as the weeks multiplied. I needed to get back to work, but this was not yet possible. I do not know what preceded the situation that I am about to describe, but I do have vivid images and I could return and mark the exact spot in our driveway where the following occurred. Something decisive had transpired between us to where Beth was deliberately shutting me out again in what I felt was an openly defiant way. I was frustrated that I was obliged to keep trying to help someone who would not let me help her in the ways that were really needed, but yet who presumed that I would always be there to provide for her worldly needs. I was looking at pure insolence and rebellion. I was incapable of appreciating that this possibly could be a phase of her emotional healing. Instead, I saw this as the person whom I had come to know.

In total exasperation I exploded with the tension that had been building up inside of me, and I wanted to grab her and shake her to try to penetrate and break down the impossible wall that prevented me from reaching her. I did just that. I walked up to her and put my hands on her frail shoulders, grabbed her firmly, and gave her one strong shake to try to reach her. I hadn't realized the strength given me by the adrenalin surging through my blood stream.

To my immediate horror her head snapped forward and then backward like a slingshot. It was almost as if her head had been barely attached to her body and had nearly come off. I hadn't realized my strength in that awful moment, and I knew with absolute certainty that I had very nearly broken her neck with deadly whiplash. She was frightened but not injured, but brutal tragedy had been so dangerously close. Having laid my hands on her once before with the spanking, this was now the end of it. I could not allow the situation to continue. I could not trust her, and I now realized that I could not trust myself. My limits had been found; they were too close; and it was over.

That very night I explained to her that we were going to have to separate permanently. She was saddened and quietly desperate and disillusioned, but she was submissive. She also had realized the dangerous situation that now existed between us, for never before had I reacted to her in such violent anger. We would sell those items that her grandmother had left in Louisiana for her, and we would try to build up as much of a financial base for her as we could. There would be no initial attempt to address the legal issues, and I would voluntarily provide modest financial support for her for some period yet to be determined. Her return to Ohio was the understood next step after we finalized her affairs with her belongings.

When all was completed, I packed and drove the U-Haul truck to return her to Ohio. Several items had not been sold, including an exquisitely carved large antique music box from Europe given to her by her grandmother. At one time there had been considerable wealth in the family, and in part it had been that wealth that had allowed the fairytale world to continue.

Beth had been offered five thousand dollars for the music box by an envious French Quarter antiques dealer—this is no exaggeration; it was a remarkable colletor's item. Our occasionally difficult financial situation had never intruded into her domain. I knew that in Ohio she would have her grandmother who still had the financial means to help her if she was unable to care for herself. She was the only granddaughter, and her brother who was also in Ohio was the only grandson. On the other side of the family her father had not been in the picture in any capacity that I was aware of since her childhood years.

In one undeniable sense I was throwing her to the wolves, but at the same time I knew that she was not going to improve with me—experience was proving this. Although I had honestly doubted that I would ever again touch her in anger, of this I could no longer be absolutely certain; and staying together was therefore an unacceptable risk. This was also an excuse aimed at my own self-justification for ending the marriage; it was the necessary proof to my conscience that we had to separate. I also had lost the feelings that I had for her. There would always remain some fondness and some appreciation, but there was not enough left between us to have a life together. In the secret corners of my mind I expected that within six months she would likely be dead or permanently institutionalized. As of this writing she is still a survivor and on her own. I had not been wrong when I had first seen something special in her; I had only been unable to reach it.

Divorce proceedings were started by me in Louisiana early in 1977 under the grounds of our having been legally separated for one year. She fought me on these grounds after she obtained legal counsel in Ohio, and I suspect that she had both encouragement and guidance to proceed in this direction. Rather than allowing me the divorce on the grounds of the one year separation, for legal positioning for the upcoming community property settlement she filed for divorce in Ohio under the specific grounds of my "gross neglect of duty and extreme cruelty". I could not deny the neglect of duty, and I could understand that she had felt cruelty at my hands. Still, it was a sad concession for me to have to make. Years of my trying had come down to this: a formal public declaration of my failure, and mine alone. I had no desire to fight the divorce, and in August of 1977 I signed the papers without protest. I wanted that part of my life over, and it was.

Chapter Eleven

Nothing to Get

With the weight of a failed marriage off my shoulders and a diving career that was starting to move into high gear, 1977 and 1978 were proving to be the best years of my life. After years of second-guessing myself after every dive that wasn't quite as good as I wanted it to be I was finally assured of my ability as an oilfield construction diver. A poor dive could always set me back, but a string of good dives would then allow me to catch my stride again. I steadily had to resist the push of the diving managers at the Santa Fe Engineering and Construction Company in Houma, Louisiana, when they kept trying to direct me into supervisory roles, for my true desire was simply to dive. I enjoyed the challenge of putting things together underwater where no one could watch me and where my mechanical aptitude and common sense approach were effective. This was where excuses failed and performance mattered. You knew if you had made a good dive, and if you did, this provided personal satisfaction.

With my finances under better control and house renovation finally able to move along at a faster pace, a brighter future seemed possible. I felt as if I had climbed out of a bottomless pit. During this period a popular self-help program was sweeping the nation, or at least it was in the circles of those inclined toward such trendy movements. Many celebrities of note, educators, and politicians alike along with hundreds of thousands of others were to find their way into Erhard Seminars Training, generally referred to with the lower case acronym *est*. The training consisted of two intense weekends, involving some sixty hours total in four days, where individuals traded their $300 (1978 rates as best I can recall) for the privilege of enduring sensory deprivation, insults, vulgarities, humiliation, scolding, interrogation, browbeating, lengthy lectures, meditation, and other publicly shared experiences for the combined four days in order to be transformed by this bizarre and hard to explain psychological shell game. It was a brief, rugged, and intense boot camp for the mind where you were to be stripped of all pretense and all previous psychological and spiritual foundations in order to achieve a new understanding of life that was intended to be and expected to be mind-blowing.

Erhard Seminars Training was the brainchild of Werner H. Erhard—a.k.a. John Paul "Jack" Rosenberg. Rosenberg had been an unhappily married young man who had subsequently abandoned his family, leaving them in Philadelphia, Pennsylvania, to then become a car salesman in St. Louis, Missouri. A name change would follow, and Rosenberg would eventually become the charismatic Werner Erhard. It was, after all, an aptly more fitting name for a mysterious and prestigious professor of personal transformation. Erhard studied many different philosophies, persuasions, and religions and formulated a program to be experienced in a two-weekend workshop designed to provide a life-changing transformation for one's thinking, understanding, and attitude.

If all of this sounds nebulous, it should. In fact, adequate descriptions of the training are quite impossible to condense into a pragmatic analysis, as a search on the Internet will confirm. How does one explain supposed cherry-picking from Zen Buddhism, Scientology, Dale Carnegie, Norman Vincent Peale, and the like when it isn't even the pieces of those persuasions that comprise *est*? I think there might have also been some basic Ayn Rand views thrown into the mix: "Reality is what it is independent of man's consciousness," although I have never seen this particular observation offered by others.

Bruce was a diving supervisor where I worked who had solid diving skills and even better supervisory skills. Before I heard of *est,* Bruce attended the training. The man had a good heart, and he was definitely a cut above those in the trade who delighted in being rude and crude. With all due respect to my former fellow divers and myself, the industry had tended to attract those individuals leaning slightly to the wild and brazen side of life. Bruce was a gentleman though, and he was inclined toward self-improvement—including a healthy awareness of life in its fullness. Somehow, he had discovered *est*. As a result he was soaring with irrepressible enthusiasm.

Bruce recognized in me someone intense who tended to weigh many things heavily. He was eager to share with me his life-changing and liberating experience, and he was not deterred when I repeatedly told him that paying $300 to spend two weekends in Houston, Texas, for some kind of awareness experience was not something that I cared to do. I didn't like group encounters, and I suspected that I had traipsed around more in my own psychological wilderness than most others had ever cared to do. There would be motel bills that I would have to factor into the cost, not to mention the investment of my time. Altogether, this didn't represent an insignificant venture for me. I would rather stay home and work on my house if I wasn't going to be offshore on a diving job.

"Please, Larry, please. Go to the training. You won't regret it; it will open your eyes. Please do this. You can't let this chance go. I can't really tell you what it is, but it will change your life." With respecting his judgment and hearing his persistent pleading along these lines, I finally agreed to go.

There were approximately three hundred of us who attended the training. I was skeptical, to say the least. People generally do not have a legitimate life-changing experience by attending a two-weekend seminar conjured up by an opportunistic former salesman. I immediately recognized some techniques routinely employed by drill sergeants in the military training of new recruits. Personal identity was about to be dismantled and reconfigured as the trainers intended, but I immediately knew that in my case they had someone in their audience whom they did not and could not understand. This wasn't an attitude of arrogance; it was simply what I knew objectively and subjectively about myself. I considered walking out almost immediately—this was not something that I was going to fall for. I would not hand my life over to anybody in the sense that this training was about to require.

The rules were many and stringent, even to the extent of severe restrictions on bathroom breaks. Unless you had a doctor's statement that you absolutely had to have frequent breaks, you would be seated with all others and have to wait for the very few allowed breaks. So began in part the process through sensory deprivation (a brainwashing technique commonly employed to break down one's resistance) to begin our transformation of thought. Each day's session ran from nine o'clock in the morning until midnight as a minimum, and we were allowed only one meal break. Having worked much tougher schedules offshore under far worse conditions, this was not exactly something that was going to break me. Additionally, we were going to be treated disrespectfully and held to deliberately unreasonable and rigid disciplines.

At our first permitted break I spoke to a fellow trainee who for lack of a better description looked like Santa Claus. This elderly gentleman was intelligent, polite, kind, and engaging. I told him that if things didn't take a turn in a hurry that I was going to quit the training. I hadn't expected his almost tearful reaction: "Oh, no, please don't leave! I have been searching all my life for answers, and this is the first time that I am beginning to see things. Please stay though the training; please stay." For a while at least, I would surrender to this man's honest and heartfelt outreach to me. As with Bruce, I could tell that he sincerely wanted this to be an enlightening experience for me. On a separate note, this man's open revelation of his own acknowledged sense of futility in a lifetime of searching stuck me as a sad and haunting commentary, and I wondered if the same fate would be mine someday.

By my simple act of being there it was obvious that there was at least some measure of my own searching for understanding and improvement, and the gentleman feared that a fellow-searcher was going to fall away and be lost. Pushing through great reluctance, I opted to remain. I didn't want my impatience or stubbornness to prevent me from receiving understanding; so I continued to let the trainers try to tear me down along with every other person present. It was obvious to me that they wanted us to suspend and relinquish control of our minds so that they could show us something unexpectedly profound in the stripped-away results.

I felt like I was in POW training 101 and that I was supposed to be intimidated by people trying to stare me down and broken by them verbally insulting me. Having held dry ice as a child until my fingers had frozen; by comparison this present intimidation was hardly compelling. I was frustrated, and I didn't see how anything good could come from this training for anyone who had ever honestly pondered his or her own self. They were trying to teach me things about myself that I already knew. Furthermore, trying to tell each of us that we created our own reality was something that I could acknowledge as true in some respects by the choices that we make in life (hardly a revelation), but I certainly knew that my choices could never alter an external reality if and when it was going to come crashing down on me. I understood what would be more scientifically described as "cause and effect", but I rejected the greater notion that we create our own reality.

I was not alone in my muted enthusiasm; the body language of some of the other participants told me that their patience was also wearing thin. But no one left. No one quit. I wondered then even more about myself: "Was I actually *that* different from everyone else that I might be the only one to leave? Was I *that* much of an outcast from society?" I resolved to try to go along and glean at least something from the experience.

Because these were scripted exercises, I refrained from lashing out at the trainer those few times that it had been an uncomfortable one-on-one. Fortunately, I was not spoken to in some of the same extremely derogatory terms that were used on other trainees. Since there were certain boundaries that I would not allow to be crossed, serious problems would have developed. The trainers were sharp, very intelligent, gifted, truly charismatic people who excelled at reading others. The two key trainers for our seminar were indeed powerful and confident personalities, and I will admit that there was something special about their presence. I suspect they might have sensed where the limits were with certain trainees, and then wisely respected those limits.

After one extended session where everyone had been led into an exercise that essentially tapped into emotional fears, many people were sobbing uncontrollably and/or screaming in a cacophony of absolute madness that sounded like a soundtrack out of hell. A hired guard who was posted outside the closed doors to the auditorium had almost been overcome by the horrendous screams that were being released by those present. Personally, I knew that they didn't really want me to act out my feelings of rage, which were my hidden driving force rather than fear.

Yet as the training progressed I was surprised to see changes in others. Initially, I thought that they might have been strategic plants—people secretly placed in the group by the *est* organization to falsely create the impression that life-changing experiences were beginning to occur. A psychologist—a fiercely proud, well-dressed man with a perfectly trimmed goatee—admitted in one session that he was an alcoholic. This was a first for him to admit this, and to do so in such a public forum was a major triumph for honesty. A withdrawn young woman who had some serious learning disabilities and much psychological baggage associated with this was freed up to share in one session that she could now, finally, accept herself for who she was. At one point during the training I had thought that she was about to be pushed over the brink into a breakdown, and I had very nearly intervened to halt the trainer when I truly thought that he was going too far with his insults. Now, however, she claimed a victory in her own simple way. We all understood that she had come to an important point in her life—she was ceasing to be a victim.

Others here and there were also slowly coming to milestones where they could admit to weaknesses and claim new strengths. People were randomly beginning to become empowered like popcorn kernels beginning to burst at a slowly increasing rate. I was bewildered to think that these people had not already covered this psychological ground in their own lives. As with the troubled young woman, people were ceasing to be victims in their lives. Yet for me, stepping back to move forward was not a solution.

What I found *est* to be attempting was the systematic dismantling of the belief that there existed some kind of a "magic answer" theory for the mystery of life—our tendency to think that there is some greater knowledge other than the simplistic notion of "what is, is". Most people do tend to think that there is some mystical purpose intertwined in our thoughts and feelings that is larger than us. Instead, *est* turns this concept on its head and in a very rude awakening tells people that by choice they create their own reality; it is as simple and complex as that. The lesson was intended to go far beyond the concept of reaping what we have sown, the lesson was about power—a personal power that shapes the reality of one's own experience of life. In the end, the training was largely about personal responsibility, and that looking for answers beyond this basic tenant was a waste of time. It struck me as a type of dry atheism. It tended for the most part to come down to: "You are who you are; what is is; what isn't isn't. Now go deal with it." Apparently this shocking revelation had never occurred to the hundreds of thousands of people who found enlightenment in the training over the years.

The catch phrase with a wink and a nod throughout the training and the one that each and every *est* graduate will likely recognize to this day is: "Did you get it?" This mysterious "it" was the perplexing and elusive riddle that both plagued and enlightened people. "It" does not lend itself to a tidy explanation. In part it is simply a revelation of personal responsibility and accepting things the way they are; it is also about how we create our own reality; it is also about whether or not "getting it" really got to you; and lastly it is that there is nothing to get, and if you got that, then you got it. If others now consider this to be bizarre, perplexing, and unworthy to be packaged as a life-changing transformation, then I am somewhat relieved even at this late date. As I said earlier, it was a psychological shell game. Nevertheless, I have to admit again to my absolute amazement and consternation that I was in the presence of three hundred people hanging on every word that the trainer would utter, even when those words would prove contradictory and absurd.

As the training was beginning to draw to a close on the fourth and final day, we were all directed to stand up. The always confident lead trainer, whom I do acknowledge was a powerful personality, presented with authority this deciding order: "Everyone who got it, sit down." Perhaps as many as a third of the trainees hesitantly sat down. I could see where this was going.

After more lecturing the same order came a second time. Now many more people took their seats, leaving perhaps only a fourth of us left standing. Those supposedly enlightened souls who were now sitting down were clearly happier and safer than those of us who were still standing. A groundswell of palpable enthusiasm was slowly building.

The lecturing resumed, and the order then came for a third time. Most of the rest of the trainees took their seats in victory. Having never liked being singled out in a group, I was now getting very uncomfortable. I took a quick inventory—there were now only seven of us still standing.

Now the trainer brought out the big guns of his culminating presentation and rambled on for a while longer. The group was nearing the climax of the night when all would share the common experience of having gotten the elusive but liberating "it". For the fourth time the order came upon us to sit down if we got it. Five more sat down, leaving one other man and me as the two remaining oddities. Had I sat down, I believe that the other man would have followed my lead. I don't think that we were still supposed to be standing at this stage. This was not quite going according to the trainer's master plan.

The trainer then walked directly up to the other man and whispered something quietly in his ear. The man hesitated briefly, and then he sat down.

During the training it was not our place to speak unless spoken to, but I looked at the last man and said in a mildly cynical and disappointing tone, "Thanks," meaning that he had obviously abandoned me to fend for myself.

The auditorium now seemed quieter than it had ever been. Every eye was eagerly awaiting the spiritual-like illumination and surrender of this last holdout or perhaps some other grand surprise so the life-changing transformation could be complete for everyone.

As he had done with the last man, the trainer came up to me to whisper in my ear. I did not know what the message might be. It would certainly have to be profound to justify the drama of the moment. I even half wondered if I had somehow passed some kind of test and perhaps even have saved the session in some inexplicable way for the trainer. I just knew that nothing said up until this point justified me taking my seat. The impotent whisper rang hollow: "There is nothing to get. Sit down."

Thoroughly convinced that I would obediently sit down after his revelation to me, the trainer immediately spun around and in bold confidence strutted toward the front center before the group. There is absolutely no way that he expected me to still be standing or that I would dare speak.

My words were direct, fierce, and challenging: "Hey! I'm not impressed with that bull____."

He turned back and studied me momentarily and countered: "It doesn't matter if you are impressed or not." For me, his confident air of authority immediately evaporated, and this man who had not long before reduced others to tears and trembling now seemed very small.

In disgust I responded briefly with some of the same vulgarities that had been visited upon us throughout the training. I had had an objection, and I had made it known. I wasn't buying what they were selling. Now, I finally did sit down, but it was hardly a victory for *est*.

My steadfast resistance had been rooted in the fact that I wasn't buying the notion that this concept of either "*getting it*" or realizing that "*there was nothing to get, so if you got that, then you got it*" was any kind of a groundbreaking revelation worthy of the description of being life-transforming. I wasn't so obtuse as to deny the validity of some of the lessons and the plays on logic that were developed during the training and the corresponding conclusions, but throughout the training and the promotional materials there had been teasers pointing to the fact that this was to be a life-changing event. The final revelation of having nothingness essentially being presented as an epiphany of thought had left me looking around the room wondering if I was an alien on this planet, and yet I was seeing glowing faces throughout as people were beginning to relax in who they were and apparently empowered as they had never been before.

But for me, unless there was some kind of blinding light of stunning revelation, I was not about to be swayed by a charismatic personality or by concocted psychobabble and forced indoctrination utilizing rudimentary brainwashing techniques. I am not that impressionable. My great-grandparents were from Missouri, the "Show Me State" that imprints that pithy slogan on their license plates, and I had seen nothing. Allowing that politics and party platforms were considerably different over a century ago, in 1899 Missouri's Congressman Willard D. Vandiver had said: "I come from a country that raises corn and cotton and cockleburs and Democrats, and frothy eloquence neither convinces nor satisfies me. I'm from Missouri. You have got to show me." I could have used Congressman Vandiver's support and wit at the *est* training seminar.

I had no desire to be the one person who was found to be different, and being found different as revealed during the training was a painful experience. This hardly meant that I was unique in a good sense. Years of solitary living in ways not understood by others followed by a failed marriage had left me pressed up against the window pane of life looking at everyone else on the other side of the frosted glass. It is impossible to convey the intensity and vibrancy of that final evening as being shared by others but from which I was excluded.

After the training concluded that last night I drove back to my motel feeling completely isolated from humanity. I truly wished that I had not attended the seminar. The negativity that I had begun to escape in my life was there again looking for a chink in my armor. Now it was official and the message was loud and clear: I really did not belong in this world. I was an insignificant and unwelcome stranger passing through. Once again, death—true non-existence—was my only real friend.

Erhard Seminars Training was a tremendously popular and successful phenomenon lasting from 1971 to 1984. It has since been replaced by another program. I have no interest in further study or pursuits of this nature.

Chapter Twelve

Visions of Light

When two fellow divers became Christians it was not necessarily a welcomed experience for the rest of us in the offshore diving ranks. With their faith came their apparently obligatory compulsion to corner the rest of us to try to engage us one at a time in religious conversations in which we were not interested, or at times they would lob spiritual shots across the bow such as when one of them would say: "I am praying for you." Such gestures were not well received by most of us.

To hear someone say that they are praying for you can be a heartwarming and supportive encouragement for those of similar convictions. However, when the promised prayer is understood to be directed at the conversion of your presumed deficient soul, the uninvited prayer can be taken as a rude intrusion of privacy—which was precisely how I took it. I wanted to tell my would-be benefactor to pray for himself. I wasn't interested, and I didn't much appreciate what I considered was the implied and condescending insult. This said to me that he presumed a superiority of knowledge; and that if I was lucky enough, someday I might reach that same lofty spiritual plateau where he now thought he resided. Their spiritual commitment also seemed to require that others be forced to read whatever literature was currently inspiring them. Thanks, but no thanks. I was not presuming in the least that either of these two men should ever want to emulate me, and I certainly did not intend to emulate them. Incidentally, it never occurred to me that they might simply be especially concerned and sincere, and not just stubbornly obnoxious.

Trouble was, both of these guys were likeable, except for when they would get off onto their respective religious tangents. I had no desire to demolish their fantasy hopes or to engage them in any kind of debate or discussion about these issues. I was an atheist, and I was thoroughly disinterested in what had now become their obsession. I only wanted to be left alone regarding these kinds of conversations. I had no desire to explain to them my years of reaching out to a phantom God who existed only in the minds of the superstitious and the religiously indoctrinated. I wasn't exactly a novice at this reaching out to God thing, and I had the deep emotional scars to prove it. In part, I honestly felt embarrassed for my deluded friends. They were starting to become a joke to the rest of us.

A recent car wreck had been an eye-opener for me suggesting that my days of carousing and excesses needed to come to a rapid halt. Belated maturity tempered by near disaster finally took hold. With me being a single and fun-loving guy again and free to pursue the nightlife, a close friend and I had enjoyed a few too many—no, make that several too many—drinks one night and had stayed until one bar's closing. During the drive that followed, I showed him some of my typically daring driving stunts that I had been quite good at as a teenager nearly fifteen years prior. As we were accelerating down a gravel road with me forcing my Ford Ranchero into escalating fishtailing maneuvers, a tie rod broke (a critical section of steering linkage), resulting in us first doing a 360° rollover and then landing in the ditch with the car again upright but now facing the opposite direction.

The roof had collapsed over Chuck's portion of the vehicle, and he was jammed down into his seat. Almost immediately I asked, "Are you alright?"

Chuck hesitantly answered, "Yeah, I think I'm okay." But he was slow in starting to move, almost too slow.

I asked again, "Are you sure you're okay?"

As he took a more thorough personal inventory he answered again that he was okay. The crushed roof that now nearly dipped to the passenger's headrest clearly indicated that he had narrowly avoided serious or deadly injury.

Ever cheerful and initially barely fazed in my stupidity, I stated the obvious: "Well, I guess we rolled, huh?"

As Chuck agreed with my assessment of the situation and we both recognized our apparent good luck, we started laughing while considering how to get out of the mangled vehicle. The windshield was of course shattered, but it was still partially in place even though sections of it were missing. The driver's side window was completely broken out, and since the roof over my area was still reasonably intact we each then crawled out my window. Once we were both safely out of the car, as a curiosity I tried to open the driver's door. When it opened freely, we enjoyed another round of good-natured laughs at having missed the obvious.

Chuck unbuttoned his shirt to shake out the remaining crystallized pieces of broken glass that had sprayed over him when we rolled and glass was shattering. His neck was stiff, and for days he downplayed his discomfort to spare me additional guilt when I sobered up and eventually came to my senses. As for my injuries, I received a small cut on my thumb. When it had firmly sunk in that I had very nearly killed or crippled my friend, I finally had to admit that it was time to put such foolishness behind me. I vowed that there would be no more escapades like this—I didn't want to hurt anyone. It was in fact the last time that I ever drove in that condition.

The only casualty of that night was my 1972 blue Ford Ranchero—the car that I had used during the extortion—the last possible piece of evidence that might link me to the now five year old crime except for the handwritten extortion demands that I had sent to South Central Bell.

Back offshore, I didn't really need or want Bob and Doug continuing to preach to me on diving jobs as they grew more intense with trying to change the rest of us. I felt that I was doing just fine with my life, car wrecks aside, without their uninvited lectures about such matters as salvation and whatever else it was that they kept rambling on about. I sure didn't need some imaginary and manipulative God who toyed with mankind like some kind of a morbid puppet-master. I quickly tuned out when the unwanted lectures would begin, eagerly taking the first opportunity to exit the one-sided conversations.

Finally though, Doug relaxed and toned down his approach after providing me with a currently popular book dealing with Christianity. Then Bob finally realized that I was not receptive to spiritual browbeating, and he took a new tack. Bob was better educated than most of us, and he had entered the diving business a little later in his life than was typical for most divers. He was new to the business, but he was not a novice at life. Our conversations—even though I did not want them to be along the lines of these religious issues—slowly began to become more of a two-way dialog. I still did not like any conversations about God, but Bob was not now compulsively forcing his views on me with curt one-liners. Also, he was articulate and I respected this.

I provided a brief assessment of my views of Christianity and of God. Bob listened without being defensive or offended. I was not being intentionally disparaging or insulting; I was being truthful. High on my list of criticisms was my opinion that Christianity was a philosophy of death—that it was all about some eventual fictitious and preposterous hope of heaven that people wanted to believe in to console themselves regarding their presently empty or otherwise deficient lives. It was about willful belief in spiritual imaginations. While it was Karl Marx who had said in part that religion was the opium of the people, I was not merely echoing his sentiments in some vain attempt to pretend to be an intellectual—especially one of his political persuasion. Instead, based on observation, I really believed that religion was a psychological pacifier that had no legitimate substance to it. It was fine for the feel-good needs of people inclined to such sentimentality, but it was in the end a destructive force in that it was essentially dishonest and it led people to build their lives on a hollow and untrustworthy foundation.

In their simplest form my arguments came down to this: it was no harder—and in fact much easier—for me to believe that matter and energy had always existed in some form or another rather than believe in the far more complex notion of a perfect God with infinite intelligence who was content to tolerate gross imperfection within His own creation. On one hand, I had been able to accept as being feasible evolution and the chance workings of impossibly complicated interactions of matter, energy, and biological mutations; and on the other I dismissed the concept of there being a Divine Designer who had instead engineered these intricate and elaborate happenings, and then arbitrarily overrode it all with an infrequent miracle here and there. For me, God was an utterly implausible alternative.

I had one secret weakness in my arguments that I could not explain, and that was the troubling existence of the persistent human conscience. I pretended to chalk that up to a random evolutionary consequence that was somehow by nature incorporated into the species to ensure survival. It was a weak argument at best. I was more than a little curious why I was not free to pursue ultimate selfishness and fully exploit or destroy whatever came my way as any personal whim might move me. I could willfully step over the line of decency and had done so numerous times in my life, but it was the very existence of that line that troubled me. Why was I not free to take whatever I wanted from others with no consideration of the costs or consequences for them?

Additionally, I had a full and confident expectation that when a person died that this was the absolute end of one's existence in all dimensions. It was an end that I personally neither feared nor dreaded and always welcomed—not the actual process of dying, but the sweet relief of finally disappearing into nothingness. Pressed, I would fight to stay alive just like the next man—that was the natural instinct of survival for any living creature. Death was simply the last door to walk through into a welcomed oblivion. Still, recollections of a long-ago suicide attempt and an existence that had seemed to extend beyond the confines of a physical body remained a mystery that I could not solve and had to deny.

In my discussions with Bob I explained that the very evidence of Christianity itself, whether past or present, undermined its credibility. The hypocrisy that I saw was pervasive. Far too many people on Sunday mornings gathered together in some kind of mutual admiration society, only then to later in the day or week resume lives that were the antithesis of supposed Christian kindness. Not far from my thoughts was the bitter memory of the Air Force chaplain at Lowry Air Force Base in Denver, Colorado, who had refused to help a young airman who was reaching out in absolute brokenness on a long ago Sunday; of the cruel wife of a minister who deeply embarrassed a shy student; of an Oral Roberts who promised healing in God's name to those who were afflicted when a young boy with asthma touched the television screen with one hand and his own head with the other just as he was told to do, believing fully that God would take away his sickness through this television preacher; and of a tearful teenager pouring out his heart to a God who preferred to remain silent, disinterested, and distant.

Curiously, the historical accounts of the abuses committed by those supposedly acting in the name of Christianity didn't mean much to me—most men were selfish and evil anyway when you got down to it with or without Christianity, so that part of the equation wasn't a concern of mine in this sense. Godless communism didn't exactly have a stellar track record either. My distrust was instead on a far more personal and practical level, even though Bob would hear only my loftier intellectual arguments and the same criticisms that any atheist might raise. That ground is hardly untilled, and the same objections span the centuries with each new atheist convinced that his conclusions would sway any truly thinking person if they were not willfully blinded by religious tradition and superstition. I need not raise all the arguments; we all have heard them, and they are tedious. Thousands of years ago Psalm 14:1 documented the objections: "The fool has said in his heart, 'There is no God.'" This is not exactly new territory.

Bob gently placed a wedge between what I considered Christianity to be—essentially the broad composite of religious behavior of those who professed to believe in God—and what basic or what might be called real Christianity really is. As he spoke I could grasp the points that he was making. He essentially reduced Christianity to being an individual relationship with God through Jesus Christ, rather than a religious system or the patchwork beliefs and behavior of all those who claimed to be Christians. I was not close-minded to what appeared to me to be a somewhat different understanding of this subject, but I did remain close-minded to the possibility that he was right in the ultimate sense and that there was in fact such a God with whom there could even be such a relationship. I was willing to consider that I had misjudged what real Christianity was if Bob was correct about what he was saying—that would account for there being people like my Aunt Jennie and Uncle Harold—but this nevertheless made no difference to me personally because I did not believe in the existence of this imagined God.

The information presented by Bob was reasonably simple to grasp, even though for me it remained completely unbelievable. In fact, he echoed many of the things that I had been taught long ago in Sunday School as a child. I had been taught about a man named Jesus who was the Son of God by way of His birth to a young Jewish woman. Although she was betrothed, she was still a virgin when Jesus was conceived by the Holy Spirit. In short: a divine miracle. I knew that this unique man had been a carpenter, and that He began a ministry that was received well by the masses but was rejected by the religious and political leaders of the day. I knew that He had performed many miracles Himself, and that He was a man like none other before or since.

I knew that Jesus Christ had been crucified on a cross as a result of the betrayal of one of His disciples and that His crucifixion was instigated by those opposed to His teachings. I knew that in one way or another His death was related to the individual and collective sins of mankind. I knew that He had risen from the dead three days after He had been crucified, and that these things had been prophesied in the Old Testament. I knew that His select group of disciples and others eventually spread His message about God's kingdom, and that based on this message churches have continued down through the ages, with all of this being called Christianity in some form or another.

I also knew the teachings about heaven and hell, knowing that somehow God was eventually going to sort out all these things, regardless of which camp we might be in. Plus, I did have to acknowledge that our calendar—the very numbering of years as either BC or AD—obviously pointed back in time to the historical Christ. Something major had to have happened back then to divide time as we know it.

But what I had never understood before was that this message was intended to have a true life-changing power within it. This message—this gospel—was to completely change the lives of those who heard it and truly believed it. This was not a psychological shell game; this was a unique occurrence in the spiritual realm. This was to be so profound that it was what the Bible called being "born again". Christianity was not merely a code of behavior; it was a living relationship with God.

Bob somehow cut through the broader concept of religion and denominations, which were many and often contrary, and brought things down to essentials. It was through a person becoming united with Jesus Christ both in His death and His resurrection that a person would then become this real born-again Christian. Nevertheless, knowledge of a Christianity that was this personal with God remained a purely theoretical and hypothetical consideration for me. I finally explained to Bob: "If you are right in what you are saying, then I will admit that I have misjudged what real Christianity is, but this honestly makes no difference to me because I don't believe it." I had no desire to submit to any religious belief system even though he confidently assured me that all this was based on the Word of God as revealed in the Bible.

Knowing that Bob was intelligent and not superstitious and with me having conceded some ground to him in these discussions, I finally decided to go ahead and expose the inconsistencies of his position. I expected this would help him understand why I could not accept what he was saying as truth—and why I legitimately had every reason to have such doubt. I did not want to humiliate him or undermine his faith; I only wanted him to see the merits and logic of my position. Having a basic knowledge of some Bible stories and teachings, I knew that the Bible spoke openly about a powerful dark creature named Satan, a fallen angel of God who was also known as the devil. Here is where superstition ran amok and where many non-believers and believers alike rolled their eyes when discussions turned to giving any credence to the existence of such a being. I knew that Bob was too bright to yield to this superstition, and when he would awkwardly have to discount this aspect it would then be a simple matter to point out that even he didn't really believe the Bible—this supposedly legitimate Word of God.

"Bob, if what you say about Jesus is true and if the Bible is really the Word of God, then by definition alone there has to be a devil." I was somewhat embarrassed for him as I knew that he would have to start to make excuses and explain that we could not take such things literally.

Instead, I was caught off guard when Bob had no reservations about agreeing that there was in fact just such a being: "Yes, absolutely, there is a devil, and he is very real."

Now I did begin to perk up; now it was time to take the gloves off and bring this religious nonsense to a halt. I had listened to more of this tripe than I had cared to and my patience was gone. In compulsive anger, my words shot out: "Well, if he is real, then I'll take him on. Let him throw his best punch."

Because of longevity and experience I was one of the senior divers at the company and somewhat looked up to, but now there was a sudden and serious maturity about Bob that I did not have, and I could feel it as he spoke solemnly: "Larry, you don't know what you are saying."

I knew immediately that Bob genuinely believed the warning that he was giving me, but the discussion had now tapped into one of the roots of my hatred and discontent. This was why I hadn't wanted him pushing my buttons. I despised this notion that there was a supposed spiritual world where cowardly beings in the shadows could destroy lives and where God stood by in amusement as humans in one dimension were tormented by the invisible corrupted forces that God Himself had created in another dimension. I despised feeling like a puppet. With no hesitation I repeated, "I don't give a damn. Let him throw his best punch." I was deaf to Bob's continuing warnings for me, and I did not back down when he solemnly recounted the experiences that his brother had suffered while experimenting with the dark side.

Our conversation drew to a close, but Bob had mentioned that he had a book detailing five case histories of demonic possession. Not only was Bob admitting to what I thought he would dismiss as superstition, he had done some serious homework on the subject. The book seemed to be as good of a place as any for me to take on this adversary, and I eventually received it from Bob. I intended at some point to move forward aggressively with my own study.

I know that Bob's prayers for me were that I would be spared from my ignorance and foolishness, that me shaking my tiny fist against spiritual principalities would draw no attacks, but rather that I would be blessed and saved from myself. Completely apart from any action of my own, I was indeed to be blessed.

It was March of 1979, and I was on the small Santa Fe construction barge named the Sioux. This barge had been a successful little workhorse for the company. Living conditions on the barge were poor and space was limited, but we worked efficiently. We had performed a subsea valve rotation and then installed a 6-inch riser—the vertical section of a pipeline that ascends from the seabed up the platform to connect with topside piping. With weather factors slowing us down, I had performed only six gas dives in the course of three weeks. Gas dives were those dives where we breathed a mixture of helium and oxygen to achieve longer allowable working times on bottom, and also to avoid nitrogen narcosis (a feeling somewhat similar to intoxication) that can occur when breathing regular air at depths approaching and exceeding two hundred feet. Because of the limited number of dives, the overall pace had been relaxed, and we were now waiting for the completion of pressure tests to confirm a successful installation.

I was in a top bunk, asleep, and it was the middle of the night. A dream began, and I saw before me the plaque that had been given to me by my father well over twenty years prior, and which I had left in Montana and given absolutely no thought to for many years. Out of the past came this memory in living color, and in my dream I saw the plaque as I had never seen it before. It was a living version of the one in my distant memory where on the left side was the picture of Jesus and on the right side was the first verse from the fourteenth chapter of the gospel of John: "Let not your heart be troubled: ye believe in God, believe also in Me" (KJV). In my dream I had time to consider the words, not in the sense of trying to sort out their exact meaning but rather to rest my thoughts on them. The picture of Jesus remained a picture, but it was far more vibrant and awe-inspiring than I had ever seen it before.

The increasing intensity of the dream transported me from a sleeping state to an awakened state, and yet the plaque remained before me. The plaque never disappeared and was now even more brilliant as the dream fully crossed the threshold into being a vision. I was now awake, and I was seeing before me something holy. I marveled at the picture of Jesus that appeared to be about six feet from me but was now taking up my full field of vision. It was somewhat different than the picture on the original plaque, for I could see the full chest of Jesus in this depiction and it was more of a frontal view than a side view, but it did remain a picture. There was no transformation that I saw in which I could claim that I saw the living Lord, but I knew fully that I was seeing spiritual energy. As I continued to look at the picture, a pinpoint of light then began radiating outward from the center of Jesus's chest, directly out from His heart. The light grew steadily brighter as it expanded towards me in a gentle but powerful enveloping explosion of love. The light itself was love, and I trembled almost violently as the oncoming waves washed into me and overwhelmed me. As I shook with awe I heard myself reverently proclaim to God, "Oh, Lord." My life changed in that instant, and I would never be the same again.

The vision departed but not the effects. I was in a condition as I had never been before. I breathed deeply but hesitantly. The room was now dark again, and I turned on my bunk light and looked around. I focused carefully to confirm that I had indeed been awake, anchoring myself back into the physical world while yet now being fully aware of the spiritual world—being aware of God and knowing that there was no choice but to believe Him. I had needed the blinding light of stunning revelation to believe, and I had been given that light. I had been as the reluctant and doubting Thomas who upon hearing that the other disciples had seen the risen Lord had himself then stated, "Unless I see in His hands the imprint of the nails, and put my finger into the place of the nails, and put my hand into His side, I will not believe" (John 20:25). There is no special place of honor for those of us who demand to see before we believe.

I dressed quietly in an almost reflective trance and left the room—I was overwhelmed with what I had witnessed and experienced. I knew that others had loved me in my life: I presumed that my parents had loved me in their own way and I was pretty sure that when I was a child my Aunt Jennie and Uncle Harold had loved me, but I had never really felt love before. This was far beyond any concept of love that I had ever considered. I was bewildered but made alive. I didn't know what to do with this new knowledge.

One thing I did know immediately: my hatred was gone. It was as if a huge malignant tumor had been painlessly removed from my soul. I was experiencing a peace that I had never known before. This wasn't a decision or a choice on my part—this was God having performed something miraculous within me.

The short hallway outside the room led directly into the barge galley. I entered the galley, continuing slowly to take in everything around me in a new way. It was a discovery of things that had always been, but I now saw everything in a new, hard-to-define way. There was now reason and purpose to this existence, and for me this was a new consideration. Continuing my slow walk of discovery, I opened the galley door that led out onto the deck where there was an adjacent workbench sometimes used by welders for small projects. Simultaneously as I opened the door a welder struck an arc and there was a blinding flash as is typical for electric arc welding. My humor was still intact as I shielded my eyes and reflected: "I guess I've seen the light." I knew it to be an understatement of eternal proportions.

As the team of departing divers boarded the crewboat following the completion of the job, I continued to wonder in amazement at what had happened to me. I spoke to no one about the vision—it was yet too precious to share with anyone, and my heart was too raw. Someone observing me and concerned because of my complete change in demeanor had asked, "Are you okay?"

When we reached the dock, we boarded company-provided ground transportation and returned to Houma, Louisiana, where the company was based and where our personal vehicles were parked. As I loaded my gear into my car, I wondered deeply if I was now a Christian. I had so much to try to figure out. I began pulling away from the parking lot, and I noticed one of the crew having difficulty starting his truck. Upon reaching the base after a job, the desire was always to get on the road and get started home as soon as possible. I hesitated, and seeing this man in need I helped him start his truck with my jumper cables. If I was a Christian, I was not about to deliberately turn my back on him; but it was more than this now: I wanted to help him.

The drive home that night left me thinking deeply and continuously about what had happened. I reached my house in Abita Springs and had a few hours of sleep before the stores in Covington opened the next day. I knew what I had to do and what I wanted to do: I went to a local bookstore and purchased a Bible. At the time there was a Christian bookstore in Covington, but I didn't even know of its existence. Instead, I went to a regular bookstore and asked the saleslady for a Bible. She reluctantly went to where a few were stored almost out of sight. I sensed her displeasure with stocking and selling the Bible—it was as if it was an unwelcome obligation to satisfy the public. No matter, I knew that this was what I needed to study.

Reading the Bible was now as it had never been in my youth. The words impacted me and created within me a hunger for more. Certainly there were many things that I did not understand, but what I did grasp had power unlike any other words I had ever read. I did not start at the beginning, but my attention went first to the book of John and occasionally to the book of Psalms. I read John 14:1, now seeing who this One was who spoke these words about believing in God and believing in Him. I looked back to long ago memorized Psalms, such as the 23rd Psalm that began: "The Lord is my shepherd." I was on a mission to learn, to sort out what being a Christian was really all about. I informed my boss that I would be taking some extended time off from work.

As I began what was to be an involved study of the Bible from a layman's practical point of view, in the back of my mind there was the lingering and troublesome challenge that remained. I had issued that foolish declaration regarding the devil, and I now had to figure out what I was going to do about this. My old nature was not inclined to run from such a challenge. There had been a couple times in my life when I had backed down from physical fights and had been left feeling like a coward for having done so, and although I knew that this was now a justifiably prudent time to withdraw in humility, I could not bring myself to do it. If I was on the verge—and I knew that I was—of discovering some of the greatest mysteries of life, then I would even venture down forbidden paths to satisfy both curiosity and understanding. A strange tingling of dread told me to retreat, but I would not.

Within weeks the foolhardy challenge that had remained outstanding finally demanded my attention. With the same ominous feeling that one has when awakening from a nightmare or when feeling the hair rise on the back of the neck when confronting something sinister and evil, one evening I picked up the book that I had received from Bob with the five case histories of demonic possession and exorcism. Alone in my house in the woods outside of Abita Springs, I knew that this act was opening a door into a dark place where I did not belong. I read the first two cases, feeling repeated chills at the permeating presence of evil. I am not suggesting that I or anyone else would experience this today or that such reading is always forbidden; I am only relating what occurred one evening under one specific set of circumstances. This is not about being able to recreate this experience in practice for me or for anyone else. This is simply part of my history.

As I closed the book and slowly placed it on the table by my chair, I knew that I had read enough. The atmosphere was heavy with dread. I knew that I had crossed a boundary that I should not have—a door had been opened.

In both of the two accounts that I had read, deliverance for the afflicted or possessed individual was achieved solely through implementation of the victory that Jesus Christ had secured through His death and resurrection. His shed blood bore witness of that victory in ways that we struggle to understand. His blood was the physical evidence of the acceptable payment and settlement for sin—there was power in its testimony. Death had no power over Him because in God's kingdom death is an aberration, a judgment, a consequence of sin, a separation from God; and yet the Son of God was sinless when He died. It was precisely because He was sinless and because He was the Son of God that He had the authority to take up

His life again in the power of the resurrection. His body had died, but His spirit had continued on.

His tomb was found empty, and many later saw the risen Lord before He ascended to be at the right hand of the Father. His crucifixion had been unjustified for Himself personally, and He therefore earned the privilege of freely giving the forgiveness that He had purchased with His own blood to others who would be joined to Him by a faith that would come to us as a gift from God.

When Jesus Christ's physical death on the cross and then His time of spiritual separation from the Father was completed, this became the prophesized substitution made for us so that we could be one with Him, and through Him be released from death's power to separate. This is a spiritual transaction made effective by the Holy Spirit in which by our belief in Jesus we are miraculously identified with Him, and we then share in His completed work on the cross through God's gift of faith to us. This is substitutionary atonement.

It is this Lord, this One who existed eternally before He entered the stream of humanity as the Son of Man, this living communication of God who is perfect in all His ways, this heavenly sacrificial lamb and yet warrior; it is this One who now alone has all authority. It is His name—when that name of Jesus Christ is understood and revered in its holy majesty and sovereignty—to which powers of darkness must concede defeat. These are not spiritual parlor games or matters for mockery, not when you understand them. It was after I was armed with a very basic knowledge of these matters but with having been given the faith to believe that I was to experience a chilling warfare.

A fitful sleep came upon me that night. The dream must have started almost right away, and the prevailing sensation was one of insidious evil and of this evil's unequivocal intention to take ownership of me. I sensed that something or someone was now somewhere within me, and the battle lines soon became clear. Whatever this force was, it was trying to twist and contort my facial expressions into vicious and vile expressions of itself. I knew that if it achieved this specific goal that it would have me in its grip.

I cannot apply logical reasoning to this conclusion—I only know that this was the defined deciding point of who would win this battle.

The fight was on. The dream rapidly gave way to an awakened state in a somewhat similar fashion as I had experienced with my positive vision, but this present experience was instead a product of a fallen and evil entity. I strained with absolutely every fiber of strength that I had to resist the force and to maintain control of my body. I had had fights in my life; I had been pushed close to my limits a few times; but I had never in my life given 100% in any fight, in any effort—something within me had always held me back. This time was different—I fought desperately with absolutely everything I had—and I was losing, and I knew it.

As in the two case histories that I had just read, I then knew that I had to call upon the Lord Jesus and somehow summon His victory. He was my only hope. This was not an overblown nightmare—I was awake and experiencing in real life the worst horror movie I had ever imagined as this creature or whatever it was continued to claw its way through my soul to take over me physically. I tried to call out to Jesus and invoke a deliverance command that I remembered from the book, but all the muscles in my face were frozen in a clenched standoff in which I was slowly weakening with exhaustion. I strained and strained and though unable to yet say the command that I knew that I must, I finally managed to utter the name "Jesus". Once I managed to speak His name, the tide of the battle slowly began to change. I continued to wrestle internally to slowly work my way up through repeated tries to speak the command that would secure my deliverance: "In the name of the Lord Jesus Christ I command you to leave." With those words eventually being spoken out loud, control was returned to me and I collapsed in sweaty exhaustion.

I do not know how long the struggle had taken. It would likely be measured in several tens of minutes, but not in hours. I prayed in humble thanksgiving that I had been rescued, and I praised the One who had delivered me from the hand of this evil enemy. As one who knows full well how preposterous this all will sound to some, I nevertheless lived it, and it happened. It was no mere bad dream. In such a time of struggle there is no formula, no set ritual, no prescribed procedure to follow other than calling out to the Lord and standing firm in the victory that He has already secured at the cross. This is not a new battle; it is reminding the enemy of the old battle that he lost. I acted only as I knew how to act in those particular circumstances. I have never doubted the authority of the Lord Jesus Christ since my first encounter with the Spirit of God when I was offshore, and after the contrary negative experience that followed I have a confidence in His victory and His Lordship that is unshakeable.

Following the negative experience it took me three days to recover physically. I was totally spent. It was nearly the same as recovering from a serious case of the flu with respect to lingering aches and complete exhaustion. It was an experience that I never want to repeat, but I do not live in fear. I know the One who has purchased my life with His life, and I am His.

The often quoted verse from John 3:16 had now become clear and distinct to me in its meaning when it stated, "For God so loved the world, that He gave His only begotten Son, that whoever believes in Him shall not perish, but have eternal life."

Chapter Thirteen

Something Wrong

Study of the Bible was no chore for me as the many weeks and soon months began to pass by. I could often doubt my understanding of any given passage that I might be reading, but I did not have to wade through a swamp of doubt regarding the ultimate divine authorship of the Word of God. I knew that any Bible that I would read was a translation and therefore subject to the skills and integrity of the involved translators, yet I was spared questioning what mankind had first been given by God as He empowered and led men to write down the information that He intended in the way that He intended. Given the committed and dedicated service of innumerable scholars down through the ages working with countless corroborating manuscripts and coupling this with links to other historical and archeological findings, I did not have to wrestle with thoughts of possible corruption of the original message and its intent. When multiple human authors separated by multiple centuries detail events covering thousands of years with this all dovetailing and pointing to and culminating in the person of Jesus Christ, then there is a consistency that for me at least defies manipulation, chance, or coincidence. Of course, I had once been blind to all this that now in hindsight seems so obvious and irrefutable.

Furthermore, this aspect of using logic and evidence to help confirm the veracity of the Scriptures was far outweighed for me by a single word: faith. I had been given the faith to believe. This faith served as a key that began to open my mind to comprehend what had before been hidden from me. Obviously, my faith cannot be the bedrock for anyone else's belief or confidence, and I don't intend that it should be. Real faith is not trying to force yourself to have confidence in something that somebody else is telling you—real faith is a gift from God that bestows spiritual understanding and assurance. Real faith has substance.

As I began to reflect back on the entirety of my life with my spiritual blinders finally off, I was able to see God's guiding hand throughout. My desperate wanting to know that there was a big God who was in control rather than some whimsical god who toyed with mankind had been resolved. I may not have been able to reconcile a mountain of lesser issues, but I did know that God was at the helm and that His personalized mercy and grace would prevail. An exasperating conclusion regarding the futility of life was replaced by the certain knowledge that an immutable divine plan was in motion. Did I understand the plan to the degree that it all made perfect sense to me? Absolutely not. I have tended to think that with one broad sweep of God's mighty hand that there instantaneously could be a perfect creation marked by nothing but love, peace, and joy. But I also knew that my limited intellect and limited perspective did not allow me a suitable vision of eternity, infinity, and God's character to even begin to understand how God was working out a far greater plan than I could possibly imagine.

Admittedly, beyond my comprehension was how tragedy and brutality, suffering and death, agony and abandonment have often been the instruments that God uses in mysterious ways to set the stage for what will be the eventual unfolding of a mystery that will leave us all silent and in awe of His wisdom, His love, and His righteousness. It is naturally far easier to imagine only acts of kindness and love as being the logical building blocks to be used in the revelation of God's perfect character than it is to see this accomplished through an apparent temporary tolerance of sin, disobedience, and turmoil.

Jesus Christ's sacrifice and accomplishments in those dark hours on the cross and during the unseen happenings in the spiritual realm for the three hidden days before His resurrection stand as the pivotal focal point in God's plan, and therein is the revelation of what really needs to be understood. The gospel of Jesus Christ is about our being reconciled to God through the death and resurrection of His Son.

God used my darkness and failure to teach me things about Himself that I could not have learned in any other way but through the very understanding that I had fallen, and that I had fallen far. The painful part of these lessons began to take hold when I began to understand that someone who was truly innocent, someone who was even far more than innocent—someone who was truly righteous—had placed His strong but gentle hand on my shoulder and held me back from the judgment that I deserved while He went forward to be my substitute. I didn't even know this One who would do such a thing, and I had rejected Him and cursed Him and hated Him, but yet He went forward for me as surely as He has gone forward for all those whom He would draw to Himself.

The darkness and failure that I knew even in my earliest years had me disliking myself and despairing of life. Granted, there were unhealthy influences that either instigated or fed these accusing feelings, but there also was some justification for this self-loathing. To describe such things as a matter of the heart places the focus on depressing feelings—on stunted or unhealthy emotions—and this is partially true. Then, to say it was a matter of the mind suggests ongoing psychological conflicts, of battles defined by thoughts, which again is true in part. To try to encompass both the heart and the mind, and even more than this, the word "soul" takes things to the next level where a more full identity begins to be developed. Further, if one sees this as primarily a spiritual dilemma, a person's "spirit" then becomes the real essence of ultimate character. Understanding these things to some degree is necessary to understanding self, but this can too easily become an indulgent if not obsessive focus on self.

This can all become a tedious and frustrating exercise in chasing down phantom or illusive symptoms, while the real malady remains obscure. There was something in me that I knew was defiant, dishonorable, selfish, greedy, mean, and dirty. Yet I also clearly knew things like respect, honor, generosity, kindness, compassion, and goodness to name a few finer attributes. In the end it might all come down to this simple observation: I was able to turn on and turn off my very shallow love as easily as a light switch, and others seemed able to do the same—and that was wrong, and I knew it.

As all this eventually firmed up into something that was almost tangible, I came to recognize an indescribable wall of division in my mind. I was on one side of the wall, and I was small. Something was on the other side of the wall, and it was significant—over there, on that other side, was the realm where everything was really playing out, and it was frustrating not to be allowed to enter the main arena where my life was being decided.

Trying to describe this wall that separated these two vague but recognized realms, which I had first tried to do as a teenager with the minister, too easily made it sound like a type of schizophrenic deviation within me. I knew that wasn't the case, but I also knew that this would likely be the conclusion drawn by others. Of course I was divided and conflicted, but not to the degree that this was a pathological and splintering psychological flaw—I understood these things too well and too coherently to dismiss them as a personality disconnect within me.

The despair that accompanied this turmoil often did cruelly suggest a personal coming meltdown or explosion, but there was something about the wall itself that whispered a convincing and powerful truth. At times throughout my life I tried to explain to the few who listened that there was something wrong within me or about me. I knew that something was not right. Well-meaning others had tried to assure me that I was okay, that I was being too hard on myself. But for me, it didn't take a high school burglary, drunken driving, loose living, compulsive hatred, or eventually extortion to convince me that something was seriously amiss—I knew this well before any acting out had occurred. In fact, those moral lapses were an imperfect and deceptively inadequate view of what I knew was wrong.

Assurances by others meant to encourage me about myself instead dismayed me—this proved that they didn't understand and that they didn't believe me, and I knew they were wrong. One honest look at humanity in general revealed to me that they were missing the point not only for me, but for themselves as well. I marveled that they could not see this. My harshest judgments were for myself, but others did not escape my unspoken criticism.

The Cuban Missile Crisis of 1962 demonstrated in no uncertain terms that the world was only the push of a button away from a nuclear holocaust when Russia and the United States were very nearly at the brink of war. Many now forget—even those of us who lived this—that there was a time when we thought nuclear war might be imminent. When you contemplate continually airborne Strategic Air Command B-52 bombers and Minuteman missiles in hardened underground silos with 100-ton blast doors all requiring only a coded message to unleash Mutual Assured Destruction (MAD as it was cryptically known), and you also understand that the other side is just as determined and capable, then you do give some time to wondering how it all might end.

When daydreaming or other random mental input prompted me to think about total world destruction linked to some waiting button, my hand would impulsively but willfully slam down on that imaginary button—and these thoughts lasted far beyond 1962. More than once others had wondered why my hand slammed down violently on something. I would have taken the world with me given the opportunity in those moments when my imagination and anger were unchecked. I found my mind to be a microcosm of an out of control world.

Contributing to the unhealthy understanding that I had of life as a child and young man was a dysfunctional family where I was shouldered with the responsibility of providing for the satisfaction and happiness of a sometimes deviant and narcissistic parent. Subjected to a mother who could seem quite cruel and perverse at times and then trying to understand a God who seemed equally disinterested in my well-being left me in a quandary. Eventually, a believed rejection by God and then coming to believe that I had been fed nothing but lies about a benevolent God was followed by a confident and bitter atheism. My sensitivity then became strangely coupled with a reactive defensive callousness, and my heart became cold as ice. With a world seemingly designed to exacerbate doubt and shortcomings and with no understanding from others, my mind turned against itself in anger because of its frustrating inability to come to grips with these things. All this set the stage for a potential total wreck of a life and a willing determination to ignore my conscience. Throughout it all there was that mysterious wall. The wall was an imperfect picture but a perfect indicator that something was wrong.

The liberating message that I soon discovered in my studies was that I definitely had been right all along—there in fact was something wrong within me. The Bible in glimpses throughout gave irrefutable evidence of the failure of human character, and when I read passages that one's pride might otherwise find offensive I instead found there to be the truth about an unhealthy condition rooted in the self that we all have. Perhaps the most thorough teaching on this subject is in the book of Romans in the New Testament where the Apostle Paul develops arguments and explains these considerations analytically. What would seem to have brought only condemnation upon me was instead life-giving. I wasn't left with the crippling knowledge that something was wrong; I was instead empowered to know how this acknowledged problem had been thoroughly dealt with by Jesus. Knowing the first half of the truth involving my failures and shortcomings—in short, sin—had given me the best possible foundation for truly appreciating the second half involving God's solution in and through Jesus Christ.

The wall had been a picture of the barrier—of the separation—that existed between God and me until the issue of sin was resolved. The wall was an effective barrier for God as well as for me, and until that wall was broken down or penetrated there could be no true relationship. My sinless perfection—clearly unattainable in this life—would not be required, for that was achieved by Someone else on my behalf solely by God's grace.

God of course is not bound by limitations and restrictions as we understand them, but He is consistent in His character. He cannot deny His own nature and welcome that which is unholy into oneness with Him any more than light and darkness can occupy the same space. Holiness is a concept that we have lost sight of, even to the extent that irreverence has now become an accepted mark of one's proud independence. But how can one who is unholy step into the presence of One who is holy? Therein was both the mystery and the understanding of the wall. Jesus Christ was the solution to the problem, and He was the only solution. First Timothy 2:5-6 spells it out clearly: "For there is one God, and one mediator also between

God and men, the man Christ Jesus, who gave Himself as a ransom for all, the testimony given at the proper time."

Taking these thoughts further regarding the wall, perhaps the easiest to understand explanation is contained in these words that Jesus spoke: "Truly, truly, I say to you, I am the door of the sheep. All who came before Me are thieves and robbers, but the sheep did not hear them. I am the door; if anyone enters through Me, he will be saved, and will go in and out and find pasture. The thief comes only to steal and kill and destroy; I came that they may have life, and have it abundantly. I am the good shepherd; the good shepherd lays down His life for the sheep" (John 10:7-11). Jesus is the door. The wall had a door, and I didn't know this.

A mere five verses after the verse in John 14:1 that had been displayed on the plaque that had hung on my wall as a child was this statement by Jesus: "I am the way, and the truth, and the life; no one comes to the Father but through Me" (John 14:6). It could not have been more clear.

That which was wrong within me was settled at the transaction of the cross, and it was mine to receive through faith. I chose to believe when I finally understood, but I never would have made that choice had not God enabled me to believe and brought me to that point where He overwhelmed me with His grace, mercy, and love. I knew that salvation involved much more than some decision that I might make of my own accord, and the Bible states this unequivocally in the book of Ephesians:

> "And you were dead in your trespasses and sins, in which you formerly walked according to the course of this world, according to the prince of the power of the air, of the spirit that is now working in the sons of disobedience. Among them we too all formerly lived in the lusts of our flesh, indulging the desires of the flesh and of the mind, and were by nature children of wrath, even as the rest. But God, being rich in mercy, because of His great love with which He loved us, even when we were dead in our transgressions, made us alive together with Christ (by grace you have been saved), and raised us up with Him, and seated us with Him

> in the heavenly places in Christ Jesus, so that in the ages to come He might show the surpassing riches of His grace in kindness toward us in Christ Jesus. For by grace you have been saved through faith; and that not of yourselves, it is the gift of God; not as a result of works, so that no one should boast. For we are His workmanship, created in Christ Jesus for good works, which God prepared beforehand so that we would walk in them" (Ephesians 2:1-10).

The relief of learning what had been wrong within me, and understanding that this was fully resolved at the cross, was a knowledge that set me free and gave me new life. As I began to live this new life many changes were to follow. The change in my nature was so extreme that at least one friend was convinced that I had lost my mind. It took nearly a year of consistent new behavior for him and other friends to accept that there really had been a permanent change in me. I had known immediately that my life would never be the same, but it took maintaining this new life for a while before others could acknowledge that there had been a genuine conversion to Christianity.

At times you hear stories of those who in their darkest moments are saved. To discredit these experiences, they are sometimes described as "jailhouse conversions", "foxhole conversions", or "deathbed conversions". These types of conversions are often eagerly dismissed by skeptics and considered counterfeit. They are especially considered suspect, often unfairly so, when an accusation of weakness or fear can somehow be leveled against a person in need who has responded to the gospel. It is easier for someone to understand and accept that a person might always have been inclined toward matters of faith, but rapid conversions during heightened stress where there is no proven track record can raise the eyebrows of skeptics who want to place limitations on God. But in my situation, I was at the top of my career with a growing confidence; I had been set free from a difficult marriage; I had no desire to find God or religion; and I was at the highest point that I had ever been in my life.

What can be difficult for people to understand is why God was silent in my times of genuine and absolute brokenness when I desperately reached out to Him with all my heart. His silence seems to contradict His promises to us in the Bible. Why didn't He comfort the heart and mind of a young boy who was begging for answers and trapped in despair? Why didn't a minister during counseling recognize the need for me to hear the message of a Savior who demolished walls and who proclaimed that He was the door? Doors allow passage through walls. Why didn't an Air Force chaplain respond to the weeping, begging requests of a young airman who was making a final plea for help? No one but God Himself could answer these questions with authority. The only possible answer that I can come up with that makes any sense to me might be as simple as this: because I really wanted to know God, then God knew that I needed first to know what it was like to live without Him. That seems a fair conclusion, and I have to leave it at that.

Why God chose to save me and why He chose that particular time I have no idea, except that I now have a greater confidence that God is every bit as big as I hoped he would be. I have been given an unusual and perhaps greater appreciation for a forgiveness that was extended to me when I was not seeking it—not even aware of it. I know salvation to be God's work on our behalf, and that brings strong assurance in times of difficulty when I might stumble or fail in some personal test. The forgiveness that saved me is also quite capable of sustaining me, and it has done precisely that.

There never was a question of who purchased my forgiveness, and the fact that this forgiveness in Him was completed. Yet as I continued in my studies I began to see that in some cases I needed to step back in time, and to the extent that I was able I needed to begin a process of reconciliation with those people whom I had wronged in my life. Such reconciliation involving confessions, apologies, and in some cases restitution in no way was an effort to try to receive forgiveness from God—that transaction was completed at the cross, and there was no way that I would presume to tarnish that miraculous achievement by Jesus Christ by adding my own efforts to His perfect sacrifice. Nevertheless, forgiveness by God did not translate into an abdication of my responsibility to others here on earth. How far this responsibility was to take me I was not sure in the beginning, but I knew that I could set no arbitrary boundaries.

Issues with relationships, including those with my parents, were clearly going to have to be addressed. This was not to be a list of various complaints and things that I needed to get off my chest, but much the opposite. It was to be a full and unconditional forgiveness given by me, a willing softening of my heart, and a reaching out to others regardless of whether or not this would be received. This was a process that continued with my parents until they passed away. There were some successes and there were some failures, and all I can do now is leave those results in God's hands. Not every story culminates in a moving scene with family members hugging one another in tears of relief and grateful understanding. Sometimes things just continue to hurt in some ways, and we find ourselves continuing on, unable to receive the healing that we desire for ourselves and for others.

After my first anniversary of becoming a Christian had passed and as I reflected more on my dealings with others throughout my life, certain situations began to stand out. Not everyone has a history of a burglary as a teenager and of extortion as an adult, not to mention a number of other untoward situations not revealed in this writing. The extortion soon moved to the front of the list. I would have gladly left this subject as closed, but that was not where God and my studies were leading me as I moved into the second year of my faith. If this faith of mine was real—and it was—then there were to be certain responsibilities that could not be ignored.

I searched out the Scriptures, trying to determine what God would have me to do about the extortion attempt that I had committed. Jesus's words in Matthew 5:23-26 seemed to speak directly to my situation: "Therefore if you are presenting your offering at the altar, and there remember that your brother has something against you, leave your offering there before the altar and go; first be reconciled to your brother, and then come and present your offering. Make friends quickly with your opponent at law while you are with him on the way, so that your opponent may not hand you over to the judge, and the judge to the officer, and you be thrown into prison. Truly I say to you, you will not come out of there until you have paid up the last cent."

Knowing that taking verses out of context from the Bible can be misleading, as well as the fact that we can misunderstand the circumstances surrounding specific verses and therefore their intent, I did not want to charge ahead blindly without having firm spiritual assurance that I was on the right course. This was a matter of ongoing prayer and of checking other relevant verses to ensure that I was seeing things properly. Yet all that I was seeing was pointing in the direction of me having to turn myself in. I knew that the Bible was not to be a cold rulebook for us and a new written law intended to be an extension of the Ten Commandments; but instead it was the living Word of God wherein we could learn of His character and His purposes and glean spiritual guidance from the teachings. Believers are told repeatedly in the New Testament that they are not under law but grace—a reading of Romans and Galatians reveals this clearly, but nowhere did I find that the Bible diminished personal accountability and responsibility. I was feeling responsibility building.

After my first several months of reading primarily only the Bible, I had discovered a local Christian bookstore in Covington, Louisiana, where I was to find a wealth of writings from many notable Christian authors: some were from far back in history; some were contemporary. One of the authors who had caught my interest for a while was a Chinese Christian named Watchman Nee (1903-1972). Mention of Watchman Nee is not necessarily intended to be a stepping stone for others for study; this is simply another piece of the puzzle for explaining how certain things came about in my life.

One evening after wrestling with the issue of my extortion attempt, my eyes settled on the bookshelf where Christian books that I had been collecting over several months were beginning to multiply. My focus fixed firmly on one of Watchman Nee's books that I had purchased but not yet read: *Not I But Christ,* which was the fourth volume in a series of six books on practical Christian living. I walked directly to the book with a gentle curiosity pushing me on. I removed the book from the shelf and opened it to some seemingly random page. The book had opened directly to the start of a new chapter, and the chapter was entitled, "Apology and Restitution." It is fair to say that in my mind I uttered a silent, "Oh, oh." There was no turning back now. The chapter offered some good guidance for when addressing the past was appropriate and when it was not, for not every prior wrong should be dredged up. Motivations and consequences must be carefully considered. My study and prayers continued for a few more days until I came to a decision.

As I knew that there had been something wrong within me from an early age that I learned later was resolved in Jesus Christ, so too I came to realize that there was something else that was currently wrong that needed to be dealt with between me and others. While forgiveness had been purchased for me by Jesus, certain responsibilities remained mine to address as I was spiritually led to do so. As a final check on my responsibility and understanding, I consulted a Christian friend whom I had recently spent time with in informal home Bible studies that he and other Christian men were conducting in the community. I explained my past regarding the extortion to him. I can still remember his bewildered expression and his words of dismay, "Larry, why did you do it?" I had no good answers, and there could be no excuses. Kirk knew that I could have no acceptable answers; his question had mainly reflected his disappointment in me and his genuine concern for me knowing the personal cost that might now follow.

It was difficult for Kirk to advise me in this situation, but as a faithful Christian brother he gave me his best understanding of what I should do. As I expected, he agreed that I should turn myself in regardless of the consequences. We both knew that this could well mean federal prison time for me.

Thoughts drifted in of there being a possible issue regarding the statute of limitations even for a felony such as extortion. It was approximately two months short of seven years since I had committed the crime, and I presumed that the statute of limitations might be five years or might be seven years. All I had to do was check the law. If it was seven years, I only had to wait a few months to turn myself in, and I could not then be prosecuted. It was practically a "get-out-of-jail-free" card. It took me only seconds to dismiss these thoughts—they never took root. If God was leading me to turn myself in, then I was not about to try to outsmart Him and presume upon His grace. I never even checked to see how the law read—that was not an issue that was guiding my decision.

Chapter Fourteen

Confession

I shut off all the utilities to the house and secured the property, preparing it for the unknown. This was uncharted territory for me, for I did not know if I would be returning this day or if I would end this day under arrest and in jail. I had routinely prepared for lengthy offshore projects in the past, so in some ways I already had an established routine for extended absences even though it had been six months since I had formally ended my diving career. However, this time instead of preparing for several weeks of possible absence, I now had to consider that I might be gone for an untold number of years. There simply was no good way to prepare for this situation other than to sell everything and dispose of personal belongings, and I did not have the time or the clear sense of purpose and spiritual leading to do this.

It had been less than seven years since I had decided to risk all without knowing how that fateful day would end—that was the day when I had performed the pick-up and escape for the extortion. Then, as now, I did not know if I would be returning, except back then I had a fair amount of misplaced confidence that I was in control. This time, I had no illusion of being in control. I committed the day to the Lord and submitted myself on my knees to His will and His purposes. With having no idea of what to expect, I locked the gate to my driveway and began the drive to the Federal Bureau of Investigation offices in New Orleans for a meeting with those whose property I had damaged in my extortion attempt and those whose lives I had threatened. I did not know if the representative from the telephone company or the FBI Special Agent I was scheduled to meet would have direct prior involvement with the case, but clearly these two men and possibly others would be representing those whom I had wronged.

On June 3, 1980, I had typed a letter to the General Security Manager at South Central Bell in New Orleans, setting the process in motion. I had taken steps to learn his name before writing the letter to ensure that the proper person would receive my confession, but for privacy concerns I will not now reveal his name. The first paragraph, unpolished and as written, had read: "This letter must necessarily be personally addressed to you in your position of responsibility and authority at South Central Bell. You may question my credibility, for what I am going to relate to you will result in serious incrimination for me. I am now asking you for your time to consider what I have to say. I regret terribly the actions I have committed which require this letter to be written."

The second paragraph, in its entirety, read: "Several years ago I committed a serious crime against your company. There was no injury to any of your personnel, but there was property damage. This was not an act of vandalism, but instead a deliberate planned attempt to extort a sum of money. The attempt was not successful. I am hesitant to relate the details of the crime in this letter, although I will provide you with any and all pertinent information when you inform me of how this should be accomplished. I would prefer to meet with you in person at any time or place you would choose. Mine is not the bargaining position though, and it is your instructions I will follow. I fully realize that this letter may leave you with no alternative but to contact law enforcement officials and that what I have today set in motion may result in my arrest and prosecution."

The letter had not been written easily, and it was important for me to try to get it right. It was difficult to explain in one page why I was coming forward at this time, but they deserved an explanation and God deserved the credit. The third paragraph continued on: "To give you an understanding of why I am now coming forward, I must necessarily tell you of certain changes in my life. I am not a 'professional confessor', nor am I psychologically unstable. However, I was a spiritually lost young man at the time of the crime, and have since been spiritually awakened. For over a year now I have been a Christian and I have sought to do as Christ would lead me. I have the Scriptural assurance of the Lord's forgiveness in this matter, but I also have the stern admonition to provide restitution to those whom I have wronged. I fully acknowledge my guilt and regret my actions. Confession and restitution are necessary matters to be dealt with. Also, if prosecution results, then I must accept this as part of the penalty."

I felt it inappropriate to ask for anyone's forgiveness—I had no right to do this and place on another person the burden of far higher standards of compassion than I had displayed at the time of the crime. I also didn't want the letter to read as if it was self-centered psychological guilt that was prompting my confession, but rather spiritual responsibility and a total awareness of my accountability. This was not to alleviate a guilty conscience even though I was still shamed by my previous actions—my guilt in this sense had been covered by the sacrifice of Jesus Christ even though there still might be repercussions for me in this world. Instead, my confession was to address my spiritual and moral responsibility.

The last two brief paragraphs combined read: "I am sorry for what I have done. I apologize with the sincerity of spiritual conviction. I would like to discuss this matter with you and provide you with any necessary information you would require for your decisions. I do not have, nor do I want, legal counsel. The terms of restitution are yours. I just don't know what else to say...I await your response."

On Friday, three days after mailing the letter, my phone rang: "Larry, this is ___ ______ with South Central Bell. I have your letter." The strong voice on the other end was resolute and clearly that of someone in authority.

When I had first sent the letter, I was not completely sure if I was providing enough information to pin down the incident. I need not have worried; there was no question during the phone call that we were immediately on the same page. The conversation was brief, almost cryptic in how we both addressed the situation. Although our discussion stayed on the perimeter of the incident, it seemed as if we were discussing something that both of us had wrestled with at length. With a hint of controlled sarcasm in his voice he mentioned that he would have preferred a handwritten letter—an obvious allusion to the handwritten extortion letters that I had sent almost seven years prior. I knew immediately what he meant, both regarding the reference to my having typed the letter of confession rather than handwriting it, and now to his having to deal with the person who had committed the crime. This was a man who instinctively knew that I would not need his subtle comments explained to me. This was also a man who understandably did not like me. He instructed me to be at the FBI offices on the following Tuesday morning where I would meet with him and an FBI Agent. No details were offered about the nature of the meeting or the possible outcome. I was told to be there at 9:00 in the morning, and that was all I was told.

The drive across the Lake Pontchartrain Causeway and into downtown New Orleans early that morning on June 10th of 1980 gave me additional time for solemn reflection. I wondered if I was going to lose my freedom and be stripped of all that I had—if I would find myself subjected to a legal system that could essentially do with me as it pleased. At the same time, I knew that I was not alone, that it was God who was directing my steps and that He could have purposes in this that I had yet to understand. I wondered if I would become one of the prisoners who would be seen as genuine in his faith and one whom others could confide in, or if I would be ridiculed as a lightweight. At the same time I wondered if they would even prosecute me at this stage. I also had no idea what the terms of restitution were going to be regarding the property that I had damaged—and I knew that if they were to bill me for investigation costs that I could be indebted for life. I was fully aware that this could be the end of my life as I knew it.

I thought of the many times that I had been shown mercy in my life that I had never even realized until God opened my eyes and my heart, whether it involved mountain climbing ventures, barroom brawls where I could have been injured far more severely, diving incidents and emergencies, multiple automobile and motorcycle wrecks, the outcome of a trial where I deserved to be caught for soliciting perjury, or having been spared from traveling the road further into a terrible darkness that I had at one time sought and welcomed. I now also knew that I had been spared capture during the extortion, having realized that nothing happens purely by chance. I knew that for some reason, God had allowed me to escape, but I was now to learn just how precarious my situation had been. At this point I knew only of the two cars that had sped past the pick-up location and of the two men in the third car who had shown up immediately thereafter to begin the search along the riverbank. I knew that the tugboat that had seemed to appear out of nowhere could have easily run over me, but I knew nothing of the men assigned to the tower for additional surveillance—or for that matter, that they were equipped with a rifle with a night scope. I also knew nothing of the circumstances surrounding what was to have been my second pick-up attempt, for which I thought there had been no response to my final demands.

I entered the government building at 701 Loyola Avenue in downtown New Orleans where at the time the FBI offices were located. I had been waiting outside an hour early; this was certainly not a meeting where I was going to show up late. With my arrival at the actual offices on the sixth floor planned to be a respectful ten minutes early, I approached the elevator apprehensively. Another man was entering the elevator at the same time as I was, and I hoped that he was not the General Security Manager from South Central Bell. Although I knew that I would be meeting him in minutes, I was more than uncomfortable in this close situation. Fortunately, the other man exited on another floor. Final seconds were used to ask God that His will would be accomplished, wherever this was to lead.

I introduced myself to the FBI receptionist, explaining that I was there for a meeting. I was told to take a seat, and a brief wait followed. Within minutes another man showed up, and our exchanged looks told each of us who the other was. Shortly thereafter we were being escorted to an office. The meeting was to be only with the FBI Special Agent, the General Security Manager, and me.

Before the meeting actually started, the FBI Special Agent left briefly and returned carrying a stack of documents. The stack was at least twelve inches high. As my eyes rested on the bulging files I was given my first awakening glimpse of the extent of trouble that I had caused. It was a sad and disappointing realization—a confirmation that my actions had created so much havoc.

I answered all questions asked of me and recounted the specific events of the extortion. Copies of my extortion letters of nearly seven years prior were placed before me, and I agreed that they were mine. As my eyes fell upon the threats and the profanity that I had used, it was a sad admission that I had written such foul ugliness. Before I had become a Christian, I had about as foul a mouth as anyone unless I was in the presence of women. Seeing my words written out coupled with the hate that was intended to be revealed painfully reminded me of who and what I had been. It had been almost seven years since I had used such language, and now it was offensively foreign and disgusting to me. I looked over the letters only briefly to confirm they were mine, not wanting to let those thoughts back into my mind.

Questioning continued to determine if I had acted alone and if there were other crimes that I had committed. Besides asking questions related to what I thought could be my potential prosecution, the FBI seemed most concerned about the transmitter that had been placed in the extortion package. Full assurance was wanted regarding what I had done with it—I was given the impression that this was not technology that they had wanted compromised. Equally of concern to the FBI was the monetary value of the transmitter. I found this a curiosity—I wasn't sure how much a small custom-built transmitter might cost, but I suspected that it was significantly less than the damage that I had caused the telephone company. I emphasized that I had destroyed the transmitter on the rocks at the riverbank as soon as I had exited the river, and that I had then thrown the pieces back into the river. When I still sensed hesitation on the Agent's part I did my best to assure him that the transmitter was completely destroyed.

To me it seemed that the South Central Bell Security Manager was more interested in an investigative sense of the overall crime than the FBI Agent. He looked me square in the eyes and told me that I was the only one who had ever attempted such a thing under his watch and not been caught. In this was the clear message: "You are damn lucky that I never got you." This was not a man who liked losing, and he clearly had no use for those who criminally placed others at risk. My conversion to Christianity was in this particular discussion of no interest to him. I had performed criminal activities with far-reaching consequences, and I could tell that he believed that the legal responsibility for my actions should rightfully rest on me with the full weight of the law.

At one point the Security Manager asked me what kind of car I was driving at the time. I answered that it was a 1972 blue Ford Ranchero. Upon hearing this, he slammed his fist down on the table, growling a frustrated, "Damn!" That he was visibly angry is an understatement. He didn't explain his frustration, but clearly his actions revealed that this represented a link to prior evidence that judging by his reaction could have tied me to the case. He had been close, and he knew it. He definitely knew my vehicle.

My confession and the questioning seemed to be building the case against me for my prosecution. My truthfulness and clear regret might have softened the Security Manager's stance against me throughout that morning, but if it did, it was minimal. Even so, it was the Security Manager who began to fill in the pieces of the puzzle that up until then had been hidden from me.

The questioning by the FBI Special Agent concluded with him asking me whether or not I would be willing to provide compensation for the transmitter that I had destroyed. I was willing to do this, but in the end this never did become an issue. Again, to me it seemed a strange priority and almost a bureaucratic obsession given the other major aspects of the case—as if the destruction of the transmitter was the crime and not the extortion itself. He then left to go to a related meeting at the United States Attorney's Office for the Eastern District of Louisiana. Here was where my fate was going to be decided. I would be waiting at the FBI office until this was resolved. I had no sense of how this might turn out. They had my confession and the evidence for a rock solid case against me, but would they prosecute? There would have been no need for a trial, as I would have willingly pled guilty.

I was aware of the statute of limitations in a general sense, but I did not know if this would apply to me in a federal case or what time factors were involved. Up until this point, nothing had been mentioned by anyone about time limitations for prosecution. As the Security Manager and I sat alone in the office and continued somewhat tense discussions, with a terse wave of his hand he indicated there would be no prosecution as he reluctantly now mentioned the statute of limitations for the first time. This legal aspect is what perhaps had angered him the most. He seemed confident that dismissal would occur, but until I heard this from the FBI I had no assurance that this would be the outcome.

At this point I knew that the Security Manager had been personally involved with the case from the beginning. In fact, he had been at the scene on August 7, 1973, and been relieved at midnight. It was three hours later when he received the frustrating call of resignation in his motel room: "We missed him. He got away."

Although I had many questions myself, it was not my place to quiz him about the events. Nevertheless, I did dare to ask him one question: "Why didn't you respond to my final letter and set up the second junction box in Gretna?"

He looked at me as if I had to have known what he was about to say. His answer made no sense to me, and I frowned in bewilderment when he revealed an impossible situation: "Because there was no such street intersection."

At the time I could not remember the actual streets for the intersection that I had designated, and I did not dare ask to look at my extortion letters again—but I knew beyond any doubt that those streets had existed. I had parked at that intersection and written down those street names as I observed them. Now this man was telling me there was no such location, but yet I had even driven back by that exact area only to discover that they had ignored my final demands. This was the key factor, the trip point, that had caused me to abandon my plans. This had kept me from attempting another pick-up at the first location. That mission was now unnecessary because of their lack of response at the second location. I was convinced that they had totally ignored all my final demands.

With all of my careful detailed planning and simply because of my natural thoroughness in essential matters, there is no way that I would have made a mistake such as this. There was a 1st Street that existed in Gretna, but how could I possibly have made up a street name like "Industrial Parkway"? Industrial Parkway is hardly a slip of the pen. Maps now reveal an Industrial Parkway some fourteen miles to the northeast of Gretna, but that was an area that I had never even visited. It was this crucial detail that had brought my extortion efforts to a close in 1973: a mysterious non-existent intersection that I had provided in a final extortion letter. Explanations fail.

I did not know when I made my final pass through the area that full-scale surveillance was in progress and that organized apprehension operations were on active standby. Their sole focus was once again at the first location at the intersection of the Harvey Canal and the Mississippi River. My third letter with its demands had not been ignored as I thought it had been. Instead, with the address for the second location being non-existent, all resources were committed to the first location. When I drove by and saw what I thought was the first junction box standing there as a lonely marker, I had made myself a perfect target for being investigated. More than once I was to hear: "You should not have gotten away."

Many of the other case particulars such as specific dates, certain addresses, true extent of damage inflicted, and other investigation matters remained unknown to me until 2007 when in the course of beginning to write this book I requested and received limited and selectively expunged records of the investigation from the United States Department of Justice under the provisions of the Freedom of Information – Privacy Act (FOIPA), request number 1093794-000. It was these records along with other personal files that have allowed me to recreate an accurate timeline of events over thirty-five years later. But it was in my discussions on June 10, 1980, with the General Security Manager and in one follow-up visit that I learned some of the amazing details of the case.

It was now explained to me that the first car that had sped past the junction box had done so at almost the exact same time that the transmitter was activated. Indeed, immediately after it had passed I had opened the junction box and had the package in hand within three seconds. This resulted in the first search vehicle initiating a pursuit of that vehicle and its innocent occupants, thereby splitting the search teams. This afforded me those few precious seconds that I needed to allow me to reach the water's edge and begin my swim out into the Harvey Canal before the second search vehicle arrived on the scene.

Information that I received in 2007 provided additional details. The first two paragraphs from the FBI report dated 8/8/73, the actual day of the crime, read as follows:

> "Junction box containing dummy package and transmitter installed at site specified by unsub [unidentified subject] at 10:30 a.m., Monday, 8/6/73, and thereafter placed under 24-hour surveillance by Buagents [Bureau Agents—i.e., FBI]. Site specified by unsub is unpopulated area surrounded by heavy underbrush and bound by extremely steep mudbanks. Site overlooks intersection of Mississippi River and Harvey Canal, an area of treacherous water currents and heavy ship and barge traffic. Street access has considerable through traffic, around the clock. Drop site was beside a paved overlook at levee terminus that is used as a "lover's lane" and by fishermen.
>
> At 2:50 a.m., Wednesday, 8/8/73, transmitter sounded indicating the package had been picked up, and Buagents were at drop site point within 25 seconds. Neither unsub nor any vehicle observed near drop site. Beeps emanating from package transmitter stopped after 30 seconds; subsequent investigation indicates that unsub swam the Harvey Canal with the package and water killed the transmission."

It had been my knowledge of electronics coupled with common sense and caution that had given me ample confidence that flooding the package would neutralize any potential electronic devices that I had considered likely to be installed. Had this not been accomplished, I would indeed have been tracked. This was one of several potential failure points for me that could easily have resulted in my capture or led eventually to my death in one way or another.

The next two paragraphs of the 8/8/73 report dealt with details that did not apply directly to my criminal activities but covered other aspects of the investigation that in hindsight are now irrelevant. But the final paragraph had stated: "Intensive investigation presently underway to identify and interview occupants of all vehicles observed in vicinity of drop site and recovery site during course of surveillance of package. Investigation being coordinated with Security Department of South Central Bell Telephone Company, New Orleans, Louisiana, in effort to identify unsub."

The reports that I received in 2007 included extensive lists of vehicles and license numbers (with the numbers deleted to protect the privacy of innocent others), descriptions of visitors to the scene, interviews with people of interest (again, with their identities protected), refusals by some individuals to take lie detector tests, and other investigative details that I know were but a small fraction of the documentation gathered during the course of the investigation. This had been treated as a major crime. Tucked within those documents was the description of a blue Ford Ranchero.

While waiting for the FBI Agent to return from discussions at the United States Attorney's Office, in the continuing conversation with the Security Manager I was to learn about the two men assigned to the tower where surveillance involved the use of a rifle scope with night vision optics. What had transpired in that tower would have been comedic had it not been so exasperating for those committed to the investigation and my capture. As mentioned previously, a man from the telephone company had been allowed there as an observer even though he was legally prohibited from partaking in arrest operations. This person had remained vigilant, but there was that one crippling drawback: he had an extreme fear of heights. On the other hand, the assigned FBI Agent was personally convinced that I would not make the pick-up, and so he had left his post and was sleeping soundly in the car below. My plan for the open-ended time for the pick-up did in fact lower expectations and attentiveness at least for this Agent.

When I removed the package from the junction box and the transmitter was thereby automatically activated, immediate surveillance of the site would have shown me headed into the Harvey Canal. A concentration of law enforcement resources downstream could then have been ordered. My escape would have been far less likely under this scenario, and my later inexplicable lapse of falling asleep a few hundred yards downstream from the Harvey Canal during the deviation from my plan would likely have ensured my capture unless I had first been able to take my own life in a final act of desperation.

Instead, because of his fear of heights the representative from the telephone company was unable to position himself where he could observe me with the night scope, leaving him the humbling option of crawling close enough to the edge so that he could toss pocket change at the car below in an effort to wake up the sleeping FBI Agent. It was not a good day for law enforcement, and it had not been a good day for the Security Manager who still nursed a grudging resentment of the apprehension failure. He did not have to tell me of these happenings, but perhaps he wanted me to know that I had not been smart, but instead been exceptionally lucky. For me, in my knowledge of God's sovereign control, I didn't consider myself lucky, but instead blessed with an undeserved mercy and grace and spared by God from getting what I deserved. As a final note about this aspect of the case, I was told that the FBI Agent assigned to the tower was subsequently reassigned to a different position in another state.

As the Security Manager saw that I was troubled by the problems that I had caused and that I had no agenda other than trying to set right a matter that I regretted causing, he was more than willing to let me bury myself in regret. I explained that one of the things that bothered me the most was that when I had disrupted phone service for a wide range of customers that I might have created a situation in which critical emergency services could not be summoned for someone in need. I wasn't requesting the assurance that this never happened, but it would have been a welcomed relief to learn this. Sensing my regret, he left me to dwell on my troubling concerns: "If I knew I would not tell you." This was not a petty retaliation; it honestly reflected how disturbed he remained at my wanton and selfish acts of destruction. His knowing that I would not be prosecuted had to have constituted for him an infuriating failure of justice.

It was at this time that he told me that they had performed background investigations on 1,500 telephone company personnel. My deliberate efforts in deception to encourage this to be an internal investigation for the telephone company had succeeded far more than I had ever imagined. Considerable resources were wasted for the investigation in this direction—both for the telephone company as well as for the FBI. The mention of this number of investigations was no flippant exaggeration of the facts of the case. An excerpt from FBI file numbered 9-2791 that I received in 2007 reads: "On August 17, 18, and 19, 1973, [deleted] FBI Laboratory Document Section, and Special Agent (SA) [deleted] in the company of [deleted] previously mentioned of South Central Bell (SCB), conducted extensive document examination of the records of South Central Bell Telephone Company, New Orleans. [Deleted] examined, according to [deleted], approximately 1,500 past and present SCB employee files for handwriting specimens similar to that of the extortionist." That one-foot stack of investigation documents still sitting on the desk before me was itself but a fraction of the documentation associated with this case.

In a separate memorandum dated 8/16/73 that reviewed certain aspects of the case, it was noted that an FBI Special Agent had requested that the FBI document examiner handling the case be authorized to proceed to New Orleans to assist in the investigation. This request dovetails with the account in the previous paragraph to reveal the considerable attention and effort given the investigation of this crime. The memorandum went on to say: "There is a threat that further tricks by the Company will result in the use of "nitro downtown." The Company feels this means an explosive device at their downtown office. No solid suspects have been developed but, due to the circumstances of the [deleted] and terminology of the letters, it is felt that the suspect could well be a present or past employee. There are some 30 such individuals who could be suspects and, in view of the time element and the fact that the Company is reluctant to turn over this volume of personnel files for submission to the Laboratory, New Orleans requests the Laboratory examiner be authorized to proceed there to conduct examinations on the scene. It is recommended the examiner proceed expeditiously to New Orleans in accordance with this request. This has been coordinated with [deleted] of the General Investigative Division."

I had wanted to be taken seriously, and I certainly had been. This memorandum confirmed that my extortion letters had indeed been a key factor in misdirecting the investigation so that it was primarily an internal one for South Central Bell. They were all looking hard for me, but they were looking in the wrong place.

That day when the FBI Special Agent returned from his meeting at the United States Attorney's Office it was confirmed: there would be no prosecution because of the Federal Statute of Limitations. The memorandum addressed to the Director, FBI, and dated 6/12/80 read in part for two paragraphs:

> "On June 10, 1980, Whited in the company of [deleted] South Central Bell Telephone Security, New Orleans, Louisiana, came to the New Orleans office of the FBI and made a full confession to SA [deleted] regarding his, Whited's, involvement in the above captioned incident. Whited advised that in 1973 he formulated and carried out a plan in an attempt to extort money from the South Central Bell Telephone Company. Whited advised that [while] carrying out this plan [he] came into the possession of an electronic device which he broke with a rock and threw into the river. Whited advised that he obtained this device from the inside of a package which he had obtained from a junction box near the Harvey Canal in the New Orleans Metropolitan area.
>
> The full context of Whited's confession and interview was presented to the U.S. Attorney's Office, Eastern District of Louisiana (EDLA). AUSA [deleted] advised that due to the Federal Statute of Limitations, the U.S. Attorney's Office, EDLA, was prohibited by law from charging Whited with this crime. On this basis, AUSA [deleted] declined this case and no further investigation is to be conducted at New Orleans."

In addition to the information that I learned from the South Central Bell General Security Manager on the day of my confession at the FBI office in New Orleans on June 10th of 1980 and in the reports later received in 2007 in accordance with the Freedom of Information – Privacy Act (FOIPA), there were a few more pieces of the puzzle filled in by another person from South Central Bell who was involved with the case. Those pieces would fall into their proper place when the matter of restitution was addressed the following week. There had been many far-reaching consequences for what was a criminal, selfish, and exceptionally foolish act.

As I drove home a free and truly liberated man following the meeting at the FBI offices I knew that God's grace had again poured over me in abundance. To have traveled the road of my life from having hated the very concept of God to realizing that He had so many times in so many ways extended unlimited mercy to me left me humbled and in awe of Him.

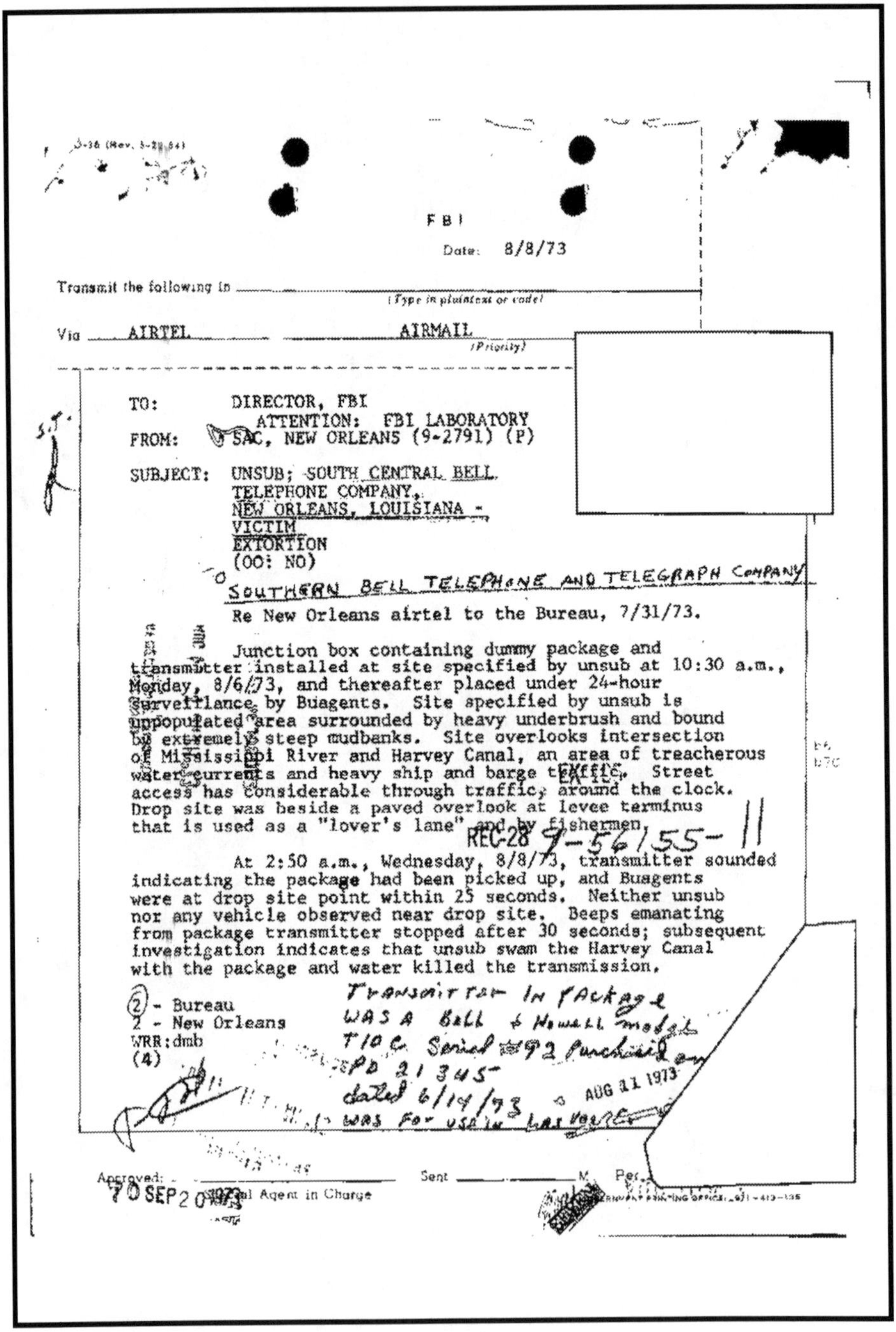

[redacted]

FBI

Date: 8/8/73

Transmit the following in ______________________ (Type in plaintext or code)

Via AIRTEL AIRMAIL (Priority)

TO: DIRECTOR, FBI
ATTENTION: FBI LABORATORY

FROM: SAC, NEW ORLEANS (9-2791) (P)

SUBJECT: UNSUB; SOUTH CENTRAL BELL TELEPHONE COMPANY, NEW ORLEANS, LOUISIANA - VICTIM
EXTORTION
(OO: NO)

SOUTHERN BELL TELEPHONE AND TELEGRAPH COMPANY

Re New Orleans airtel to the Bureau, 7/31/73.

Junction box containing dummy package and transmitter installed at site specified by unsub at 10:30 a.m., Monday, 8/6/73, and thereafter placed under 24-hour surveillance by Buagents. Site specified by unsub is unpopulated area surrounded by heavy underbrush and bound by extremely steep mudbanks. Site overlooks intersection of Mississippi River and Harvey Canal, an area of treacherous water currents and heavy ship and barge traffic. Street access has considerable through traffic, around the clock. Drop site was beside a paved overlook at levee terminus that is used as a "lover's lane" and by fishermen.

REC-28 9-56155-11

At 2:50 a.m., Wednesday, 8/8/73, transmitter sounded indicating the package had been picked up, and Buagents were at drop site point within 25 seconds. Neither unsub nor any vehicle observed near drop site. Beeps emanating from package transmitter stopped after 30 seconds; subsequent investigation indicates that unsub swam the Harvey Canal with the package and water killed the transmission.

2 - Bureau
2 - New Orleans
WRR:dmb
(4)

Transmitter in package was a Bell & Howell model T10C Serial #92 Purchased on PO 21345 dated 6/14/73 was for use in Las Vegas

AUG 31 1973

Approved: ______ Special Agent in Charge Sent ______ M Per ______

70 SEP 20 1973

Document from FBI Investigation

UNITED STATES GOVERNMENT

UNITED STATES DEPARTMENT OF JUSTICE
FEDERAL BUREAU OF INVESTIGATION

Memorandum

TO : DIRECTOR, FBI (9-~~56155~~) 46155

DATE: 6/12/80

FROM : SAC, NEW ORLEANS (9-2791)(P)

SUBJECT: CHANGED
LARRY A. WHITED;
SOUTH CENTRAL BELL TELEPHONE COMPANY,
New Orleans, Louisiana - VICTIM;
EXTORTION;
OO: New Orleans
Southern Bell Telephone and telegraph Company

b6
b7C

Title marked changed to reflect name of subject as Larry A. Whited, previously carried as "Unsub".

9-56155-3

Re New Orleans teletype to Bureau, 8/1/73; SA [redacted] telephone call to New Orleans from Laboratory, 8/2/73; and New Orleans airtel to Bureau, 8/8/73. New Orleans report to Bureau dated 6/28/74. 9-56155-20

On June 10, 1980, Whited in the company of [redacted] South Central Bell Telephone Security, New Orleans, Louisiana, came to the New Orleans Office of the FBI and made a full confession to SA [redacted] regarding his, Whited's, involvement in the above captioned incident. Whited advised that in 1973 he formulated and carried out a plan in an attempt to extort money from the South Central Bell Telephone Company. Whited advised that carrying out this plan came into the possession of an electronic device which he broke with a rock and threw into the river. Whited advised that he obtained this device from the inside of a package which he had obtained from a junction box near the Harvey Canal in the New Orleans Metropolitan area.

LA V-43 DE-28 9-56155-21

The full content of Whited's confession and interview was presented to the U. S. Attorney's Office, Eastern District of Louisiana (EDLA). AUSA [redacted] advised that due to the Federal Statute of Limitations, the U. S. Attorney's Office, EDLA, was prohibited by law from charging Whited with this crime. On this basis, AUSA [redacted] declined this case and no further investigation is to be conducted at New Orleans.

2 - Bureau
1 - New Orleans

23 JUN 14 1980

JDJ:ebc
(3)

68 AUG 14 1980

Buy U.S. Savings Bonds Regularly on the Payroll Savings Plan

Document from FBI / Confession & Legal Closure

Chapter Fifteen

Restitution

On Tuesday, June 10, 1980, I left the FBI offices in downtown New Orleans knowing that I had acted in accordance with and in obedience to God's will. Having been set free legally and spiritually, I knew that I had been especially blessed. I was experiencing an extra assurance coming upon me because now fear, second-guessing, and looking over my shoulder would not be a problem when it came to my past criminal behavior and future spiritual walk. There would always be the consequences of regret, but this regret kept me focused on Jesus Christ and the forgiveness that He had purchased for me with His life. That which might have crippled me with guilt instead pointed me to grace and mercy and allowed me to begin to understand His godly kind of love.

These spiritual thoughts that tended to float somewhat above happenings in the physical world also remained firmly anchored to the reality that was immediately before me. Two days after the Tuesday meeting, on Thursday, June 12, 1980, my phone rang again with the second and final call from the South Central Bell General Security Manager: "Larry, we have come up with an amount for the damages that you caused, and I know that you will be pleased. On Monday morning two of us from the company will drive over to your house. Have a cashier's check for us made payable to South Central Bell in the amount of $8,955." And so started and ended the conversation. He did not ask for directions to my house hidden deep in the woods; he did not ask if I would be able to come up with the amount; and he had nothing else to say once I acknowledged the amount. I had my marching orders.

It had not surprised me that I had caused that much damage, and I did in fact know that the amount determined by the telephone company could have been much higher, but I did not have $8,955 conveniently sitting in a checking account waiting for withdrawal. I knew that the telephone company was not going to be interested in excuses from me—they expected payment in full at the time specified. Coming up with that amount of money by Monday morning left me in a quandary. By this time I did have home equity comfortably exceeding this amount, but I had aggressively been using my savings to complete the seemingly endless project of house renovation so that I could sell the house and move on to a future that as yet remained uncertain.

I had a good working relationship with a local bank after eight years of financial history, and my first thought was that it would be an easy matter to see the bank president with whom I was on a first-name basis and take out a loan using the house as collateral. The father of the then current bank president had been the one to walk through the rubble of the house when I first wanted to buy it, and as the bank president at that time he had personally approved the first loan in a matter of hours. I thought that my eight years with the bank had earned me a somewhat privileged consideration for a sufficiently collateralized loan. I was wrong. I was told that the bank could not approve a loan on such short notice.

Panic was not setting in because I was still overwhelmed with a sense that God was intimately involved in all the details of what was transpiring, but I did seriously wonder how it was that I would be able to come up with the required amount for restitution. Events then began to unfold like clockwork. First, I called a separate out-of-state financial institution where I had my savings funds and requested an immediate transfer to my local checking account. During those years, this had always required a minimum of two to three days for a transaction to be completed, and with the weekend coming up I was concerned. However, this time the transaction was to take only one day. It was a good start, but I was still far short of what I needed.

Three years prior I had helped a friend who had a dream of making it in the entertainment business as a singer and songwriter. As anyone knows who has knocked on that door, it is a tough one to open. Being no music critic myself, I nevertheless thought that he had the raw talent necessary to become a success. He and his wife with their two young boys had no way of meeting the financial costs of producing a recording. They had shyly asked me if I could help them get started. It was no small matter for me, but I decided to do more than they expected: I would loan them the entire amount that they needed. It was a loan without a contract, and the terms were generous: "Pay me back when you can." Their dreams never were realized after completing the recording, and three years had since passed with no payments being made. I had not pressed for payment, but we understood that the loan still existed.

Because of a diving incident a few years prior in which he had been improperly decompressed resulting in injury, a lawsuit had subsequently followed. Delay after delay had occurred, and expectations had been repeatedly dashed when the planned settlement failed to materialize. I made a call to him and learned that the settlement check had cleared only a few days earlier. Yes, he could pay back the loan. On Friday I had a check from him. Still, I was short, although I was getting close.

Taking inventory of what I could quickly sell for cash, my weapons were the obvious choice. On Friday afternoon I drove to Gretna, Louisiana, to sell an assault rifle and a semi-automatic pistol that I still owned from my dangerous years. That rifle, an AR-15 with various 20 and 30-round magazines, was still one that I could enjoy shooting for target practice, but it now had a higher purpose. A gun store in Gretna where I had previously conducted business offered me a fair price for the two weapons, and I gratefully accepted their offer. I cannot remember what other sources I tapped into, but by Saturday morning I had collected nearly $9,000, leaving me about $40 more than I needed to settle my debt with the telephone company.

On Saturday morning, June 14, 1980, I walked into Citizens Bank and Trust in Covington, Louisiana, and in minutes left with a cashier's check made payable to South Central Bell in the required amount of $8,955.00. I was now ready for the Monday visit by the General Security Manager and the other representative who would accompany him. The check was a significant sum for me to part with, but it was part of the price for my past criminal actions. I had not been billed for any investigation costs. If I had been, I expect that the amount would have been staggering. I had been shown considerable mercy and treated more than fair.

The words came back to me from Matthew 5:23-26 where Jesus had taught: "Therefore if you are presenting your offering at the altar, and there remember that your brother has something against you, leave your offering there before the altar and go; first be reconciled to your brother, and then come and present your offering. Make friends quickly with your opponent at law while you are with him on the way, so that your opponent may not hand you over to the judge, and the judge to the officer, and you be thrown into prison. Truly I say to you, you will not come out of there until you have paid up the last cent."

The offering that I was presenting at the altar was my life, for I no longer owned myself in the way that I once thought I did. Wrestling matches would of course continue and still do, with love-driven obedience being on one side and selfish independence and all that it entails on the other, but at the end of it all I knew that Jesus Christ had purchased my life with His. If I intended to acknowledge His lordship over my life, then His words had to mean something to me beyond some kind of mystical perfection reserved for a hypothetical spiritual ideology that I could conveniently choose to accept or reject. His words had in fact seemed quite specific to me. He expects us to attend to those situations in which someone else has been wronged by our behavior and is still in some way negatively impacted by our previous actions.

Monday came quickly and on June 16, 1980, I waited at home for the two South Central Bell representatives to arrive. I heard them drive up to the house, and I went outside to meet them. The General Security Manager remained as firm, authoritative, and businesslike as he had been the week before at the meeting with the FBI. The person who accompanied him was another professional, and both men automatically commanded respect. It was the second man who soon opened up another line of communication with me, and he began to speak openly about God having been involved in what had occurred.

His words to me were: "I knew at the time that God's hand was somehow in this. There is no way that you should have gotten away. I knew that God was involved." It was a repetition and confirmation that my escape should have failed on all practical counts—a point that by then I knew beyond any doubt. He also had meant that the story had broader reaching implications than simply being a daring nighttime escape—there was something more spiritually profound transpiring in the hidden background.

We went inside, and this allowed the men to see how I lived—perhaps best described as modestly. With the renovation still underway and with me personally doing all the work, I expect they soon realized that I was not living a life of ease and great wealth. It would have been obvious that the check that I would be handing over represented a serious financial setback for me, and I think this contributed to their now being more generous in their opinion of me than I deserved.

A manila folder was produced, and in it were duplicate copies of a typed release for my indebtedness to South Central Bell. I handed over the cashier's check before I even read the prepared release. The release read as follows, with the General Security Manager's name deleted for reasons of privacy:

> "Received of Larry A. Whited, Eight Thousand, Nine Hundred Fifty-Five Dollars ($8,955.00) for payment in full for damages to the facilities of South Central Bell Telephone Company, New Orleans, Louisiana, which damages were caused exclusively by Larry A. Whited during the months of July and August 1973, as specified in South Central Bell Security Department File 7-55.
>
> By signature affixed below, the undersigned, [Deleted] as an agent of South Central Bell, hereby declares that Larry A. Whited's indebtedness to South Central Bell relative to damage to the facilities of South Central Bell in New Orleans, Louisiana, perpetrated in July and August 1973, as set forth in File 7-55, is resolved."

Below the two paragraphs outlining the details of the settlement were signature spaces for the Security Manager, the other representative who accompanied him as a witness, and me. The document was dated June 16, 1980. To my knowledge, not one lawyer had been consulted regarding the matter of restitution. Perhaps there had been someone consulted on the telephone company's behalf, but I had obtained no legal counsel concerning either my confession or the restitution that followed. The duplicate copies were signed by all, and I was provided one for my records. I also retained a copy of the cashier's check.

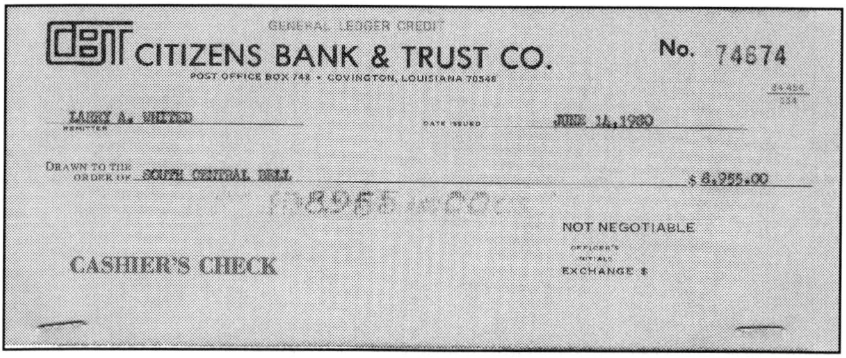

Cashier's Check / Restitution

With the business of restitution out of the way, the visit became less strained. Some of our talk was unrelated to the extortion attempt, but still it found its way into the conversation—especially for the other representative. The man obviously had a strong and committed belief in God, and because of this he could better understand and appreciate the situation now as things had come full circle.

To reaffirm how dangerous my situation had been, I was told that for the second demand—the one that I thought had been completely ignored—they not only had been waiting for me at the first location; but helicopters, boats, and other resources were assigned and on alert. They were not ready in a loose sense; instead they were standing by and fully prepared to spring into immediate action. It was again that mysterious street intersection for the second drop-off point that did not exist that had led me to assume that no action had been taken at the first location either. Not only had I been wrong, but I had been miraculously and mercifully wrong. I maintain to this day that I could not have written down that street intersection wrong. I saw the street signs, and I wrote down what I saw. I simply had seen what was not there—there is no natural explanation that can satisfactorily explain this.

A few more details were offered regarding the investigation and things that had transpired the night of my escape, with everything coming back to the fact that I should not have gotten away. In truth, I had never escaped in God's eyes, and no one ever does. That is why there is no such thing as a perfect crime, no such thing as a cold case file. Settlement of this matter had happened in time in this life so that this need not be a pending judgment against me in the next. I had found—I had been given—the solution to my sins in the sacrifice of Jesus Christ on the cross. Matters of restitution were not matters of forgiveness for me, but they did reveal that genuine forgiveness had done its work in me and had left me with a new outlook on life.

The second man knew that God had performed a work in my life, and this revelation had brought him joy—this was evident in our developing conversation and in the warmth and kindness that I felt being extended to me; and, yes, even forgiveness. I hope that he had the liberty to share this story with others if the appropriate situation had ever arisen. We had shared a common understanding in our knowledge of God's grace, and this shared bond between spiritual brothers was refreshing and encouraging for both of us. On the other hand, my liberty to share this story publicly would not come for many years—I had to have the spiritual assurance that telling this was the right thing to do, and I knew that I would have to touch on other subjects that were especially sensitive not only for me but for others. In fact, I had to wait until certain others could no longer be impacted by my words.

Our visit ended that day with me eager to continue walking in obedience to God's will. There were other matters that remained outstanding, and these too would need to be addressed. Some matters would be relatively easy to address other than working through my shame; some matters would be much harder. Relationships were to be the most difficult challenges.

The next matter regarding my former criminal behavior was the burglary that I had performed in high school in Red Lodge, Montana, almost seventeen years earlier. I knew the man whose sporting goods store I had broken into. His son was only one year behind me in school. To make things even worse, the man was a friend of my parents, not to mention that he had also been the Carbon County Sheriff.

A personal visit would have been the best way to address this, but at the time this would have involved a roundtrip of approximately 3,000 miles. I again prepared a letter of confession and apology. In this letter I tried hard to bring forth the message of the gospel of Jesus Christ, and in hindsight I think that I tried perhaps too hard. We generally know when words are strained and forced, and I fear I crossed that line in my letter to him. If he had noticed this, he was gracious in not correcting me. He received with great kindness what I had to say. He did admit that at the time the loss was a costly one for his family as those were lean and difficult years for them, but he did not have one unkind word to say to me in his return letter. For years he had suspected someone else, so this was an important matter to have resolved. I had sent a check to cover the items taken, and wish now that I had sent more. It was the man's kind acceptance of my apology that hurt me more than the guilt of the crime—I had treated this man so poorly, so unfairly. He, in turn, extended forgiveness to me. As I had written earlier concerning this, the curious thing about grace is that it sometimes hurts as it heals.

Other issues were also addressed where I had wronged people, yet I was especially careful not to turn confessions and apologies into an obsession in which every rock had to be overturned to find where potential grievances might be lurking. There were no specific checklists or tests that I could use to determine if something should be left in the past or if it was required to be brought into the open; but in general I felt that if someone might be nurturing a grudge against me or possibly unfairly thinking that an innocent party had wronged them when in fact it had been me, then I likely needed to act. But if by bringing up a subject I was causing a healed wound for someone else to be opened up again so that I might come away feeling better while others directly or indirectly were then left with troubling thoughts, then that was a signal to leave the situation alone. Where God had healed and sealed a matter, I was to leave it alone. This was not a mission to bring me personal peace at the expense of others—it was a mission to prevent me from being a stumbling block for others and to ensure that there was nothing else that God wanted me to address before I "presented my offering at the altar" as had been the teaching in Matthew 5:23-26.

Fortunately, my criminal past was limited. In a matter of days, the confessions, apologies, and restitution matters that required my immediate attention had been resolved. By no means did I apologize to every person whom I had ever wronged, but the line had to be drawn somewhere. There is a point at which people begin to look at you a little suspiciously if you start recounting every misstep of your past. I found that in being open and honest before God that He was quite capable of leading me to that point of conviction where I needed to act. In Hebrews 10:17 He also says, "And their sins and their lawless deeds I will remember no more." If God is willing to forget, then I know there is a time for me to do the same.

Conversely, and this is another involved subject where formulas cannot be rigidly applied, I found no teachings in the Bible and no spiritual leading directing me to systematically seek out those who had wronged me and whom I might have reason to seek an apology from or even possibly other compensation. Jesus does provide guidance for dealing with a spiritual brother who has wronged us (Re. Matthew 18:15-17); but this is not a license to demand an apology or retribution—this is about the restoration of Christian fellowship.

For one thing, a coerced apology means less than nothing if it is not offered from an understanding heart that has taken responsibility. Otherwise, it is only a forced humiliation, and that brings no healing. Not seeking or demanding this satisfaction of fairness for myself also made sense to me in another way; for I knew that the last thing I wanted from God was strict fairness carefully measured out on the scales of justice. It was mercy, grace, and forgiveness that I needed—not impartial justice based solely on the rule of law. If an exacting justice were to reign in this life, then I was condemned.

I remembered well those years of wanting to obtain my own brand of justice and retribution while conveniently ignoring my own sins—my conscience had rightfully condemned me in the blatant hypocrisy.

Forgiveness is perhaps nowhere more complicated than when it comes to relationships. In Matthew Chapter 18, verse 21, Peter had wondered: "Lord, how often shall my brother sin against me and I forgive him? Up to seven times?"

Peter had been looking for that rule, that law, which pinned down the full extent of his responsibility. In response, Jesus said to him, "I do not say to you, up to seven times, but up to seventy times seven" (Matthew 18:22).

The answer obviously was not to quantify a literal number, but rather to point out that we cannot arbitrarily set limits on the forgiveness that we are willing to extend. Jesus then used Peter's question as a stepping stone to further address the subject of forgiveness, teaching Peter and the other disciples that those who are forgiven should extend the same grace given them, and in turn forgive others.

God's healing forgiveness flowed into me when in my vision and conversion my malignant hatred was washed away. Without compulsive hatred controlling me, forgiveness for others was finally possible. "Of course," was the obvious answer when faced with the question of whether or not I should forgive someone. But herein can also be a difficult thing to understand: there can still remain a righteous disapproval of corrupt actions, for forgiving is not to be confused with excusing.

Forgetting a matter may follow the act of forgiving, with this forgetting linked to giving up the willingness to harbor resentment or vindictiveness. This does not necessarily translate into non-memory. Once forgiveness has truly been given, we lose the right—if one can call it that—of reminding the other person of how they have hurt us. It does not necessarily mean that we personally can or must mentally forget that we have been hurt. Life is more complicated than that.

Forgiveness of others is not the triumph of our own good will, but it is instead a profound recognition and confession of what our own forgiveness cost God, and of our being joined with Him in extending that same grace to others. It is in another realm altogether. Forgiveness in this sense is not natural; it is supernatural. It comes from the heart of God, and it cost God the Father the sacrifice of His Son.

Ideally, confessions, apologies, and restitution will lead to reconciliation—coming to peace with the other person. This may involve taking steps to try to make it easier for the other person to forgive us, while at the same time being careful not to presume that they will be able to do this. Also, if we are to receive the same genuine outreach for forgiveness from others, then we are called to forgive. Indeed, our forgiveness for others in a spiritual sense is given apart from any efforts by them to seek our forgiveness. Our identification with Christ requires this.

On the heels of this open-ended forgiveness come the tales of horrendous abuse and unimaginable horror inflicted on others by those who have been overcome by evil. We consequently look for the rule or for the exception to the rule to know what response is justified. This writing was never intended to unravel and resolve those kinds of difficult issues, and no brief comment can bring healing or achieve justice for those so terribly wronged. I only know that forgiving others first comes from understanding that we ourselves have been forgiven.

Chapter Sixteen

Reflections

Uncle Harold passed away on September 15, 1970, when he was sixty-three years old. In a letter to our family following the funeral that we had all attended, Jennie had started her letter of thanks to us with the following: "Although this is a beautiful morning, I'm so sad and lonely—our home is so empty without Harold."

Her beautifully handwritten letter went on to acknowledge those who in one way or another had extended kindness to her during this difficult time. Jennie, in her own sorrow, immediately saw in others their acts of kindness and appreciated this so much. The emptiness had torn at her from every direction, but she had pressed on.

As was customary in rural North Dakota communities like Buffalo where Harold and Jennie lived, when a loved one passed away those with a close connection to the family would send cards with condolences—often including a small check intended to be used in some way to honor the one who had died. With Buffalo in 1970 having a total population of two hundred and forty people, one would expect a modest number of these much-appreciated tokens of respect and friendship. Instead, donations in Harold's name poured in to the Heart Fund, cancer funds, facilities for troubled children, and other charitable organizations.

Jennie's letter had continued on: "I went to the post office this morning—sent 335 cards and I wrote on each one of them." These were cards of appreciation to recognize those who had either said or contributed something to honor Harold. Jennie would not allow such kindness and respect to pass without responding in true, personal gratitude. Such was the character of Harold, and such was the character of Jennie. To have this number of people to thank means that far more lives were touched by Harold and Jennie than the town even held. At the funeral we had begun to understand this, and it was humbling. It was also wonderful in a sad way as we realized even more the loss.

Kathy and I had received boundless love and much help from Harold and Jennie. With this precious pair not able to have children of their own, their hearts had opened wide to us and to others. With Kathy being four years older than me, the first years of her life were spent either living with or next door to Jennie and Harold. Those were the years when Harold became so attached to Kathy—he truly delighted in his little niece who was so preciously sensitive and responsive to the love given her. That love would prove to be an anchor for her young soul when the hard times would soon come.

In Jennie's letter she had mentioned Harold's brother, Lou, who had kindly helped her, and it was not surprising for us to learn later that Harold and Jennie had also been especially kind to Lou's sons. That was part of what was so precious about Harold and Jennie—whoever they loved knew that the love was genuine. You didn't have to compete for their love; they gave it freely. They offered a special refuge for Kathy and me where we did not have to live under a cloud of criticism—it was an oasis of acceptance.

Jennie closed her letter to us by saying, "I couldn't begin to thank you for all the kind things you have done and said for Harold. I will only mention a few. First, for sharing your love with Kathy and Larry—they were so dear to him and he truly loved them so much; for the flowers, all your telephone calls, your kind words in your letters and cards; for all the help you gave me—but most of all for loving him too. My heart is so heavy and sad. I miss him so much."

Jennie, we all miss him, and we miss you.

It was nineteen years later in September of 1989 when Jennie was eighty-one years old that the call came that she was in the hospital. The prognosis was not good: she very likely had only a few months left to live. We wondered if it might be as many as six months, but we had no way of knowing. I believe we all tended to think that it could be as soon as a month, perhaps two or three.

I was living in Washington State at the time, in the Seattle area; Kathy was in Indiana; and Jennie was in a hospital halfway between in Fargo, North Dakota. As we monitored the situation long distance in the hours after first receiving the news, it was difficult to consider how it might be best to time our visits. The reports from the doctors did not indicate that anything was likely to happen immediately, and Jennie herself did not think that it was necessary to come right away. She knew she was dying, but she didn't want our lives to be unnecessarily disrupted for her.

I felt it was Kathy who most needed to be with Jennie, for both of their sakes. While my relationship with Jennie had remained strong over the years and was lifted to a new plateau when I became a Christian in 1979, I knew that she and Kathy had always shared a unique bond between them extending all the way back to the early years in North Dakota when Kathy would sleepwalk from our house to Jennie and Harold's—drawn simply by their unconditional love and devotion.

When we first heard the news about Jennie, our thoughts went to our wanting to be there with her. I absolutely wanted to be there to see Jennie again before she died, but I knew that Kathy *had* to be there—that it was critical for the two of them to have some final time together with nothing but love being shared. I cannot recall the exact timing of this, but it was within a brief day or two of first hearing about Jennie that I received the undeniable spiritual leading to encourage Kathy to make the trip to see Jennie now, not later. By "now", I knew that this meant as soon as possible. I could not explain why, but I knew there was an urgency. I was not one to try to impose my views on Kathy (I was, after all, a younger brother), but I stressed that she needed to go be with Jennie now.

Kathy listened to my concern and made the arrangements to fly to North Dakota without delay. I remained in Washington, waiting to hear her firsthand report. Kathy flew to North Dakota to be with Jennie on Sunday, September 24, 1989.

I received the first full report from Kathy on Monday evening regarding Jennie's condition. Things did not seem to be at a crisis stage, but she knew that there would be no improvement for Jennie in the sense that Jennie could ever hope to return home again. Her life was coming to a close. I asked about what the feeling was for when I should go to see Jennie. Kathy and Jennie had discussed this, and Jennie had recommended that I wait for a while longer until things turned worse for her. Based on this and the fact that the doctors had not indicated that Jennie's condition was critical with respect to her day-by-day status, I decided not to make any immediate plans, but to wait. I wanted to see Jennie while she was still lucid, but it appeared that there was still plenty of time for this.

The next day on Tuesday morning when I was at work, thoughts of Jennie would not leave me. This was an especially close time for me with God, intensified I know because of Jennie's situation. I desired with all my heart to be sensitive to His leading. This was beyond something that I could figure out—who can time death? I prayed as I worked. That morning, without receiving any kind of an emergency call from Kathy or any other news, I was given another clear spiritual leading just as I had received for Kathy when I knew that she needed to make the trip now. This, now, was my time. Kathy had had some personal time with Jennie, and now it was my time to go.

The spiritual leading that I was experiencing was so definitive that I notified my boss that I would have to leave work immediately. I first considered that I would drive from Seattle to Fargo, and this would have been my first choice. This would have been a two-day drive for me under normal conditions. I could make it to Fargo by late Thursday. But the leading that was upon me was stronger than this: I would have to fly. After leaving work, I prepared for the trip and made my flight arrangements. I would be taking a Wednesday morning flight, arriving later that same day. I let Kathy know of my decision. Still, Jennie's condition was stable. There was nothing suggesting that there were pressing medical reasons for me to be this determined.

On Wednesday, September 27, 1989, I made the flight to Fargo. After renting a car, I drove straight to the hospital. I was able to see Jennie right away, and I knew that this would be my last opportunity to visit with her.

Kathy and I visited, and then I left to make arrangements to stay at a motel. Kathy would stay with Jennie throughout the early evening, and then I would stay with her for a few hours. A few other relatives were coming and going as well; everyone wanted more time with Jennie—and that is just what it was: a time to be with Jennie. Although it was a hospital setting, the time there conveyed the feeling of visiting someone in a nursing home who was confined to bed for her final weeks or months. This was not a time for physical healing; this was a time for a slow goodbye.

It was perhaps between 9:00 and 10:00 Wednesday night when everyone left. I now was alone with Jennie. She drifted in and out of sleep. When she was awake she was fully aware of her surroundings, and we were able to visit. I was able to convey again to her some of what she and Harold had meant to me throughout my life. For Kathy and I to have both come to her at this time was a seal on a life well-done. Certainly we were not the only ones there to share our love and respect, but we did have a special relationship where aunts and uncles, nieces and nephews are concerned.

Perhaps an hour had passed, and I asked Jennie, "Do you want to pray?"

Our family was never a family to pray openly about anything other than when someone might offer grace at a meal or when in a church setting everyone might join in and say the Lord's Prayer. Jennie and I had never prayed together even after I had become a Christian, except when during a few prayers of thanksgiving at meals these prayers started to venture a little further into God's kingdom. Now I was asking this frail little woman who was in the final stage of her life if she wanted to pray. I expected that she would want to, and this was an opportunity for us to acknowledge God together. The enthusiasm of her response surprised me: "Pray? Oh, yes!"

I prayed first, struggling somewhat it seemed to enter the presence of God. Of course He was there; God is everywhere, but words were being hunted in my mind rather than flowing out of an inner fullness as they sometimes did. I honored God in my prayer, praising Him and thanking Him for the salvation that Jesus had purchased for us with His life. I thanked Him for Jennie and Harold, acknowledging their love and faithfulness. It was not an especially emotional prayer; it was a deeply respectful prayer, but I had to work to find the words this time.

Jennie had been a faithful church member of the First Reformed Church in Litchville, North Dakota, where she had moved from Buffalo after Harold had died. This was not a church known for any type of demonstrative behavior. One's faith where Jennie attended services was for them generally a quiet personal matter, revealed in one's faithfulness and in one's character.

When I had finished praying, Jennie began. Never have I heard anyone pray as she did. While I had struggled to enter the presence of God in my prayer, Jennie was immediately before Him. I was there, but I was on the outside, and I was privileged to hear Jennie pour out her heart to God in such praise and thanksgiving that I knew this was coming out of a heart now totally filled with the love of God. This was holy ground, and I could only listen in awe as Jennie, now with raised arms, praised God with all of her being. Jennie and God were communicating on a level where I was not then allowed, and I knew that I was blessed to be able to witness this. God knew Jennie, and Jennie knew God.

Jennie's prayer concluded. I am now unable to remember if we spoke again after this. I expect that we did for a few brief moments, but it was her prayer that I would remember—not her specific words, but the purity and intensity of that moment of heaven on earth. Sleep came upon Jennie, and with tears in my eyes I continued to stay in her room to contemplate the power that I had witnessed. Midnight approached, and about midnight with Jennie sleeping peacefully I left for my motel room.

Kathy's call came in the early morning hours. Jennie had passed away a few hours after I had left her. The impact of what I had witnessed again flowed over me as I realized all that had transpired. Kathy was initially heartbroken that she was not by Jennie's side to be with her when she died, but as I relayed the events of only a few hours earlier she was comforted. Jennie had not been alone.

Epilogue

This writing has covered some varied territory. It is, among other things, a tribute to my Uncle Harold and Aunt Jennie who extended a selfless love to my sister and me and to so many others. Although their lives were confined to a small North Dakota farming community, they touched many lives and were a beacon of hope for so many. It is a recognition of my father for his many letters to me down through the years, which although they were usually about the common things of everyday life, were nevertheless an outreach of his own heart in his own way. I am thankful that I was able to sincerely thank him for those letters before he passed away. It is a recognition of my mother who was unable to handle her own past of being a scorned child by her father and who unwittingly passed along the very pain, criticism, and rejection that had crippled her emotionally, thereby ensuring the very rift that she feared between her and her children. I am thankful that I was able to try to repair the damaged relationships with my parents, and I am sad that in many ways I failed. It is a recognition of my sister who has fought in the same trenches as I have, but who has had a family of her own in which she has tried desperately to ensure that she would not pass along the legacy that she received. This writing is also a tribute to other family and special friends who left space in their own lives for someone who otherwise didn't quite belong in this world. With gentleness, this writing is also a recognition of life's "wounded birds" who believe that they are alone in their agony as they suffer in ways that seem designed to crush the very life out of them.

More than this though, this writing is about a sovereign God who did not abandon me to myself and to the miserable eternity that I deserved. Thank you, Lord, for so great a salvation; thank you for deliverance, thank you for a forgiveness that cost you so much, thank you for blessings beyond measure that I know I have yet to begin to recognize and appreciate.

As I lay down my pen in these early morning hours after reflecting on more than I can possibly understand, I hope that from this writing more good comes than harm, more healing than hurt, and more compassion for some than they otherwise would have received. That child who through behavior or words is reaching out for help may truly need help and understanding. Left to himself, he may well choose the wrong road. Left to the enemy of his soul, he certainly will. But for God, there would be no hope.

You are invited to visit the author's website:

http://riversintolight.com